SCHOPENHAUE
AESTHETIC STA

With its pessimistic vision and bleak message of world-denial, it has often been difficult to know how to engage with Schopenhauer's philosophy. His arguments have seemed flawed and his doctrines marred by inconsistencies; his very pessimism almost too flamboyant to be believable. Yet a way of redrawing this engagement stands open, Sophia Vasalou argues, if we attend more closely to the visionary power of Schopenhauer's work. The aim of this book is to place the aesthetic character of Schopenhauer's standpoint at the heart of the way we read his philosophy and the way we answer the question: why read Schopenhauer – and how? Approaching his philosophy as an enactment of the sublime with a longer history in the ancient philosophical tradition, Vasalou provides a fresh way of assessing Schopenhauer's relevance in critical terms. This book will be valuable for students and scholars with an interest in post-Kantian philosophy and ancient ethics.

SOPHIA VASALOU is Visiting Research Fellow at King's College London. She is author of *Moral Agents and their Deserts* (2008), and editor of *Practices of Wonder* (2012).

SCHOPENHAUER AND THE AESTHETIC STANDPOINT

Philosophy as a Practice of the Sublime

SOPHIA VASALOU

CAMBRIDGE
UNIVERSITY PRESS

CAMBRIDGE
UNIVERSITY PRESS

University Printing House, Cambridge CB2 8BS, United Kingdom

Cambridge University Press is part of the University of Cambridge.

It furthers the University's mission by disseminating knowledge in the pursuit of
education, learning and research at the highest international levels of excellence.

www.cambridge.org
Information on this title: www.cambridge.org/9781107570252

© Sophia Vasalou 2013

First published 2013
First paperback edition 2015

A catalogue record for this publication is available from the British Library

Library of Congress Cataloguing in Publication data
Vasalou, Sophia.
Schopenhauer and the aesthetic standpoint : philosophy as a
practice of the sublime / Sophia Vasalou.
p. cm.
Includes bibliographical references and index.
ISBN 978-1-107-02440-3 (alk. paper)
1. Schopenhauer, Arthur, 1788–1860. 2. Aesthetics. 3. Sublime, The. I. Title.
B3148.V37 2013
193–dc23   2013000438

ISBN 978-1-107-02440-3 Hardback
ISBN 978-1-107-57025-2 Paperback

Additional resources for this publication at www.cambridge.org/vasalou

To H.

Contents

Acknowledgements

This book first took shape a few years ago and slumbered for some time before it was reanimated to assume its present form. During this period, it changed roof twice, from Gonville and Caius College in Cambridge to the European College of Liberal Arts in Berlin, before moving on. I owe to the former – with its almost uninhabitable liberties – the environment that allowed it to take shape. I owe to the latter – with its daring adventures across disciplines and spirit of serious play – the environment that gave me the resources to enrich it, and made its slumber fertile. I owe to the readers of this work for Cambridge University Press, anonymous and eponymous, the generosity that made reanimation and enrichment possible.

Introduction

Wonder: a starting point – a category for investigation?

There are many different senses in which one might talk of a philosopher's starting point, and of what it means to look for it. But surely one of the most important senses is that in which Aristotle spoke of wonder as the beginning of all philosophy – "it is owing to their wonder that men both now begin and at first began to philosophize" – picking up in his *Metaphysics* on Plato's earlier remarks in the *Theaetetus*: "this feeling – a sense of wonder – is perfectly proper to a philosopher: philosophy has no other foundation."[1]

Both remarks were set to reverberate throughout later philosophical tradition and become a staple in its self-understanding. Yet there is clearly no one kind of wonder from which philosophy begins, any more than there is one single question with which philosophy would rightly be occupied. This is already evident from the contrast between the wonder on which Aristotle's and Plato's remarks are respectively focused – the one a wonder characterising men's outwardly turned gaze to the cosmos and unexplained natural phenomena, the other a wonder provoked by conceptual phenomena and arising through the complex manoeuvres of Socratic dialogue (and thus, we may remark, one already internal to philosophical activity). Aristotle's, it has been said more generally, is a wonder that seeks to explain, and after supplying inquiry with its beginning seeks its own dissolution; Plato's a wonder that also accompanies inquiry as its affective tone and indeed stands not only at its beginning but at its end, informing the reverential vision it seeks out.[2]

---

[1] Aristotle, *Metaphysics*, trans. W. D. Ross (Oxford: Clarendon Press, 1928), 982b13–15, and Plato, *Theaetetus*, trans. R. A. H. Waterfield (London: Penguin Books, 2004), 155d.

[2] See the discussion in Sylvana Chrysakopoulou, "Wonder and the beginning of philosophy in Plato," in S. Vasalou, ed., *Practices of Wonder: Cross-Disciplinary Perspectives* (Eugene, OR: Pickwick, 2012); and for further nuance Andrea W. Nightingale, *Spectacles of Truth in Classical*

That philosophy can take its beginning from a wonder belonging to different kinds, similarly, is a proposition to which Schopenhauer, who was familiar with the remarks of both of his predecessors, would extend his own support when qualifying the motivating passion of inquiry in his main work. For the "more specific character ... of the astonishment that urges us to philosophise," he would write in the *World as Will and Representation*, is "at bottom one that is dismayed and distressed." And the reason for this, Schopenhauer would suggest, is that it receives its fundamental provocation from the spectacle of suffering, and human evil.[3] Here, indeed, we may no longer be comfortable speaking of wonder, and like Schopenhauer's translator E. F. J. Payne – who exhibited some vacillation, translating the same word (*Verwunderung*) now as "wonder," now as "astonishment" – we may need to talk, with Schopenhauer, of an astonishment; an estrangement; a kind of horror.

Yet even if we recognise that particular philosophies and individual philosophers take their starting point and are carried forward within their inquiry by responses of wonder, or astonishment, or perplexity that are different in kind and object, it might now be queried whether anything substantial could be gained by posing a systematic question concerning the type of astonishment at work in a particular philosopher's undertaking. For passions might stimulate inquiry, and passions might sustain it, but an investigation of these passions would seem vacuous or otiose, deflecting our attention from the content of the inquiry itself, which ought to form the real object of our investigation. It might thus appear doubtful that a concern with the specific character of a thinker's astonishment – whether the astonishment he begins from, the astonishment he seeks to produce, or indeed the false astonishment he seeks to dispel – could function as a meaningful handle for investigation.

That an explicit concern with wonder can, however, serve in such a meaningful role is a view that has begun to receive growing support in recent times, through a variety of works that have taken wonder, and a concern with the different kinds of wonder, as a category for approaching their subjects. One thinks of Lorraine Daston and Katharine Park's magisterial history, *Wonders and the Order of Nature* (1998), which plots the changing place of wonder in science and philosophy between

Greek Philosophy (Cambridge University Press, 2004), Epilogue, esp. 257ff. See also on this point Mary-Jane Rubenstein, *Strange Wonder: The Closure of Metaphysics and the Opening of Awe* (New York: Columbia University Press, 2008), ch. 1.
[3] Arthur Schopenhauer, *The World as Will and Representation*, 2 vols., trans. E. F. J. Payne (New York: Dover Publications, 1966), II:171 (hereafter cited as *WWR*).

the High Middle Ages and the Enlightenment, and in doing so tracks important intellectual transformations, notably in the practice of scientific inquiry. In philosophy, one thinks more recently of Mary-Jane Rubenstein's *Strange Wonder* (2008), which focuses on the renegotiation of wonder by Heidegger and his successors, and shows the renegotiation of the grounding mood of philosophy to be twinned to a deeper reconsideration of its task.

There are philosophers, to be sure, who have been preoccupied with the mood of their activity more strongly than others. Among recent philosophers, Heidegger is a case in point. Wittgenstein is another, for a concern with wonder would appear as a leitmotif in his later philosophy, and it would do so in the context of a similar preoccupation with the need to reorient philosophical inquiry and define its proper standpoint. The concern with wonder would thus be therapeutic in kind, aiming to heal false forms of philosophical wonder – the tendency, for example, to shroud the workings of the mind in an aura of mystique thick with its own presuppositions – and to promote a truer wonder directed to those things that are precisely "hidden because of their simplicity and familiarity" (*PI* §129), such as the phenomena of ordinary language.[4] With Heidegger, with Wittgenstein, with Plato, an explicit thematisation of philosophical mood would seem to promise itself as a fruitful grip. What, then, of Schopenhauer?

It will be one of the main tasks of the work that follows to suggest that a concern with the specific character of Schopenhauer's philosophical wonder forms an illuminating category through which to calibrate the way we read his philosophy; and that it offers an equally important handle for deciding how to engage it. For in seeking to engage Schopenhauer's philosophy, commentators have often found themselves faced with a recurring predicament, one that no doubt mirrors a more general predicament with which the history of the philosophy confronts its readers, yet that in Schopenhauer's case seems to surface with particular tenacity. In approaching philosophers of the past, we are often naturally driven towards an effort to draw them into a conversation that will take place in our language, one that will speak to our concerns and answer to our standards. And in the context of present-day philosophy, this has often meant: standards in which the quality of argument carries the strongest privilege.

---

[4] *PI* = Ludwig Wittgenstein, *Philosophical Investigations*, trans. G. E. M. Anscombe, P. M. S. Hacker, and J. Schulte, rev. 4th edn by Hacker and Schulte (Oxford: Wiley-Blackwell, 2009).

It is this prevailing understanding of philosophical excellence that has been expressed in many of the most distinguished efforts to engage Schopenhauer philosophically in the recent past; one thinks of the work of D. W. Hamlyn, Bryan Magee, Christopher Janaway, or Julian Young, to mention but a few. The focus, within such efforts, has often fallen on core aspects of Schopenhauer's philosophical scheme, to take these critically to task and assess them for their coherence or justificatory force. Yet it is an approach that has often appeared to be brought into tension by the success of its own techniques, which reveal Schopenhauer's claims to be vulnerable to multiple stress fractures upon the lightest probing. And in placing the coherence of Schopenhauer's philosophy in doubt, such approaches simultaneously raise a question concerning Schopenhauer's claim to serious philosophical attention, and to gaining a hearing from a contemporary audience that has after all many contenders among whom it must distribute its finite energies.

This has not been the sole type of reading that Schopenhauer's works have called forth, and there has been a different body of reactions, more motley in kind and intellectual orientation, which have often shared few positive features other than attesting an attunement to Schopenhauer's philosophy in which the quality of its argument is *not* the most important concern. One thinks, here, of shorter glosses like Iris Murdoch's meditative discussion of Schopenhauer in her *Metaphysics as a Guide to Morals*, or Terry Eagleton's fiery account in *The Ideology of the Aesthetic*. One thinks, likewise, of some of the later works of his German readers, such as Rüdiger Safranski's compassionate biography or Arthur Hübscher's scrupulous yet wistfully admiring intellectual history. One thinks, inescapably, of the impassioned and mercurial reactions of Schopenhauer's best-known reader, Nietzsche.[5]

It is against the background of this larger question about how the philosophy of Schopenhauer should be engaged that the present study unfolds, and its task can be understood as an effort to spell out more explicitly this alternative type of attunement. Or more accurately, and more modestly: to spell out what I take to be one of the most illuminating ways of specifying it – and this, indeed, is as an attunement to a wonder of a very particular

---

[5] I am referring to Iris Murdoch, *Metaphysics as a Guide to Morals* (London: Penguin Books, 1993), 57–80; Terry Eagleton, *The Ideology of the Aesthetic* (Oxford: Blackwell, 1990), 153–72; Rüdiger Safranski, *Schopenhauer and the Wild Years of Philosophy*, trans. E. Osers (Cambridge, MA: Harvard University Press, 1991); and Arthur Hübscher, *The Philosophy of Schopenhauer in its Intellectual Context: Thinker against the Tide*, trans. J. T. Baer and D. E. Cartwright (Lampeter: Edwin Mellen Press, 1989).

kind. My main argument rests in the simple claim that Schopenhauer's philosophical practice, to be adequately characterised, needs to be located within the framework that his own aesthetics makes available, and more specifically, within that particular aspect of his aesthetics that consists in the experience of the sublime. Schopenhauer's philosophical standpoint can be understood as an exercise in vision that Schopenhauer's own analysis of the sublime – with its peculiar configuration of the terrible and the exulting, and its peculiar constitutive insight – provides us with the best structure for approaching.

Locating Schopenhauer's standpoint in this context, I will argue, allows us to place his philosophical undertaking in clearer light on many levels. It allows us to understand the philosophical subject that Schopenhauer's work constructs for itself, and to thematise revealingly the relationship between the subject and the content of its philosophical representation. It allows us to grasp the task of philosophy more distinctly and to rewrite it as one that has a therapeutic of wonder at its heart – a therapeutic of the passions that is simultaneously a therapeutic of the subjectivity that underpins them. It allows us, similarly, to recognise the dialectic of pride and vulnerability as the subtext and affective backbone of Schopenhauer's philosophical undertaking. And it allows us, finally, to understand our own reactions to Schopenhauer's philosophy, despite or indeed because of its terrible content.

With this reading of Schopenhauer's philosophical vantage point in place, one may confront in new terms the question concerning how this vantage point stands to be constructively engaged. My proposal will be that for this to be done, Schopenhauer's standpoint needs to be anchored in a broader context, and to be aligned with an epistemic ideal boasting a longer philosophical lineage. More specifically, the vantage point *sub specie aeternitatis* that Schopenhauer constructs in his work needs to be connected to a privileged notion of ascent that had been etched deeply in the thinking of ancient philosophers – among Platonists, Stoics, and Epicureans – and had found direct expression in the imaginary of "flights of the soul" and in the more programmatic cultivation of what Pierre Hadot has described as a "view from above" or "cosmic consciousness." Connecting Schopenhauer's standpoint to this history, however, involves connecting it to a strongly *ethical* context, given the profound ethical significance and indeed transformative power with which the occupation of this standpoint was vested in ancient philosophy.

Yet it is more specifically, I will argue, the thick ligaments tying this standpoint to one particular element of the ancient ethical outlook – namely, to the virtue of greatness of soul or *megalopsychia* – that provide us with the richest resources for approaching Schopenhauer's standpoint. It is an approach that would offer itself as an appropriation conditioned by critique, seeking to place Schopenhauer in a kind of dialogue with the ancient ethical tradition that responds to Alasdair MacIntyre's understanding of the "continuities of argument" that constitute traditions in general. Locating Schopenhauer's vantage point within this longer tradition enables us, on the one hand, to articulate the value of this standpoint more clearly and thus find the motives for its appropriation, tying its value to its capacity as a location of self-knowledge. At the same time, it enables us to critically approach Schopenhauer's specific articulation of this standpoint as an expression of ethical choice, and of a specific kind of character – a character for whom self-knowledge is sterile, for whom the "view from above" is constituted as a "view from nowhere," for whom ascent fails to lead to redescent and re-engagement. And to the extent that Schopenhauer's modification of the ancient standpoint is in great part our own – a modified standpoint expressing, it has often been said, the "homelessness" of a newly disenchanted, freshly secularised world – to critique its character is to open the possibility of asking how this peculiarly modern space can be differently negotiated. My own proposal, located against MacIntyre's revisionary account of the virtues, will take the form of an argument (or an adumbration of one) that the ancient philosophical understanding of greatness of soul, taken as a character trait that regulates the attitudes of hope and despair with which we respond to epistemic uncertainty, offers itself precisely as an ethical ideal for negotiating that space.

What follows is a brief overview of the stages of the argument chapter by chapter. The main task of the first chapter is to set the stage by providing an overview of Schopenhauer's philosophy, focusing on the characterisation of Schopenhauer's standpoint as "subjective" or "inward-looking," and singling out Schopenhauer's account of aesthetic experience for special attention. Chapter 2 launches into the main argument, taking as a point of departure Schopenhauer's discussion of the fear of death and his proposal for resolving it. A closer examination of Schopenhauer's discussion reveals the presence of an "objective" or "outward-looking" standpoint within his account, one that is rich in visual elements and carries more positive valence than Schopenhauer's programmatic avowal of the subjective standpoint of philosophy prepares us to assume. Studied more carefully, this objective standpoint turns out to be affiliated to the privileged mode of surveying that Schopenhauer understood as aesthetic in kind. The conclusion that Schopenhauer's philosophical standpoint participates in the aesthetic is supported by a more systematic survey of the evidence, including the so-called "argument" from analogy that plays a pivotal role in Schopenhauer's development of his metaphysical position.

Chapter 3 picks up where the previous chapter left off to qualify its reading further, focusing on a narrower set of "physiognomic" features within Schopenhauer's work that construct a philosophical standpoint offering a holistic representation of the world in its infinite vastness from a location seemingly outside it. This standpoint, I argue, stands to be linked with Schopenhauer's discussion of the sublime, and participates in its basic structure, in which the mind overcomes the world through an act of understanding that reveals the world in its dependence, and the mind as the true object of sublimity. In the double act of cognising the world and pronouncing judgement on it – "it ought not to be" – the mind asserts its dominion over the world to which it had formerly appeared vulnerable. This understanding of Schopenhauer's standpoint, which meshes with a privileging of the notions of "height" and "ascent" pervasive in Schopenhauer's outlook, reveals the philosophical subject in a transformed identity in which the embedded viewpoint of individuality has been transcended.

Chapter 4 turns to confront the question how Schopenhauer's philosophy stands to be most fruitfully approached. Having placed this question in the framework of a larger concern with the way we approach philosophers of the past, I offer a conspectus of some of the most important recent efforts to engage Schopenhauer philosophically for an English-speaking audience, and of the challenges these have faced given the limitations of Schopenhauer's arguments and of his positions considered as rationally justified claims. Yet these limitations, I suggest, on the one hand need to be located against Schopenhauer's own disavowal of argument in his philosophical method and conception of philosophical excellence. On the other hand, they point us to another way of reading Schopenhauer's claims, namely as expressive in nature, both in the narrower sense of an expression of personal character, but also in the broader sense of an expression of far-reaching social and spiritual conditions that still define our present. A closer critical examination of the content and grounds of Schopenhauer's pessimism provides further evidence in this regard.

With this ground covered, Chapter 5 restates the question – how (why) read Schopenhauer? – and proposes to look for an answer specified in ethical terms. After considering some prominent ethical readings Schopenhauer's philosophy has received in the past and addressing their peculiar challenges, I suggest that a more promising way of approaching Schopenhauer ethically can be identified by looking towards the aesthetic reading of Schopenhauer's philosophy offered, and more specifically towards its "sublime" vantage point. Yet this requires that we connect this vantage point to one receiving wide expression in ancient philosophy, where the notion of "ascent" had carried a similar privilege, surfacing in the works of Plato and his successors among the Stoics and Epicureans with varying degrees of distinctness and strength as an imaginary of cosmic flight or holistic representation. This imaginary, and the capacity for moral and intellectual transcendence revealed in it, was in turn linked to the ethical ideal of grandeur or greatness of soul. It is this ideal, I suggest, that provides us with the resources for a critique of Schopenhauer's standpoint, one that presents itself as a critique of its ethical character.

It is the task of Chapter 6 to place this critique within the horizon of an appropriation, and to articulate an alternative ethical proposal in positive terms. This proposal rests on taking the core tension to lie in the notion of dignity or self-esteem, and to centre on a dialectic between mastery and vulnerability that is a dialectic between pride and humiliation. Schopenhauer's philosophical decisions, in such terms, can be read as expressions of a desire for mastery that involves an intolerance of vulnerability and its enforced passivity. An alternative decision would lie in a different negotiation of vulnerability, and of the dialectic of dependence and transcendence, and would include an embrace of epistemic vulnerability directly opposed to the intellectual closure typifying Schopenhauer's philosophy. Opened up by such an act of intellectual humility, the philosophical vantage point *sub specie aeternitatis* becomes a space in which different responses are possible. Looking to the tradition of greatness of soul can enable us to articulate more distinctly the notion of hope – a hope for the good that I follow MacIntyre in understanding as a quest for the good – as the content of an alternative way of responding, and as a virtue whose exercise might allow this vantage point to fully regain its ancient character as a location for "questing" and self-knowledge.

CHAPTER I

A riddle and its answer

The inward turn of philosophy and the metaphysics of the will

He has come to be known to us as the philosopher of pessimism; the philosopher who brought up life for question only to utter a "No" as his adamantine response. But for Schopenhauer, it all began with a look inward. My aim in this chapter will be to consider that inward look, taking it as an opening to Schopenhauer's philosophy. Having called up Schopenhauer's philosophy in broad outlines, the stage will be set for the narrower questions about its character that will form the heart of my concern.

In what sense might one then speak of an inward look in considering Schopenhauer's philosophy? To this question, seasoned readers of this region of philosophical history would no doubt respond by pointing to Schopenhauer's immediate context, and to those of Schopenhauer's predecessors to whom he himself would be most vocal in professing his intellectual debts. For it was Kant's philosophy that had provided Schopenhauer with his most formative apprenticeship, and it would be as an heir and claimant to Kant's legacy that Schopenhauer would persist in presenting his own work. And among the most potent elements in this intellectual bequest would be the "Copernican revolution" that Kant had effected in proclaiming that, contrary to traditional philosophical understanding, it was not our knowledge that conformed to objects, but objects to our knowledge. Properties that had formerly been ascribed to things themselves and to realities outside our minds – such as time and space – in fact constituted nothing but the forms of our knowledge and the conditions of our experience.

This ground-shaking thought would form the kernel of Kant's transcendental idealism, and it was linked to a revised understanding of what the task of philosophy was, and what it could hope to be. Traditional metaphysics, blind to this insight, had used the categories of understanding

9

to investigate matters that lie outside our experience, aspiring to answer questions about God, the soul, or immortality. Kant's notion of critical or transcendental philosophy counterposed the claim that the sole ambition of philosophy must henceforth lie in investigating the forms conditioning our experience, of which we have *a priori* knowledge. This inversion of philosophical focus – setting the ground spinning by redirecting inquiry away from objects of knowledge to their representing subject – was in turn linked with a distinction counting equally among Kant's most significant and indeed provocative conceptual bequests, namely, the distinction between phenomena and noumena.

For while we may be confined to the phenomenal realm, and while we can never get past the way things appear to us in order to discover the reality of how things are in themselves, we still possess such a notion – a notion of "how things are in themselves," and not *merely* how they appear relative to the forms of our knowledge. The very notion of the phenomenal seems to presuppose the notion of the noumenal as its non-intuitable basis and as the ground against which it is possible to distinguish it. Or as Kant put it in his second Preface to the *Critique of Pure Reason*, without such a notion of the noumenal, "we should be landed in the absurd conclusion that there can be appearance without anything that appears." Hence, although we may not "*know* ... objects [of experience] as things in themselves, we must yet be in a position at least to *think* them as things in themselves."[1] It was a distinction that would occupy a crucial place in Kant's account of practical reason and his view of human freedom and the possibility of moral agency.

Schopenhauer hailed this distinction as "Kant's greatest merit" (*WWR* I:417), and embraced wholeheartedly Kant's inversion of philosophical standpoint and its central insight that "the beginning and the end of the world are to be sought not without us, but rather within" (*WWR* I:420–21). This thought was the cornerstone of transcendental or critical philosophy, which Schopenhauer defined as "every philosophy that starts from the fact that its nearest and immediate object are not things, but only man's *consciousness* thereof" (*PP* II:9),[2] and whose beginnings – the first blossoming of an "*inwardly*" directed philosophy" that starts "from the subject as that which is immediately given" – he located as early as Descartes (*PP* II:17; cf. *WWR* II:4).

[1] Immanuel Kant, *Critique of Pure Reason*, trans. N. K. Smith (Basingstoke: Palgrave, 1929), Bxxvi.
[2] *PP* = Arthur Schopenhauer, *Parerga and Paralipomena*, 2 vols., trans. E. F. J. Payne (Oxford: Clarendon Press, 1974).

This, then, was the inward turn that Schopenhauer would be among many to inherit from Kant's work. Yet like many others, he would soon experience the abatement of what his biographer Rüdiger Safranski refers to as the first "euphoria" that accompanied the discovery of the "world-creating ego" – a euphoria, after all, that, having arisen in the space created by the destruction of old intellectual securities about the human capacity for understanding the world, already harboured the possibility of something darker.[3] Like many, Schopenhauer would soon begin to chafe at the imperative of confining oneself to mere knowledge of the subjectively conditioned world, and would return to that mesmeric divide set up by Kant between phenomena and things-in-themselves to study it more carefully. And leaning closer, he would discover that it let in a draught.

For Kant had declared traditional metaphysics, conceived as an inquiry into what lies beyond the forms of our knowledge, to be impossible. Yet Schopenhauer now declared this to be a premature defeat. How, after all, could such philosophical quietism be accepted so long as one remained alive to one's deepest philosophical responses? For "the world and our own existence present themselves to us necessarily as a riddle" (*WWR* 1:427); and this riddle cannot simply be abandoned. It was not, however, metaphysics of the traditional sort that Schopenhauer was interested in pursuing, or rehabilitating. For on the road Kant had opened, there was no turning back. Yet what was required was to see that this road did not end in blockade; that from Kant's central insight, the wholesale abdication of metaphysics did not follow. And that required placing in question Kant's account of what metaphysics must involve and rejecting it as unjustifiably restrictive. As Kant would have it: "The source of metaphysics cannot be empirical at all; its fundamental principles and concepts can never be taken from experience, either inner or outer" (*ibid.*, quoting Kant's *Critique of Pure Reason*). This description Schopenhauer took to be a question-begging one; and his counter was given in the claim that an understanding of what underlies the phenomenal – namely, the noumenon or thing-in-itself – was eminently possible, precisely through an examination of experience itself.

The remark just quoted already contained the germ of Schopenhauer's proposal; and in fleshing this out, we move closer to a stronger specification of the "inward turn" of Schopenhauer's philosophy and what we may term its "subjective" or inward-looking character. For it could not be by examining the world as the obsolete "objective" philosophy had

---

[3] Safranski, *The Wild Years of Philosophy*, 111, and see generally ch. 7.

attempted to do that the knowledge of its inner nature could be acquired. To the extent that such an outward-turned philosophy relied on our representations of the world, it remained captive to the forms of knowledge that condition these representations – namely time, space, causality, and the fact of being object for a subject – and could not go beyond them. "In consequence of all this," Schopenhauer asserted,

> on the path of *objective knowledge*, thus starting from the *representation*, we shall never get beyond the representation, i.e. the phenomenon. We shall therefore remain at the outside of things; we shall never be able to penetrate into their inner nature, and investigate what they are in themselves, in other words, what they may be by themselves. (*WWR* I:195)

It was not by looking "outwards" to "the vastness of the world and the infinitude of its beings" (*PP* II:16) that we could therefore get to the unconditioned. Rather, this was to be accomplished by examining "inner" experience or what Schopenhauer elsewhere terms "facts of self-consciousness." The claim was that there was a particular mode of access that the subject had to himself that was non-representational and transcended the division between subject and object, and that could take us past the phenomenal to show us what lay beyond. This access, declared Schopenhauer with a firework display of his characteristic *élan*, throws open before us "a subterranean passage, a secret alliance" that places us "as if by treachery" (*WWR* II:195) within the seemingly impregnable fortress – the thing-in-itself – that we had hitherto tried unavailingly to storm "from without."

This was the background to Schopenhauer's heady claim to have discovered, through just such an examination of inner experience, that the inner nature of the world is *will*. It was a heady, startling claim – and a claim whose very grammar would seem to defy its intuitive absorption. Yet Schopenhauer's discovery was ultimately grounded in the remarking of a fact so ordinary and familiar as to seem perfectly unremarkable. He called it "the most intimate fact of self-consciousness" (*WWR* II:183); and that is the fact that we will.

Our first reaction to this claim might be to pose a question that would echo one earlier framed by Stanley Cavell when describing Wittgenstein's actuating philosophical astonishment. "What motivates Wittgenstein to philosophise," Cavell writes, "what surprises him, is the plain fact that certain creatures have speech at all, that they can say things at all." Yet "it is not clear," he continues, "how one might go about becoming surprised by such a fact."[4] What surprises Schopenhauer, we might say, is that we

---

[4] Stanley Cavell, *The Claim of Reason: Wittgenstein, Skepticism, Morality, and Tragedy* (Oxford University Press, 1979), 15; the continuation of this remark suggests an answer to this question. Cf.

will at all; but persisting in our echoing resumption of Cavell, we may now ask: how might one go about being surprised by such a thing? What would it mean to think it away, or step back from it far enough to then be capable of being struck by it?

Central to that act of remarking and to Schopenhauer's metaphysical discovery was what we might call a thought experiment, which proceeded by summoning a purely objective viewpoint and applying it to the human body and its actions. It was "objective" in being specified as the vantage point of an observer whose only access to the world was that of having it as object of representation (as object for subject). Now, if we were to imagine a world in which we only existed as representing beings – only as "knowing subjects" – to whom the world was available or "significant" only in so far as it crossed the threshold to becoming perceived through the mediation of our forms of knowledge, "this body [would be] a representation like any other, an object among objects." Considered in this manner, it would be the case that

> [the body's] movements and actions are so far known to him in just the same way as the changes of all other objects of perception; and they would be equally strange and incomprehensible to him, if their meaning were not unravelled for him in an entirely different way. Otherwise, he would see his conduct follow on presented motives with the constancy of a law of nature, just as the changes of other objects follow upon causes, stimuli and motives. He would be no nearer to understanding the influence of the motives than he is to understanding the connection with its cause of any other effect that appears before him. (*WWR* I:99)

But this, Schopenhauer continues, is a counterfactual state of affairs:

> All this … is not the case; on the contrary, the answer to the riddle is given to the subject of knowledge appearing as an individual, and this answer is given in the word *Will*. This and this alone gives him the key to his own phenomenon, reveals to him the significance and shows to him the inner mechanism of his being, his actions, his movements. (*WWR* I:100)

We are invited, then, to imagine a counterfactual state of affairs in which we look upon "our" acts objectively as representations.[5] We watch "our" hands stretch out towards items piled on the dinner table, the veins in "our" neck bulge when another strikes "our" face; we watch a body

---

Wittgenstein's "Lecture on ethics," *Philosophical Review*, 74 (1965), 11, which provides the basis for this attribution.

[5] Given the sequence of this reasoning, Schopenhauer's use of "our" or "his" to refer to the conduct or body in question is rather paradoxical, as John E. Atwell points out in *Schopenhauer on the Character of the World: The Metaphysics of Will* (Berkeley and Los Angeles: University of California Press, 1995), 84–85.

regularly approach the naked body of another, or note a pulse regularly quicken as a body steps out before dozens of spectators on a stage. Across time, such correlations (assuming that one could even succeed in characterising them in purely objective terms) are reliably sustained. Yet into the causal nature of these concatenations as they unfold before our eyes, we have no more insight than into the sequence of any other natural events taking place in the world around us – the magnet that pulls the metal to itself, the ball that traces an arc in the air and returns to the ground, the moon that moves inexorably in its orbit. From that perspective, actions seem to follow one another with a lawlike constancy that might provoke in us the same astonishment we now sometimes experience at the terrible infallibility of natural laws (see *WWR* I:133–34). One is a phenomenon to oneself like any other, one's actions as strange as the sequence of any other natural events.

The objective vantage point summoned here is one of which the first book of the *World as Will and Representation* might be seen as providing an extended discursive expression, in so far as it takes the aspect of the world as representation as its exclusive focus. Writing in this context, Schopenhauer introduces the notion of the body as "object proper," which seems to anticipate and form the foundation of the thought experiment conducted at the opening of the second book. The knowledge we have of our body as "object proper" is one in which we know our own body as a "representation of perception in space," and thus as a representation like any other, through the material provided by the senses to the understanding, "as by the eye seeing the body, or the hand touching it" (*WWR* I:20).

"The eye," "the hand," "the body" – generalising idioms of philosophical diction, perhaps, but also ones that, in the context that follows, come to carry the ghostly import of a body not yet rescued from the domain of brute fact and claimed as a centre of experience. It is this ghostly picture of an eye seeing a body without yet knowing it as the body from which it sees, and a hand touching flesh that it does not yet know will yield feeling it will experience as its own – it is this picture that is at the heart of the experiment in objective vision just described, in which it is not the body as static object but the body in time (in its actions and movements) that forms the proper subject of the experiment.

And what this objective vantage point is designed to do is to make the perceived connection between motives and action appear occult, and thus make us feel the need for a mode of access to ourselves that would go beyond the phenomenon. Or rather, it is designed to make us see with sudden clarity the mode of non-representational access that we actually possess and that we merely imagined away in this process. Having estranged one's actions through this vantage point, one has in fact estranged one of two separate modes of access to the body. For "the body is given in two entirely different ways ... in intelligent perception as representation ... [and] as what is known immediately to everyone and is denoted by the word *will*" (*WWR* I:100). In seeing ourselves from an objective observer's point of view, we momentarily abstract from the latter, in order to then restore it when struck by the strangeness of our own bodily actions. We then recover the fact of our willing that grounds our subjectivity – that is to say, our access to our body from the inside. And by willing, Schopenhauer specified, we are to understand "not only willing and deciding in the narrowest sense, but also all striving, wishing, shunning, hoping, fearing, loving, hating, in short all that directly constitutes our own weal and woe, desire and disinclination" (*WWR* II:202). It is these psychological facts – intimate and immediate facts of self-consciousness – that give meaning to our actions and render them inexplicable. Or as Schopenhauer put the claim more strongly: it is these psychological facts that *are* our actions. For these two are distinguished through our mode of epistemic access, but they are identical in reality.[6]

---

[6] See the discussion in *WWR* I:99–103. My construal of this key moment in terms of a thought experiment that foregrounds introspective access might not go unchallenged, as it would seem to conflict with certain other interpretations, notably Julian Young's in *Willing and Unwilling: A Study in the Philosophy of Arthur Schopenhauer* (Dordrecht: Martinus Nijhoff, 1987). Young construes the "discovery" of the will effected in moving from the objective to the subjective viewpoint in terms of a person's *character*, this being what, "from the subjective point of view, underlies the regularities in our behaviour in just the way in which, from the objective point of view, character does" (53). Yet this proposal cannot be right, most obviously because the notion of character does not offer an access to oneself in which one's actions do *not* seem to "follow on presented motives with the constancy of a law of nature." As Young himself notes, to grasp one's character is to see oneself precisely in a *nomological* light, in a way that is achieved not through privileged introspective access but through observation also accessible to third persons (see his limpid discussion of this point at 57–59). Schopenhauer has stressed the language of first-person or experiential access throughout: in talking of our access to "what is known *immediately* as will" (*WWR* I:100); in saying that "the body occurs *in consciousness* in quite another way" (*WWR* I:103); in his claim to start from direct and intuitive knowledge (*WWR* I:452), which knowledge of character is not; in his remarks about access "from within" and about the study of "inner experience" to gain metaphysical insight; in his remarks about the concept of will proceeding "from the most immediate consciousness of everyone" (*WWR* I:112), or about "the *inward* observation we have of our own will" (*WWR* II:196) (all emphasis added). Compare Georg Simmel, *Schopenhauer and Nietzsche*, trans. H. Loiskandl, D. Weinstein, and M. Weinstein (Urbana and Chicago: University of Illinois Press, 1991), 22: "the will as radical interiority"; and Patrick Gardiner's remark, *Schopenhauer* (Harmondsworth: Penguin Books, 1963), 56. See also Moira Nicholls' critical remarks in "Schopenhauer, Young, and the Will," *Schopenhauer-Jahrbuch*, 72 (1991), esp. 148.

This insight might be put more broadly as the observation that we have a particular vantage point on the world, that there is a bit of world to which we relate in a special way, and not merely as object to subject. This special way, which at the same time constitutes the ground for our individuality, is by possessing it as our body. The world does not appear neutrally or objectively as it might otherwise have done, because we experience it as subjects that can be affected by pain or pleasure. The body is after all nothing but a sum total of potentialities of pain and pleasure. And that is another way of saying: to be embodied is to will. Willing is not something we do, but something we are, for our embodied condition leaves us no choice as to whether to will or not, and to will certain worldly events as against others. Put differently – and anticipating Schopenhauer's more saturnine denouement – to have a body is to have an inalienable vulnerability, and be subject to the grim necessity of experiencing the action of the world on oneself as something that has positive or negative value. Given the body, there is no possibility of neutrality in the world. At the root of it all, then, is the realisation that one is not "a winged cherub without a body," but rather "he himself is rooted in [the] world," his knowledge "given entirely through the medium of a body, and the affections of this body ... the starting-point for the understanding in its perception of the world" (*WWR* I:99).

This, then, was Schopenhauer's claim – and it is a claim that, in locating the starting point of reflection in the human being and the human body, has often been seen as Schopenhauer's most original philosophical contribution. Schopenhauer's momentous next move was to announce that what we had discovered within our consciousness by means of a non-representational access must constitute the thing-in-itself that lies beyond phenomena altogether, and to declare the will to be the inner nature of all things, and the whole visible world to be nothing but its objectification. Underpinning this heady claim was a movement that appeared to carry a stepwise or sequential character, proceeding from the individual subject's discovery of their own inner nature to first extend this insight, via a rejection of solipsism, to other human beings. If one's own nature is will – if willing is "the key to his own phenomenon" (*WWR* I:100) – the fact that one has privileged access to a single phenomenon offers no reason for thinking that the inner nature of other phenomena should be any different from one's own. In the next stage, this insight was extended to all other beings, and rejecting any notion of human uniqueness, the key to the human phenomenon became the key to the whole world. Moving forward in this manner, one came to recognise all natural phenomena, whether organic and inorganic, whether plants or animals, down to the basic forces of nature – "the force that turns the magnet to the North Pole," as much as "the force that appears in the elective affinities of matter as repulsion and attraction, separation and union, and finally even gravitation" – as sharing the same inner nature, and one recognised them "as that which is immediately known to him so intimately and better than everything else, and where it appears most distinctly is called *will*" (*WWR* I:110). It was this climactic moment that gave meaning to Schopenhauer's epigrammatic admonition that "we must learn to understand nature from ourselves, not ourselves from nature" (*WWR* II:196).

About this moment of recognition or transition, there will be more to say later.[7] Yet what is more important for our immediate purposes is to take stock of what kind of claim Schopenhauer's central metaphysical "discovery" – as I have persisted in calling it – was *not*. For certainly it was a "discovery" in the sense that an insight now existed that had not been present before – an insight, as we will see in a moment, with enormous implications. And a "movement" certainly appeared to have taken place in effecting it. Yet this movement was not – philosophical movement, after Kant, could no longer be – the one familiar to us from established philosophical custom. It was not a matter of crafting arguments or proofs, or offering rational demonstrations, moving forward from a set of premises to an entailed conclusion. For all proof and explanation belonged to the reason-giving framework that constituted the principle of sufficient reason, which had application to the world of representation and concerned the relationship between different representations. To get beyond the representation, as philosophy hoped to do, one had to do away with explanation, and in doing so entirely overhaul the notions of "discovery" and "movement" involved.

It was a movement not "forward," strictly speaking, but a movement upward – and a movement characteristically deriving its impetus and starting point from something very close to home, and to immediate experience. The task of philosophy was to effect an epistemic transformation so that something known existentially or experientially – by what Schopenhauer called knowledge of perception (*anschauliche Erkenntniß*) or feeling – was "raised" to an articulate and communicable form – what Schopenhauer called knowledge of reason (*Wissen* or *Wissen der*

---

7 See Chapter 2.

Vernunft).[8] What this view of philosophy implied, Schopenhauer stated explicitly when he wrote: "it might be said that everyone knows without further help what the world is." "But this," he continued,

> is a knowledge of perception, is in the concrete. The task of philosophy is to reproduce this in the abstract, to raise [*erheben*] to a permanent rational knowledge successive, variable perceptions, and generally all that the wide concept of *feeling* [*Gefühl*] embraces. (*WWR* I:82)

Thus, the identity of the movement of the body with the act of will that stood at the heart of Schopenhauer's metaphysical claim could never be *proved*; it could merely be raised to rational apprehension (*WWR* I:102).

To our starting question, then, about the inward-looking character of Schopenhauer's philosophy, two answers have already come into view. One element of this character, as we have seen, consisted in the inward turn effected by Kant in articulating the thesis of transcendental idealism, which reoriented attention to the subject to account for the appearance of objects in the external world. But then there was Schopenhauer's further claim – entailing a separate turn inward, one that proposed to go deeper than Kant's, and in doing so led to a partial overthrow of its constraints – that we could look within us to discover, not only the forms conditioning the appearance of the world, but the very inner nature of the appearing world: the thing-in-itself. And this we could do by looking inward to the psychological facts of our self-experience – foregrounded by the thought experiment of a purely objective gaze – to which the forms of our knowledge did not (or did not wholly) condition our access.

---

[8] In referring to these terms (*Erkenntniß*, *Wissen*, as also *Anschauung*), I am following Payne. Since the core of this book was first written, a new translation of Schopenhauer's main work has begun making its way into print (ed. and trans. J. Norman, A. Welchman, and C. Janaway [Cambridge University Press, 2010]), which incorporates the decision to mark a clearer distinction between *Wissen* and *Erkenntniß* by rendering the former as "knowledge" and the latter as "cognition," and to translate *Anschauung* consistently as "intuition" rather than "perception." While it is important to effect a clearer demarcation of different terms, neither decision takes place without sacrifice; and in both cases, the greatest loss appears to concern the notion of epistemic warrant or achievement involved. "Cognition," for example, seems to focus attention on the epistemic process rather than its objects in a way that weakens the notion of achievement at stake ("I know" is an achievement as "I cognise" isn't), and undermines the accomplishment Schopenhauer packs into the apprehension ("cognition") of the Ideas. Similarly, given the broader meaning the term "intuition" carries, the abandonment of "perception" for "intuition" calls away from the direct visual confrontation of the concrete world Schopenhauer envisages and the kind of authority or epistemic warrant (cf. *WWR* I:35) attaching to it. These are ordinary-language criticisms of course, and it is a substantive question to what kind of audience a translation of Schopenhauer's works should be pitched, and how the linguistic needs of different audiences should be balanced. Yet given the above, and as this translation remains incomplete, in the present work I continue to rely on Payne's translation, and my own language in discussing Schopenhauer's views continues to gravitate towards Payne's.

It is an understanding of Schopenhauer's avowed standpoint that we must hold on to, for we will be returning to it to locate the resources for our investigation. But before doing so, we need to follow that inward look to its denouement – and to that fuller, and darker, philosophical vision that, turning outward again to the world, Schopenhauer unpacked out of that grounding knot of inner experience to offer a sweeping account of the entire panorama of existence. A panorama; yet a panorama animated throughout by a secret pulse whose nature Schopenhauer had just declared fathomed. And it was a pulse calculated, upon closer consideration, to provoke – horror. To feel this fully, all one need to do is pause over the notion of "will" forming the linchpin of Schopenhauer's vision, to grapple with the sources of one's discomfort at Schopenhauer's unconventional usage.

For to say that one may "recognise" what in oneself one calls "will" as the force operating in minerals and crystals, creeping plants and beasts in the field, or the forces of nature, clearly involves a decision to give the word "will" a very special employment. It is a usage that would appear to strain language.[9] But more important, in this context, is the way it strains self-understanding. For to apply the same term to gravity, rushing waters, and shooting plants, as well as to the doings of human beings, would seem to be to ignore the fundamental way in which human willing differs from those other cases. For human desire, unlike forces of nature, does not simply "pull" or "push," or brutely knock us around; it operates in the daylight of consciousness, and, equally importantly, in the light of reason. The movement of human desire responds to reasons; it is minded. And even if for some desires – such as those connected to the needs of the body – this might seem less obvious, for many others – whether the desire to learn a language or follow a particular calling, to take up sports or politics, to give a hand at the local soup kitchen or join the local Zen Buddhist community – its truth would seem incontrovertible.

Yet far from ignoring this seeming difference, Schopenhauer's employment of the word "will" can now be seen as a deliberate *bouleversement* of its claims, inverting the relationship of priority between reason and the will in ways that Schopenhauer knew were calculated to send tremors through human self-understanding. For if reasons or grounds may seem

---

[9] Schopenhauer's main discussion of his choice of term can be found in *WWR* I:110–12. For discussion of this choice and its strains, see for example Atwell, *Schopenhauer on the Character of the World*, 102–5; Gardiner, *Schopenhauer*, 151–52; Young, *Willing and Unwilling*, 64–66; and Christopher Janaway, "Will and nature," in Janaway, ed., *The Cambridge Companion to Schopenhauer* (Cambridge University Press, 1999).

to exist for particular desires, what must be noted is this: "*that* I will in general, or *what* I will in general" is a groundless fact (*WWR* I:106). The will itself is not only without reason, but "without consciousness" (*WWR* II:201), and it is only in man that it contingently ascends to self-awareness, a self-awareness that always then arrives after the event. The essential nature of the will – a will that constitutes us, too – is mindless. Deep at our core, push and pull – a brute pulse – forms our own essential reality. Forget weary old disputes about the distinction between animals and humans, and the relative dignity of man; every conceivable divide in the order of being has henceforth been abolished. What is essential to man – a sense of longing perpetually etched into our awareness – is something that "man has … in common with the polyp" (*WWR* II:204).

And this is to say: the torch of reason has been knocked off its place on the pyramidal apex, and the world has been plunged, to put it poignantly, in the dark of night. With reason and consciousness declared a contingent accretion to the will, the inner nature of the world reveals itself as a blind force of energy, striving without purpose. "In fact, absence of all aim, of all limits, belongs to the essential nature of the will in itself, which is essential striving." So, too, within us: "Every individual act has a purpose or end; willing as a whole has no end in view" (*WWR* I:164–65). We ourselves, it thus turns out, are nothing but embodiments of an insatiable force intrinsically incapable of satisfaction, contentment, and rest. This indeed is expressed in the phenomenology of our lives in a way that lends itself to a confirmation of metaphysics through experience. For aren't we always driven by desire? Always irresistibly striving for goals that we attain only for new ones to immediately mushroom in their place, led forward in a never-ending Sisyphean march? Satisfaction always seems like *now* it will finally arrive – after this goal has been met, after that one; but satisfaction always eludes us, and we continue to thirst on with insatiable desire and a bottomless sense of need. And in those rare moments when our desires are finally satisfied, boredom swiftly ensues to cause new malaise. We think we know why we strive. But in reality we strive because we *are* striving. "Every attained end is at the same time the beginning of a new course, and so on *ad infinitum*"; and this is the reason why: "eternal becoming, eternal flux belong to the revelation of the essential nature of the will" (*WWR* I:164). Beings whose nature it is to will are condemned to suffer.

Fated to suffer; revealed to be brute to the core, our being pulsing to the same beat as the stirrings of the polyp and the sap that rises in plants. Philosophy has always seen itself as being in the business of discovering truth. The riddle of existence, in Schopenhauer's view, had been solved. Yet after philosophical truth has been achieved, one is entitled to ask: where *to*? Or again: can this truth be lived, and enter fruitfully into our mode of living? To this question, Schopenhauer's answer took two forms, both of which appeared to modify the above view of the relationship of the human mind to the world, suggesting that the light of awareness – whose importance appeared to have been all but extinguished once assimilated into the rhythms of mindless being – had not entirely lost its place and its significance. And it was a significance all the more numinous given the view of reality that framed it, lending to the operations of the mind an aspect salvific in kind.

Yet it was not, indeed, a matter of consenting to live in the light of this truth; or of finding a way of being in a world thus described. The discovery of its true nature in fact could only lead, not to a re-embrace of the world or a more "fruitful" way of being in the world, but rather to its radical denial. Having discovered the nature of the world by looking inward, and looked outward to behold the suffering that formed its inevitable adjunct, one could only turn away from the whole spectacle in revulsion. Having succeeded in seeing the identity of the will in all phenomena, one

> knows the whole, comprehends its inner nature, and finds it involved in a constant passing away, a vain striving, an inward conflict, and a continual suffering ... that knowledge of the whole, of the inner nature of the thing-in-itself, which has been described, becomes the *quieter* of all and every willing. The will now turns away from life. (*WWR* I:379)

And to turn away from life meant to turn away from the very will pulsing within one, withdrawing one's consent to being even while remaining rooted to the body, continuing to be in the world without being of it. One's inner life was henceforth to be a still life of resignation, composure and will-lessness (*WWR* I:379), and one's outer life a consistent effort to suppress one's will and mortify bodily desire, particularly sexual desire, to the point of self-torture and self-castigation.

At the end of this road, and thus at the summit of Schopenhauer's philosophy, stood an apocalyptic vision that made plain the special – if deeply grim – place that human beings were still capable of occupying in the world of nature. For should this road be followed consistently by all – should this maxim, in Kant's idiom, become universal law – the human species would cease to reproduce and pass away; with it would pass away the animal kingdom; and with it, the world-creating subject of representation, and then the "rest of the world would of itself also vanish into nothing" (*WWR* 1:380). By bringing the will to self-knowledge in their person, and by allowing this self-knowledge to lead to the self-abolition of the will in their person, human beings had it in them, then, to bring about the redemption of the entire world.

This drastic "ascetic" solution was hard to achieve, and harder still to sustain. A second road, however, stood open – an offer of temporary, if not permanent, salvation. This was the "aesthetic" solution, which proposed aesthetic contemplation as a temporary means by which suffering could be suspended, and the human subject be "lifted" above the strivings of the will. In spelling out this proposal, Schopenhauer forged a seminal rapprochement – he would claim it, more strongly, as a synthesis – between the teaching of Kant and the teaching of the philosopher who would register as the second most prominent influence on his thought, Plato. For the centrepiece of his view of aesthetic contemplation was a notion that Schopenhauer explicitly identified as the brightest philosophical jewel adorning Plato's crown, namely, that of the "Forms" or "Ideas."[10]

It was a notion, it must be said, with which Schopenhauer would exhibit no less creative liberty than he had with the ideas of Kant, and readers of Plato might find difficulty recognising his image in Schopenhauer's appropriation. This will be immediately evident at the level of content, where one will fail to discover in Schopenhauer's construal any trace of those Ideas that played the most distinctive role in Plato's philosophy, such as the magnetic Idea of the Good in the *Republic* or the Idea of Beauty in the *Symposium*. Schopenhauer's Ideas tracked, not moral or evaluative notions, but rather the seams of the natural world.[11] The Ideas, generally characterised, consisted of "the definite species, or the original unchanging forms and properties of all natural bodies, whether organic or inorganic, as well as the universal forces that reveal themselves according to natural laws,"

---

[10] For Schopenhauer's stronger claim of synthesis, see *WWR* 1:170–76.

[11] For discussion of some of the differences between Plato's and Schopenhauer's understanding of the Ideas, see Hilde Hein, "Schopenhauer and Platonic Ideas," *Journal of the History of Philosophy*, 4 (1966). (And see now also Frank C. White, "Schopenhauer and Platonic Ideas," in B. Vandenabeele, ed., *A Companion to Schopenhauer* [Oxford: Wiley-Blackwell, 2012]. This excellent volume of essays unfortunately became available to me too late in the preparation of this work to be meaningfully engaged.) Our understanding of how deeply some of these differences cut, however, will certainly be influenced by a tension present in Plato's own works between an emphasis on the perceptual notion of vision in connection with the Ideas and an emphasis on rigorous intellectual training of a different kind. See briefly Julia Annas, *An Introduction to Plato's "Republic"* (Oxford: Clarendon Press, 1981), 238–39; and for a recent account placing renewed emphasis on visual perception, and more specifically aesthetic perception, as a means for accessing the Forms, see Nightingale, *Spectacles of Truth*.

which relate to the many individuals of this world "as the archetype ... to its copies" (*WWR* I:169).

But to understand the role of these "archetypes" in aesthetic experience, one needs to gain a clearer view of their place in Schopenhauer's metaphysics. Schopenhauer encapsulated this by describing the Ideas as "grades of the objectification of the will." Put briefly, the Ideas occupied an intermediate stage between the thing-in-itself – the will – and the plurality of particular things of this world in which the will becomes object for knowledge. These individual things exist only for our knowledge, which is governed by the four forms of time, space, causality, and that of being object for subject – the division between object and subject constituting "the first, universal, and essential form of the representation" (*WWR* I:25) in so far as every representation presupposes it. The first three forms were subordinate to the last, and were seen to be aspects of what Schopenhauer called the "principle of sufficient reason." Taken together, they acted "like a prism" – to use Robert Wicks' suggestive metaphor – "separating into fragments the undivided Will, and with kaleidoscopic patterning organize[d] the shards into a comprehensive pattern."[12] Yet as Schopenhauer's characterisation of Ideas as "grades" suggests, the fragments were distinguished in a hierarchical manner. The term "grade" was meant to capture the character of an ascent – an ascent of the essentially unconscious, striving will that wended its way upwards through the forces of nature, the inorganic world, and the plant kingdom, then through conscious animals, to culminate in the consciousness of human beings, whereupon "it finally attain[ed] to reflection for the first time with the appearance of reason" (*WWR* II:160).[13]

Within the framework just outlined, Schopenhauer drew a finer distinction, to claim that it is in fact the first three forms of knowledge that are responsible for the appearance of things as individuals. This distinction was at the heart of a claim that it was possible for these three forms to be lifted; and that what we then perceived would be no longer individual things, but the Ideas that constitute their eternal archetypes. The Ideas were intermediate between the will and the plurality of particulars in the sense that a single form of knowledge – that of being object for

12 Robert Wicks, *Schopenhauer* (Oxford: Wiley-Blackwell, 2008), 83. The inspiration for this metaphor can be seen in *WWR* I:153 ("a magic lantern"), or *WWR* II:504 ("the multiplying glasses" of time and space).

13 See Terri G. Taylor, "Platonic Ideas, aesthetic experience, and the resolution of Schopenhauer's 'great contradiction'," *International Studies in Philosophy*, 19 (1987), 46–47, for an interpretation of Schopenhauer's hierarchical view of the Ideas.

subject – separated them from the former. As such, the Ideas represented the purest objectification of the thing-in-itself.

To understand the relevance of this point for the nature of aesthetic experience and its salvific potential, however, we need to make a characteristic Schopenhauerian move, turning away from the object to consider its representing subject. For the differences in the object of knowledge corresponded to – strictly speaking, indeed, *consisted* in – differences in the knowing subject. The changes in one – from particulars to Ideas – corresponded to changes in the other. In perceiving the Ideas – the "purest" phenomenal object – one was transformed into the purest subject, "the pure subject of knowing," or what Schopenhauer also referred to as the "supporter of the world," which "does not lie in space and time" but is rather "whole and undivided in each representing being" (*WWR* I:5). It was a change, in fact, that constituted a dramatic self-transformation; and this can be fully appreciated by identifying more clearly the aspect of one's being one left behind, in a way that makes its connection to the problem of suffering plain.

For suffering comes through the body, and that is to say, through our existence as individuals. Now the mode of knowledge that we have as embodied individuals is one that is fundamentally a knowledge of relations; and that is because it is an interested knowledge, one fundamentally subservient to the will. Driven by the needs and desires of our embodied existence, what we know is always particular things in particular times and places, and how these affect us or impact on our self-interest. *This* road, which I must take for work, *this* tree in my neighbour's yard, which obstructs my sea view and I must ask him to prune, or which bears good figs in the summer. Schopenhauer's claim was that this mode of interested knowledge could be overcome, by rising from a perception of individual things to a perception of their Platonic Ideas, and this by prising them free from all relations to contemplate them in their supreme singularity as eternal forms. In achieving this vision, one gained a respite from the demands of the will. And it was an aesthetic vision that by the same token left one transformed, no longer an individual seeing the world through the prism of one's interests, but looking out to the world freely from the vantage point of one's thinnest, yet also grandest, status as a subject that represents the world – a conscious being.

The kind of transformation involved is evocatively captured in a key passage of the *World as Will and Representation* that offers a striking image of the aesthetic moment, one suffused with the significant language of "ascent."

Raised up by the power of the mind, we relinquish the ordinary way of considering things ... Thus we no longer consider the where, the when, the why, and the whither in things, but simply and solely the *what* ... [we] devote the whole power of our mind to perception, sink ourselves completely therein, and let our whole consciousness be filled by the calm contemplation of the natural object actually present, whether it be a landscape, a tree, a rock, a crag, a building, or anything else. We *lose* ourselves entirely in this object ... we forget our individuality, our will, and continue to exist only as pure subject, as clear mirror of the object, so that it is as though the object alone existed without anyone to perceive it, and thus we are no longer able to separate the perceiver from the perception, but the two have become one, since the entire consciousness is filled and occupied by a single image of perception. If, therefore, the object has to such an extent passed out of all relation to something outside it, and the subject has passed out of all relation to the will, what is thus known is no longer the individual thing as such, but the *Idea*, the eternal form. (*WWR* I:178–79)

"Raised by the power of the mind" – yet this, we should note, was a salvific effect produced by a "light of awareness" that, as in the act of resignation that responded to the realisation of the world's true nature, constituted not an exercise of reason, but an act of cognition that was intuitive or perceptive in kind. The supreme value Schopenhauer attached to art, finally, derived directly from the above account. For while the Ideas could be perceived in nature, they could be perceived in a heightened and more effective form through the medium of art, whose aim Schopenhauer identified as the communication of Platonic Ideas that the artist – endowed with superior aesthetic vision – had distilled from particular things and sought to express.

Aesthetic contemplation

This, then, was the way in which one could respond to the metaphysical truth about human existence to render the latter – if only temporarily – liveable. The aesthetic solution, it will be clear, was the only response that could count as a "positive" proposal for a way of being in the world in light of the answer to the riddle of the world, even if it was a proposal that appeared to bear the character of a grudging compromise, and even if what it proposed as a way of being in the world consisted in an irruption of absence, or what we might call a temporary death. It will be one of the main aims of the discussion that follows to suggest that the aesthetic vantage point has an important role to play in Schopenhauer's own philosophy – a role that may indeed lead us to reappraise our understanding of what is "grudging" or even "temporary" in the contemplative act involved. Given the importance of the aesthetic viewpoint in the following, it is worth pausing over Schopenhauer's aesthetics to bring it into clearer view. My account here does not aim to be comprehensive, and my strategy will be to focus on certain distinctive features, and even more so, certain definitive tensions.

The linchpin passage of the *World as Will and Representation* we have just left behind (1:178–79) can serve us here as the best point of entry. For in many respects, this passage seems to present us with a compelling paradigm for understanding aesthetic experience on Schopenhauer's terms. It is a picture of disarming simplicity: the individual stands before an object, excised from its relations to the world, and loses himself in the image; the environing world disappears. Studied more attentively, however, this picture turns out to be a deceptive one, and its simplicity yields to qualifications with an important effect on how we construe Schopenhauer's account. For let us consider how aesthetic objects appear in this picture. They are (a) predominantly understood as natural kinds and (b) actually present to the observer. Both points are encapsulated in Schopenhauer's remark about "let[ting] our whole consciousness be filled by the calm contemplation of the natural object actually present, whether it be a landscape, a tree, a rock, a crag."[14] The stress on the actual presence of the contemplated objects seems to be reinforced later on in the same passage where Schopenhauer speaks of our consciousness as being filled by a "single image of perception."

Yet this, clearly, cannot offer us the whole story. For without thinking twice, the focus on natural objects already needs to be qualified to include the artistic representations of these objects. And once art has been brought into view, the exclusive focus on seeing ("a single *image* of perception") comes immediately into question, given Schopenhauer's well-known keen interest in music and the aesthetics of hearing rather than sight. Yet the focus on seeing is undermined by an additional consideration, which

---

[14] I truncate this remark to sidestep the questions raised by Schopenhauer's reference to buildings, which would seem to contradict the initial claim that aesthetic contemplation takes natural kinds as its object. It definitely appears as an anomaly in the list, and its inclusion seems even odder given that Schopenhauer denies the existence of Ideas corresponding to manufactured objects (*WWR* II:365). Yet the most plausible explanation of its inclusion lies in connecting the aesthetic experience of man-made buildings to the contemplation of the "lower" Ideas these exemplify. This is suggested by Schopenhauer himself in his discussion of architecture, where he writes that it is the lowest grades of the objectivity of the will – such as gravity, cohesion, rigidity or hardness, "those universal qualities of stone" (*WWR* I:214) – that are brought to our perception by architecture and are involved in our aesthetic apprehension; it is these that would thus represent the natural kinds in question.

Schopenhauer's discussion of the individual arts helps bring out. For a single Idea, Schopenhauer explains, can become the object of different arts under different aspects, as sculpture considers human beings under the aspect of movement, painting under the aspect of visual form, or poetry under the aspect of the character expressed in human actions. And it is the last aspect that points to something that Schopenhauer elsewhere makes explicit, namely, that certain Ideas require temporal development for the full manifestation of their nature. Aesthetic contemplation of these Ideas could hardly be conceived in terms of images fully present to the instantaneous gaze.

The Idea of an entity – as Schopenhauer emphasises in *WWR* I:181–82 and elsewhere – is constituted by what is essential to it. Yet even what is essential to a stone seems hard to divorce from the way that a stone acts under particular conditions – from dispositional terms, thus, that bear an ineliminable temporal reference.[15] And if this holds true of stones, it holds even truer of living beings. It would take more than an hour's contemplation of the sleeping form of dog to understand its nature, and far more than either to understand the nature of a human being seen at a cross-section of any given activity. Animate beings *can* be characterised through their external form, but certainly *must* be characterised through the character they display in their actions, in order for the Idea they manifest to be fully grasped. Many of these points are condensed in Schopenhauer's remark that

> to appear at the higher grades, [the Idea] requires a whole series of states and developments in time, all of which, taken together, first achieve the expression of its true being ... The plant ... does not express the Idea of which it is the phenomenon all at once ... but in a succession of developments of its organs in time. [In the case of the animal] this is first completed through the animal's actions, in which its empirical character, the same in the whole species, expresses itself and is the complete revelation of the Idea ... In the case of man, the empirical character is peculiar to every individual. (*WWR* I:155)[16]

---

[15] And if we do not grant the intelligibility of considering a stone in abstraction from its behaviour, we might find it equally hard to understand several of Schopenhauer's other lower-level examples, notably his inclusion of forces of nature among the Ideas (e.g. *WWR* I:155); for it is difficult to see how forces of nature could be understood in abstraction from their observed effects over time. Something similar could be said concerning Schopenhauer's remark about clouds, when he states that "the figures they form" are inessential to them, whereas by contrast, "that as elastic vapour they are pressed together, driven off, spread out, and torn apart by the force of the wind, this is their nature, this is the essence of the forces objectified in them, this is the Idea" (*WWR* I:182). This, of course, has given us a description of temporally extended behaviour; without it, could we even comprehend what "elasticity" – or any other dispositional property – would mean?

[16] Cf. *WWR* I:156–57, 223.

This, indeed, serves as a serious qualification to the way we read Schopenhauer's claim that "the Idea lies outside time" (*WWR* I:159) and that an Idea's "unfolding or development, because drawn apart in the forms of the principle of sufficient reason into a multiplicity of many-sided phenomena, is inessential to the Idea" (*WWR* I:182).

An important difficulty stalking the above discussion, it must be remarked, is the tension into which it brings a distinction on which Schopenhauer himself placed enormous emphasis in his aesthetics, namely that between rational and intuitive or perceptual knowledge, which corresponded to a distinction between abstract concepts and Ideas. For to talk of Ideas in terms of what is "essential" to beings, as Schopenhauer himself gives us licence to do, seems to make available a way of approaching aesthetic objects that would steer us into more familiar epistemological territory, allowing us to move away from a notion – the Platonic Idea – that commentators have often concurred in viewing as one of the most indigestibly exotic elements of Schopenhauer's aesthetics. Retaining Schopenhauer's distinction would require drawing a sharp and difficult line between "grasping the essential" seen as a rational process produced by abstraction from plural particulars, and the non-rational perception of the Idea.[17] And once our understanding of aesthetic experience is revised in the way just indicated, the boundary between rational concepts and intuitively

[17] This tension frequently clings to accounts of Schopenhauer's aesthetics. Atwell's account in *Schopenhauer on the Character of the World*, for example, is dissatisfying because it equates Ideas with "the essential aspects of particular things" and identifies the contemplation of the Ideas as the discernment of these aspects (146–48), without addressing the problematic distinction between conceptual and intuitive modes of construing this discernment. His use of the terms "type" versus "token" to characterise the relationship between Ideas and particulars (151–52) draws Schopenhauer towards a contemporary idiom calculated to obscure this distinction, undermining Atwell's own interest in arguing for the importance of the Ideas in Schopenhauer's work. Similar remarks apply to Dale Jacquette's discussion and his suggestion that imagination "generalizes perceived natural forms into typified abstract ideas," in his "Schopenhauer's metaphysics of appearance and Will in the philosophy of art," in Jacquette, ed., *Schopenhauer, Philosophy, and the Arts* (Cambridge University Press, 1996), 8; cf. 17. As Jean-Marie Schaeffer notes (*Art of the Modern Age*, trans. S. Rendall [Princeton University Press, 2000], 192–93), some of Schopenhauer's examples present special challenges to a preservation of this distinction. This connects to another persistent controversy, as to whether the Ideas have a necessary role to play in Schopenhauer's aesthetics – questioned by numerous readers. In addition to Schaeffer, see Bryan Magee, *The Philosophy of Schopenhauer* (Oxford: Clarendon Press, 1997), 238–40; Christopher Janaway, *Self and World in Schopenhauer's Philosophy* (Oxford: Clarendon Press, 1989), 278–79, and "Knowledge and tranquillity: Schopenhauer on the value of art," in Jacquette, ed., *Schopenhauer, Philosophy, and the Arts*; Gardiner, *Schopenhauer*, 203ff. A notable exemplar of this current is Young, who introduces the debate through a question as to whether Ideas are identical to or distinct from ordinary objects (*Willing and Unwilling*, 92–93), and proposes to describe the difference between particulars and Ideas in terms of different ways of attending to a given object – as a matter of "selective attention" to the essential as against the inessential.

known Ideas begins to look even less hermetic. For if time is a concept of reason – a form that belongs to the principle of sufficient reason – one might justly wonder how the perception of an entity that involves temporal progression could fail to be "rational" on Schopenhauer's terms.

For our immediate purposes, however, such questions can be put aside. For already, the above has yielded one important amendment to our initial view of aesthetic contemplation, suggesting that the aesthetic object cannot be understood as an image of perception present to the observer's instantaneous gaze, but must transcend the present through time. Yet this form of transcendence is joined by another, one that derives from attending more closely to the aesthetic experience of natural objects from the perspective of their artistic representation, or more specifically, from the perspective of the artist – the "genius" – responsible for producing them. The defining characteristic of the genius, in Schopenhauer's view, was simply a gift for seeing the world from a will-less or objective point of view – an "objective tendency of mind" (*WWR* I:185) – and thus a gift for perceiving particulars under the aspect of their Ideas, and then expressing these in artistic form. Schopenhauer would add a crucial further brushstroke to his representation of the genius, however, when naming a heightened power of the imagination (*WWR* I:186) among his constitutive intellectual traits.

The aesthetic need for imagination Schopenhauer put down, on the one hand, to the inadequacy of individual objects, which are "always only very imperfect copies of the Idea that manifests itself in them" (*WWR* I:186). Whether Schopenhauer was entitled to a distinction between perfect and imperfect copies – which would only seem coherent if Schopenhauer's Ideas, like Plato's, were assigned to a separate ontological sphere – is a question that has been debated.[18] Yet it was this that formed the ground for Schopenhauer's claim that these imperfections could be overcome by the use of the imagination, which "extends the mental horizon of the genius beyond the objects that *actually present themselves* to his person, as regards both quality and quantity" (*WWR* I:186–87; emphasis added).

A second reason why imagination came into demand stemmed from an element of chance or contingency that we might call "aesthetic luck." For the experience of a given individual will always be confined to a

---

[18] Hein, "Schopenhauer and Platonic Ideas," 139–41. For more detailed discussion of the role of imagination in Schopenhauer's view of the Ideas, see Cheryl Foster, "Ideas and imagination: Schopenhauer on the proper foundation of art," in Janaway, ed., *The Cambridge Companion to Schopenhauer*.

finite number of perceptions; and to Schopenhauer, this seems to have
carried the troubling implication that no individual could directly perceive all the particulars to which correspond permanent Ideas within
a given life, so that "the knowledge of the genius would be restricted
to Ideas of objects *actually present* to his own person" (*WWR* I:186;
emphasis added). The solution, for Schopenhauer, lay in ascribing to the
genius the preternatural ability of his imagination to "extend his horizon far beyond the reality of his personal experience, and enable him to
construct all the rest out of the little that has come into his own actual
apperception, and thus to let almost all the possible scenes of life pass by
within himself" (*WWR* I:186).[19]

This claim might strike us as an outlandish one; and the problem giving rise to it might seem as compelling or uncompelling as any of the
problems associated with human finitude. I might never see snow if I live
my life in a village in sub-Saharan Africa, or in the days before television
or zoos, I might never get to see a white tiger or meerkat in the flesh as
a European town-dweller. But then why should my failure to map the
full spectrum of the Ideas trouble me any more than my multiple other
cognitive or experiential limitations? Part of this cavil, of course, reflects
a resistance to engaging Schopenhauer's notion of the Ideas – and his cognitive ideal more broadly – on his own terms. And indeed, putting such
critical impulses aside, it seems to me that the most constructive way of
engaging this particular point is precisely by seeking to locate it more
meaningfully within this cognitive ideal, reading it as an illuminating
token (and, in terms of our account, also a foretoken) of the mental cast
that Schopenhauer made central to his salvific epistemology, and of the
persona his philosophy set up as its epistemic hero.

For if the paradigmatic picture of aesthetic experience from which we
started – a man faces an object, and loses himself in the image – seems to
present us with a contemplator riveted to the realities before him, what
should be noted is that the emphasis on imagination presents a contemplator who, significantly, transcends these realities. The aesthetic subject
leaves reality behind as "defective" and "feeble" (*WWR* II:379), overcoming

---

[19] This train of thought might illuminate an otherwise perplexing passage found in *WWR* I:180, where
Schopenhauer moves from the simple model of subject–object, person-facing-tree/crag/rock aesthetic contemplation (*WWR* I:178) to say that in contemplating we "picture to ourselves the *whole*
of the Ideas, or grades of the will's objectivity, passing though it successively" (emphasis added). It
is not clear to me how this grand cataloguing vision follows from the previous discussion, but perhaps Schopenhauer has in mind a certain deployment of the imagination such as the one discussed
in the main text.

its limitations by accessing the plenitude of reality, ranging freely over it with his mind. It is telling, in fact, having begun from the image of a man riveted to a tree or a rock (*WWR* I:178), to note the evocative words with which Schopenhauer would elsewhere sing the praises of the man of imagination, who can "call up spirits" at will instead of standing before reality in obsequious attendance, contrasting him with the "man without imagination," who is "related to him as the mussel fastened to its rock, compelled to wait for what chance brings it, is to the freely moving or even winged animal" (*WWR* I:178). A more striking image of freedom could hardly be found; nor, indeed, a more direct contrast with our starting passage. For while this image of the winged contemplator harmonises most felicitously with Schopenhauer's pervasive language of "rising" and "ascent" – the individual, he tells us, "soars aloft in this [i.e. aesthetic] contemplation" (*WWR* II:180) – it is in sharp conflict with the image of aesthetic contemplation present in our initial paradigm. As such, it reveals the drastic modification the notion of "actually present" objects has undergone, as several of the above quotations have already made plain.

What it also brings to light, however, is another important tension, pointing onward to yet another modification of our starting paradigm; and this concerns the way we understand the nature of the observer's contribution. For Schopenhauer speaks of "losing" oneself in the object, of "sinking"; elsewhere he talks about the way natural beauty "snatches" us out of ourselves. ("Whenever it presents itself to our gaze all at once, it almost always succeeds in snatching us ... from subjectivity," *WWR* I:197). Aesthetic experience, here, appears like an event that occurs to the contemplator from the outside, as it were. The subject need not act; the objects undertake the entire action for him. The metaphor of the "mirror" Schopenhauer repeatedly deploys in characterising the contemplating subject (a "clear mirror of the object") seems calculated to convey the same notion of passivity. Elsewhere, this glacial metaphor is replaced with the more sensuous metaphor of a sexual union between eye and object – a metaphor in which we may recognise the idea of a "procreative marriage between mind and nature" which, as M. H. Abrams has shown, formed a potent motif (one strongly charged with religious meaning) for several Romantic poets.[20] Yet in Schopenhauer's hands, this metaphor serves to entrench the subject's passivity, distributing the active functions to the

[20] See Meyer H. Abrams, *Natural Supernaturalism: Tradition and Revolution in Romantic Literature* (New York: W. W. Norton, 1973), esp. ch. 1. The sexual metaphor serves to cement – or in Schopenhauer's diction, to "precipitate" – the notion of a mutual infusion of object and subject that is an important motif in the discussion; see e.g. *WWR* I:178–80 ("the two have become one").

object and allocating to the contemplator a passive role: "the object in general, as that which is the male, practises a constant act of procreation on the subject, as that which is the female" (*PP* II:428).[21]

This representation of the observer's passivity is no doubt particularly serviceable to Schopenhauer's interest in upholding the claim that aesthetic experience excludes desire or volition. And yet this representation – one that would cast the ascent to aesthetic contemplation as an "in a way inexplicable" transition or spontaneous ecstasy – coexists, as several commentators have remarked, rather uneasily with other elements of Schopenhauer's account.[22] The most important of these, indeed, we have already seen. For Schopenhauer's emphasis on the imagination was accompanied by a strong accent on the subject's active contribution to the aesthetic process. In this context, we may recall that Schopenhauer had used the tell-tale notion of "constructing" – the genius is enabled "to construct all the rest out of the little that has come into his own actual apperception" – in speaking of the work of the imagination. And it is indeed relative to that extraordinary aesthetic subject that is the genius, and relative again to artistic expression, that Schopenhauer strikes the note of activity most strongly. For in that context, it is no longer beautiful objects that snatch the person, but the artist himself who snatches objects: art, writes Schopenhauer, "plucks the object of its contemplation from the stream of the world's course, and holds it isolated before it" (*WWR* I:185). What was elsewhere described as a kind of "falling" or "sinking" into an object present right before our eyes is thus seen to demand a much more active contribution. And it is a contribution, after all, that Schopenhauer's characterisation of the aesthetic object – as one released from its enmeshment in the world to be held up to the gaze – will have made us feel early in his account, in raising a question about the means by which this release could be effected.

Schopenhauer's initial template for aesthetic experience, I have been suggesting, needs to be modified in important ways; and one of the unifying themes of these modifications concerns a tension between presence and transcendence. Aesthetic objects are not present to the instantaneous

---

[21] Compare *PP* II:492, and the organic metaphors in *WWR* I:235.

[22] The phrase is Atwell's, picking up on Schopenhauer's own remarks, in *Schopenhauer on the Character of the World*, 141. Atwell stresses some of the active aspects of aesthetic perception in 150–51. For further discussion of the distinction between passive and active construals, see Paul Guyer, "Pleasure and knowledge in Schopenhauer's aesthetics," in Jacquette, ed., *Schopenhauer, Philosophy, and the Arts*, 117–22. Kai Hammermeister, in *The German Aesthetic Tradition* (Cambridge University Press, 2002), bemoans Schopenhauer's failure to distinguish clearly between passive and active elements, and concludes that Schopenhauer's discussion remains ambivalent between the two (118–19).

gaze – for they transcend the present through time; the objects present to the outer gaze are transcended through the inner gaze of the imagination, and through the activity of the subject.[23] So far, I have been focusing on Schopenhauer's general account of aesthetic experience. Yet it is by turning to that subset of aesthetic experience that forms the emotive heartland of Schopenhauer's account – the sublime – that the elements and tensions just outlined can be brought into view most sharply and most significantly. And given the crucial role the notion of the sublime will play in my later argument, it is worth articulating the issues with some attention. For if the notion of "transcendence" or that of "overcoming" – an overcoming of the poverty of the present by the free movement of the genius' mind – was present in Schopenhauer's general account, though somewhat muted and equivocal given its conflict with other elements, it is pushed to the very foreground in the experience of the sublime, where it presents itself as the principal headline.

For the experience of the sublime depends, in the first instance, on an act of self-conquest. Whereas in the merely beautiful, the "significant forms" of natural objects veritably "invite us to a pure contemplation of them" (*WWR* 1:201), in the sublime something different holds: the immediate effect of the forms of objects is not attraction, but repulsion. The objects confronting the subject in the sublime are ones that stand in a hostile relation to human beings, posing a threat to human beings in general, even if not a direct threat to the particular subject beholding them – for a real concern with personal safety would provoke a contraction of self-interest and movement of the will that would instantaneously cancel out the aesthetic posture. Yet while not immediately threatening to the individual, one's awareness of their threatening relation to human beings – of their disvalue to oneself *qua* embodied being – is such that a struggle is required in order to overcome one's resistance and confront them. One

---

[23] Even this broader statement of aesthetic experience will of course seem limited to the extent that it focuses on the visual, to the notable neglect of music. Music possesses a special though maverick position in Schopenhauer's account, as it is said to provide a copy, not of the Ideas, but of the will itself – hence indeed its special status (see Schopenhauer's discussion in *WWR* 1:255–67). Critics have suggested that the case of music reveals Schopenhauer's aesthetics to be an amalgam of conflicting conceptions. In Schaeffer's view, there are no less than three such conceptions at work, one of which corresponds to the contemplation of the Ideas and is illustrated by the visual arts (the "cognitive" conception), while another is connected with the will and is illustrated by music (the "expressive" conception): *Art of the Modern Age*, 207–8. In these terms, my account has focused on the "cognitive" conception; I hope the discussion that follows will do much to justify this focus. For more on Schopenhauer's view of music, a good starting place is Malcolm Budd's critical discussion in *Music and the Emotions* (London: Routledge & Kegan Paul, 1985), ch. 5, and the essays in Jacquette, ed., *Schopenhauer, Philosophy, and the Arts*.

must "consciously turn away" from one's will and "tear himself" from its relations to elevate oneself above it, in an act of overcoming that is then preserved linguistically in the sublime – *das Erhabene*, from *erheben*: "to raise," "to lift" – and internally as a sense of exaltation (*WWR* I:201–2).

Schopenhauer's articulation of the sublime was indebted to Kant's earlier discussion in the *Critique of the Power of Judgment* – whose account of the sublime Schopenhauer indeed singled out as its finest moment (*WWR* I:532) – but also to the longer history of seventeenth- and eighteenth-century aesthetic and literary discussions of the sublime catalysed by Boileau's 1674 translation of (pseudo-) Longinus' *Peri Hypsous*, to which Kant himself had been responding. Schopenhauer's first debt was plainly visible, for example, in his appropriation of Kant's distinction between the mathematically and dynamically sublime, the first produced by spectacles of enormous magnitude, the second by spectacles of nature's enormous power. It was also a broader debt, however, that was evident in the examples that Schopenhauer would use to illustrate both categories, which presented nature at her most vast, disordered, and powerful. Tempestuous weather, dark stormy skies, precipitous cliffs towering above, the rush of foaming water, desolate deserts, the wailing wind – this is nature at its most terrible, and it is this display of raw might, metabolised through an act of self-overcoming, that gave rise to the dynamically sublime. And it was the starry sky at night, stretching out above in its infinite vastness, that provided the mathematically sublime with its paradigm case. This, of course, was a spectacle that had occupied a special place in the Romantic "aesthetics of the infinite,"[24] one in turn immortalised by Kant in the famous words closing his *Critique of Practical Reason*: "Two things fill the mind with ever new and increasing admiration and awe … *the starry heavens above me and the moral law within me.*"

Yet what is worth registering more strongly in this connection is a rather more particular set of debts. For integral to Schopenhauer's discussion of the sublime, as it had been to Kant's before him, was a dialectic already prefigured by the theme of "overcoming" highlighted above. And this was a dialectic that had taken the experience of power and impotence, mastery and vulnerability, as its central spine. Confronted by displays of the terrible might and magnitude of nature, as human subjects we are struck by a sense of nature's power and our own vulnerability and dependence.

---

[24] The phrase is Marjorie Nicolson's, from her *Mountain Gloom, Mountain Glory: The Development of the Aesthetics of the Infinite* (Ithaca, NY: Cornell University Press, 1959). For the eighteenth-century development of the sublime from its rhetorical origins, see Samuel H. Monk, *The Sublime: A Study of Critical Theories in XVIII-Century England* (Ann Arbor: University of Michigan Press, 1960).

"[T]he irresistibility of [nature's] power certainly makes us, considered as natural beings, recognise our physical powerlessness," Kant had written in his *Critique of the Power of Judgment*. Yet "at the same time," he had continued, "it reveals a capacity for judging ourselves as independent of it and a superiority over nature ... whereby the humanity in our person remains undemeaned even though the human being must submit to that dominion."[25] In the first moment we are impressed by nature's power; in the second we rise to overcome it through a power we discover in ourselves that transcends it. And what this sequence crucially reveals is that this resurgence also arrives as a self-discovery: a discovery of (and by identifying with it, already an ascent to) an aspect of ourselves that is distinct from the one threatened by nature's might, and stands above it.

What Kant had in mind was our character as rational beings participating in the realm of the noumenal and capable of responding to the moral law. Our superiority over nature – our "dignity," which experiences of the sublime are grounded in and also prepare us for – is constituted by our moral vocation, through which we are capable of resisting the power of nature and independent of its dominion. Schopenhauer would dismiss Kant's moralised construal of human dignity and the "higher" self at stake with an impatient flick of the hand, yet he would preserve much of the architectonic structure that had supported it. Both the dialectic of power, and the metaphysical discovery and self-discovery at its heart, would be distinctly present in Schopenhauer's characterisation of our response to nature at its dynamically sublime. The storm howls; the sea roars:

> Our dependence, our struggle with hostile nature ... now appear clearly before our eyes. Yet as long as personal affliction does not gain the upper hand, but we remain in aesthetic contemplation, the pure subject of knowing gazes through this struggle of nature ... and comprehends calmly, unshaken and unconcerned, the Ideas in those very objects that are threatening and terrible to the Will.

Yet what the subject discerns through this tempest is not the Ideas alone; it is not the aesthetic objects *sensu stricto* that constitute the most important insight it contains. It is rather oneself in their mirror – oneself as the subject they entail – as the next moment reveals more clearly:

> Then in the unmoved beholder of this scene the twofold nature of his consciousness reaches the highest distinctness. Simultaneously, he feels himself as individual, as the feeble phenomenon of the will, which the

---

[25] Immanuel Kant, *Critique of the Power of Judgment*, trans. Paul Guyer and Eric Matthews (Cambridge University Press, 2000), §28, 145.

> slightest touch of these forces can annihilate, helpless against powerful
> nature, dependent, abandoned to chance, a vanishing nothing in face of
> stupendous forces; and he also feels himself as the eternal, serene subject
> of knowing, who as the condition of every object is the supporter of this
> whole world, the fearful struggle of nature being only his mental picture
> or representation; he himself is free from, and foreign to, all willing and all
> needs, in the quiet comprehension of the Ideas. (*WWR* I:204–5)

The discovery of the Ideas in the tumulting spectacle is thus a discovery
of their correlate in oneself that transcends it: one's identity as the pure
subject of knowing, on whom the world depends. And this, of course,
is nothing but a restatement of the truth of transcendental idealism.
Aesthetics has forged a pathway to metaphysics. In this process, the attrib-
ute of sublimity – in Schopenhauer now, as earlier in Kant – shifts from
the objects of the external world to the subject that holds them in his gaze.
The same pattern is seen enacted in the mathematically sublime, in a rich
passage worth quoting in full.

> If we lose ourselves in contemplation of the infinite greatness of the uni-
> verse in space and time, meditate on the past millennia and on those to
> come; or if the heavens at night actually bring innumerable worlds before
> our eyes, and so impress on our consciousness the immensity of the uni-
> verse, we feel ourselves reduced to nothing … transient phenomena of will,
> like drops in the ocean, dwindling and dissolving into nothing. But against
> such a ghost of our own nothingness … there arises the immediate con-
> sciousness that all these worlds exist only in our representation, only as
> modifications of the eternal subject of pure knowing. The vastness of the
> world … now rests within us; our dependence on it is now annulled by its
> dependence on us. All this, however, does not come into reflection at once,
> but shows itself as a consciousness, merely felt, that in some sense or other
> (made clear only by philosophy) we are one with the world. (*WWR* I:205)

As in the dynamically sublime, the mathematically sublime is an aesthetic
experience that yields metaphysical insight. To see objects aesthetically is
to see them in their dependence on our act of seeing – a "seeing-as" that,
as Schopenhauer makes clear, consists in an intuitive grasp of metaphysical truth that philosophy must then render reflective.[26]

---

[26] Kant had felt equally compelled to distinguish between different levels – intuitive as against
reflective – at which the truth of his analysis could be established, defending his view against the
charge of being excessively "far-fetched and subtle" by suggesting that the principle articulated is
evinced in our judgements even though "one is not always conscious of it": *Critique of the Power of
Judgment*, §28, 146. Note also that while the achievement of metaphysical insight may have special
significance in the sublime, Schopenhauer takes this kind of insight to inform aesthetic experience
in general: *WWR* I:181.

With the above in view, we may now return to the narrower angle we had earlier brought to Schopenhauer's general aesthetic account, questioning the nature of aesthetic objects and the subject's contribution. Now it will be clear that an emphasis on active contribution forms an ineliminable aspect of Schopenhauer's characterisation of the sublime, given the way this foregrounds the subject's act of self-overcoming. The subject must *tear* himself from his will, must *turn away* from it, and in doing so make an active contribution to aesthetic experience that unfolds this time at the level of volition rather than cognition. The acknowledgement of this type of contribution is not, it must be said, a move free from tension within Schopenhauer's scheme. For if aesthetic experience demands a suspension of the will, as Schopenhauer avows, what is the source of that active struggle – a struggle that Schopenhauer indicates must be sustained throughout, given the sublime's dependence on the constant presence, and continual overcoming, of its darker chord? Put differently, by what faculty, in this exhaustive dichotomy of will and intellect, is the transcendence of the will to be accomplished?

The most meaningful way of parsing this problem, in this case, is as a difficulty accounting for the presence of a key element in the experience – namely, emotion or affective response. For in Schopenhauer's view, all emotions represent movements of the will (*WWR* I:101, 107); and thus a perfectly will-less or disinterested aesthetic contemplation ought to involve their wholesale suppression, as Schopenhauer elsewhere explicitly stipulates (e.g. *WWR* II:367). It is notable, however, that Schopenhauer often cannot refrain from using strongly positive terms to characterise aesthetic experience, as when he speaks of the "delight" and "pleasure" objective perception occasions, of its "extremely gratifying" nature (*WWR* I:200), or its capacity to make us "positively happy" (*WWR* II:368). And if we turn to the sublime in particular, we will notice that Schopenhauer explicitly speaks of the sublime as a feeling (*das Gefühl des Erhabenen*, *WWR* I:201) – a point that instructively recalls us to the fact that an emphasis on passion had been integral to Longinus' genetic discussion.[27]

Yet even without this explicit gesture, the experience of the sublime would seem utterly incomprehensible without reference to its emotional texture given the nature of the dialectic – a dialectic of power and

---

[27] See Longinus, "On Sublimity," trans. D. A. Russell, in Russell and M. Winterbottom, eds., *Ancient Literary Criticism* (Oxford University Press, 1972), 461 (8.1), in the context of an overview of the five sources of sublimity.

vulnerability – that structures it. We cannot experience our nothingness without blinking; we cannot discover our supreme freedom from
the world without an upsurge of release or excitement, of ex*u*ltation to
match ex-*a*ltation in the physical sense. Ascent *must* be a felt experience
here. With the dialectic structuring the sublime in view, it is evident that
it is the notion of dignity or self-esteem that provides the happening of
the sublime with its main dramatic theme. The dialectic of vulnerability
and mastery, dependence and transcendence, could hardly be understood
in other terms. Surveying oneself against the infinite or powerful world,
one's self-worth suffers devastation. Conquering psychological pain, one
shoots upwards to coolly contemplate this scene. In doing so, one leaves
the demeaned husk of one's individuality behind to behold the world as
a representing subject; one thereby experiences an exultation that registers the recovery of self-worth – no longer the worth, however, of oneself
under one's aspect as an individual, but under one's universal aspect as a
conscious subject. Without the language of emotion, this drama of dignity in upheaval would make little sense.

Some commentators have taken the emotional content with which the
sublime is vested to signal the debacle of Schopenhauer's account of this
experience. So Terry Eagleton: "the more exultantly the aesthetic subject experiences its own nullity before the object the more, by that very
token, the experience must have failed."[28] A more constructive response
to this particular perplexity has been articulated by Julian Young, who
has suggested that we distinguish between two types of emotion – emotion associated with individual subjectivity, and "disassociated" or
"impersonal" emotion associated with higher supra-individual subjectivity – and that we take the emotion present in aesthetic experience to
embody the latter kind.[29]

---

[28] Eagleton, *The Ideology of the Aesthetic*, 164.

[29] Young, *Willing and Unwilling*, 88–91; it is a proposal significantly formulated with a focus on
Schopenhauer's discussion of the sublime. Paul Guyer has argued for a related revision to the view
of Schopenhauer's aesthetics, which would give a place to positive pleasure in aesthetic contemplation, in "Pleasure and knowledge"; the sublime likewise plays an important role in his discussion. Young's proposal is interestingly reminiscent of one articulated by Troels Engberg-Pedersen
in connection with the Stoics, arguing a similar type of distinction between individual or personal
("ordinary" or "unreformed") emotions and the "enlightened" emotions experienced by the Stoic
sage, who shares Schopenhauer's denigration of the passions yet is also seen to embrace certain
types of emotions. See his "Marcus Aurelius on emotions," in J. Shivols and Engberg-Pedersen,
eds., *The Emotions in Hellenistic Philosophy* (Dordrecht: Kluwer Academic Publishers, 1998), 305–
37. A different set of questions about the role of emotion in aesthetic experience emerges in connection with music, where, as Budd suggests, the expression of emotion plays an essential role in
Schopenhauer's understanding; see his discussion in *Music and the Emotions*, ch. 5.

Whatever difficulties it might occasion for Schopenhauer's account in its wake, however, what should be retained is that Schopenhauer's emphasis on the struggle internal to the sublime entails an important accent on the subject's active contribution to the experience. Yet this, it may now be added, is certainly not the only level on which this accent is sounded; and we can readily see this by considering how the objects of the sublime relate to our earlier discussion of the simple view of aesthetic objects as "images of perception" that are "actually present" to the observer. Some of the objects of sublime experience, to be sure, would appear to fit that simpler bill without having to bend too far. This would hold particularly true of the examples adduced to illustrate the dynamically sublime: towering mountains, steep cliffs. Foaming waves and stormy skies might slowly begin to stretch the boundaries of the visual, introducing a temporal extension demanding transcendence of the present. One subset of the examples employed by Schopenhauer to illustrate the mathematically sublime might also appear capable of being accommodated within the boundaries of that simpler paradigm – one thinks of Schopenhauer's account of enclosed spaces in grand edifices, like St Peter's in Rome and St Paul's in London (*WWR* I:206), where the object seems fully available to the present gaze.

Yet the greatest aberration – and the one that exercises the strongest boundary-stretching effect – is presented by that exemplar of the mathematically sublime with a claim to constituting its most significant paradigm: the vision of the starry sky, and the spectacle of the world's infinite vastness. The word that Schopenhauer uses in this connection is *betrachten* (*WWR* I:205), which Payne translates as "contemplate," a term equivocal between a more narrowly visual and a more broadly cognitive signification. It is also translatable, however, by the verb "to see," "to look at," "to regard." And it is this second, narrower translation that would seem to harmonise most naturally with Schopenhauer's basic aesthetic paradigm. Yet if we stick to this second construal, now, what does it mean to "see" the vastness of the world, or the "infinite greatness of the universe in space and time"? What does it mean for "the heavens at night [to] *actually* bring innumerable worlds before our eyes"? For we do not *see* the whole world, as we stand rooted to our particular spot – we only see a limited part of it. We do not see an infinite universe – only dots of light at a distance.[30]

---

[30] I am aware of a debt to Malcolm Budd's discussion of the Kantian sublime in my formulation of this thought; see his "The sublime in nature," in P. Guyer, ed., *Kant's "Critique of the Power of Judgment"* (Lanham, MD and Oxford: Rowman & Littlefield, 2003), 135–37.

Only a few lines above, however, we seem to have been given the key for addressing such queries. For moments before his central passage on the contemplation of the sky, Schopenhauer had introduced the mathematically sublime by referring to "our imagining a mere magnitude in space and time"; his central passage had then seemed to follow as a natural continuation. What this suggests is that the experience of the mathematically sublime is provoked by an awareness of the vastness of the world that depends on an act of imagination – and thus an active contribution from the subject – to be achieved. Payne was right: "contemplation" – in its more capacious signification, allowing for more complex cognitive possibilities – was the best linguistic call.

In the above, I have sought to present a thumbnail sketch of Schopenhauer's account of aesthetics, and one of its organising themes has been a suggestion that, studied more closely, Schopenhauer's account reveals a significant tension between competing images of the aesthetic process. This is a tension that the contrast between presence and transcendence offers a particularly illuminating set of terms for characterising. Earlier in my discussion, I suggested that the concern with transcendence reflects something important about Schopenhauer's epistemic ideal and its heroic embodiment in the genius gifted with an objective gaze and capable of roaming at will ("freely moving or even winged") over the plenitude of reality. Schopenhauer's discussion of the sublime turned out to express a similar fascination with a possibility of transcendence, offering us an even more powerful notion of "ascent."

There will be more to say about the themes visited above in what follows, and more comment to make concerning their significance. Already, however, these ingredients have provided many of the resources that my argument requires to take off. Yet the more specific starting point of my own argument lies elsewhere. It will be the task of the next chapter to locate it; and it may no longer come as a surprise that the plot should take its starting point – once again – from a point of tension. Real or apparent? Let us consider.

CHAPTER 2

Philosophy as: *aesthetic*

Confronting the fear of death: Schopenhauer's methods in conflict?

In the last chapter, I suggested that an inward turn defined the standpoint of philosophy for Schopenhauer in two related senses. Philosophy was inward-looking in turning to the subject to understand the mode of appearance of external objects. But philosophy was also inward-looking in turning to the self-experience of the subject to find a pathway that led beyond appearances, and to the thing-in-itself. In both cases, doing philosophy meant turning inward: away from the representation; into the depths of what lies within.

Yet that, I will be suggesting in this chapter, cannot provide us with the whole story about how philosophy is done. To find the sharp point of a wedge into a fuller account, there can be no better way of proceeding than by turning back to consider the moment that gives philosophy its beginning. And this is a moment that Schopenhauer, remaining faithful to the experiential commitments of his philosophy, would identify in profoundly existential terms. The search for an understanding of reality, it has sometimes been said, is grounded in the sense of human vulnerability. "The search for certainty and for the ultimate ground," as Leszek Kołakowski remarks – for "a world of which the origin, rules and destiny we can grasp" – is "the expression of the experience of human fragility."[1]

It was this intuition that Schopenhauer was expressing in his turn when he put down the origin of metaphysics to the problem of suffering; and more specifically, to the anguish produced by the prospect of our own death (*WWR* II:161). Standing behind our fear of death – of our non-being – as the ground of its possibility was the crucial human ability, both blessing and curse, to be surprised at our own being. "No beings,

[1] Leszek Kołakowski, *Metaphysical Horror* (Oxford: Blackwell, 1988), 15 and 27.

41

with the exception of man," Schopenhauer opens his essay "On Man's Need for Metaphysics" to say, "feel surprised at their own existence, but to all of them it is so much a matter of course that they do not notice it." It is only as the will – the inner being of nature – reaches reflection in human being that this surprise becomes possible to it. Nature "then marvels at its own works, and asks itself what it itself is. And its wonder is the more serious, as here for the first time it stands consciously face to face with *death*" (*WWR* II:160).

It was this existential confrontation that Schopenhauer placed at the root of metaphysical inquiry, and implicitly his own. It has been said indeed that the problem of death constituted Schopenhauer's deepest motivating concern, and the problem against which his philosophy was measured for its success. It is death, Michael Fox writes, that "ultimately preoccupied Schopenhauer," forming "the hub of the wheel from which all of his various doctrines radiate like spokes ... The confidence with which Schopenhauer assessed his own contribution to philosophy can and should be seen as giving expression, in part, to his satisfaction at having overcome the fear of death through systematic, rational reflection."[2]

How, then, had the fear of death been overcome? Yet in approaching this question, something more needs to be said concerning the presence of this fear in our lives. For the fear of death may provide philosophy with its starting point when it arises; yet how often does it in fact do so? Death, for all the engrossing interest philosophy has historically taken in it, in other ways appears to be singularly absent from the concrete present of our ordinary experience. We go about everyday life as if death simply did not concern us. As if this "internal human relation to mystery – to that which resists comprehension"[3] was not internal at all; as if, to use Schopenhauer's phrase, we were eternal: "everyone lives on as though he is bound to live for ever" (*WWR* I:281). Other philosophers,

---

[2] Michael A. Fox, "Schopenhauer on death, suicide and self-renunciation," in Fox, ed., *Schopenhauer: His Philosophical Achievement* (Brighton: Harvester, 1980), 146–47; though whether this philosophical reflection should be described as "systematic" and "rational" in kind will be a key question in the discussion that follows. For discussion of Schopenhauer's starting point, see David E. Cartwright, "Schopenhauer on suffering, death, guilt, and the consolation of metaphysics," in E. von der Luft, ed., *Schopenhauer: New Essays in Honor of His 200th Birthday* (Lewiston, NY: Edwin Mellen Press, 1988), and Michael A. Fox, "Schopenhauer on the need for metaphysics," in von der Luft, ed., *Schopenhauer: New Essays in Honor of His 200th Birthday*. For more on Schopenhauer's view of death, see also Dale Jacquette, "Schopenhauer on death," in Janaway, ed., *The Cambridge Companion to Schopenhauer*.

[3] The expression is from Stephen Mulhall, "Wonder, perplexity, sublimity: philosophy as the self-overcoming of self-exile in Heidegger and Wittgenstein," in Vasalou, ed., *Practices of Wonder*, discussing Heidegger.

like the Epicurean Lucretius, might have here proposed subtle psychological interventions for discerning the fear of death that pervades our seemingly carefree everyday existence.[4] More recent philosophers might offer the thought that this fear, or its conditioning awareness of death – for all its constitutive role as an "internal relation" – must be an achievement. But for Schopenhauer, the next step lies elsewhere.

There is in fact a noticeable tension that runs through Schopenhauer's remarks concerning the epistemic availability of the notion of our own non-existence. At times, Schopenhauer speaks of this prospect as a firm epistemic possession: "man alone carries about with him in abstract concepts the certainty of his own death." Yet "this," he immediately continues, "can frighten him only very rarely and at particular moments." And in the next moment, the initial positive affirmation has given way to something far weaker: "it might be said that no one has a really lively conviction of the certainty of his own death" (*WWR* I:281). This denial assumes more categorical tones elsewhere, as when Schopenhauer refers to our "deep conviction of the impossibility of our extermination by death" – a conviction so deep that our own death may indeed be for us "at bottom the most incredible thing in the world" (*WWR* II:487). If we can represent our death at all, this is because of the temporal nature of our consciousness. Yet this representation seems to constitute not only an extraordinary event, but indeed a veritably unattainable one. The prospect of our own death is fundamentally inconceivable to us.

Yet it is precisely by attending to this tension more closely that the resolution to the fear that stimulates philosophical inquiry can be identified. For a fear of death may indeed only supervene at extraordinary moments – and all we can say is that this is when philosophy will need to be done. Yet philosophy will respond to our need in a manner that calls precisely upon the truths already reflected in our resistance to being provoked to this fear, and our limited capacity to fully assent to our representation of this eventuality. If we ordinarily live in a state of unquestioning absorption in the present, and if everything in our phenomenology suggests an absence of doubt concerning our continued existence, this phenomenology can be subjected to interpretation. On closer examination – an examination that raises "mere feeling" to "reflectively appropriated insight" according to philosophical procedure – it turns out to contain precisely the metaphysical truth we require for our consolation. For our phenomenology,

---

[4] See the interesting discussion in Martha C. Nussbaum, *The Therapy of Desire: Theory and Practice in Hellenistic Ethics* (Princeton University Press, 2009), ch. 6.

Schopenhauer would suggest – or rather, that aspect of our phenomenology that registers as the dominant chord – is simply an expression of our true inner nature. Our sense of endlessness reflects a primitive certainty that "there is something positively imperishable and indestructible" in us and a "consciousness of our original and eternal nature" (*WWR* II:496, 487). And this, of course, is in the first place our inner nature as will; and on another level, our nature as representing subjects whose supra-individual consciousness conditions the world.[5]

It is not, thus, that one lives "as *though* he is bound to live for ever" – but rather it is *in fact* the case that one does. For our true nature does not reside in our character as individuals, which can be affected by temporal events. Individuals, indeed, have no real existence; they exist only in the knowledge of a representing subject, which is conditioned by time, space, and causality. Untouched by the course of time and underlying the succession of appearances, by contrast, "our being-in-itself ... exists in an everlasting present" (*WWR* II:479). When we suddenly call up a larger temporal perspective and the representation of our death impresses us with its inevitability, the anguish we experience belongs to us in our identity as individual beings that are phenomena of the will. The tension between the two "certainties" – the certainty that we will die, the certainty that we cannot – thus turns out to be a tension between two different ways of experiencing ourselves: as individual phenomena, and as will. Appreciating this distinction involves recognising that "the greatest equivocation lies in the word 'I' ... According as I understand this word, I can say: 'Death is my entire end'; or else: 'This my personal phenomenal appearance is just as infinitely small a part of my true inner nature as I am of the world'" (*WWR* II:491).

Our astonishment at the finitude of our consciousness, which arises only infrequently due to the inertia of our truer nature, is ultimately grounded in an illusion – the illusion of the *principium individuationis*. To that extent, one's horror at one's prospective non-existence is as ill-founded as the wonder with which every new individual greets his present existence, finding himself "so fresh and original, that he broods over himself in astonishment" (*WWR* II:501). From the true metaphysical perspective, there is neither freshness to be found nor decay; the concepts of duration and extinction themselves "are borrowed from time that is merely the form

---

[5] The passage just cited (II:487) is in fact referring to the second aspect more directly. It comes on the heels of a remarkable thought experiment that consists precisely in an effort to imagine oneself away through death, and whose failure serves to confirm the truth of transcendental idealism (see 486–87).

of the phenomenon," so that "the constant arising of new beings and the perishing of those that exist are to be regarded as an illusion" (*PP* II:269).

Dispelling this illusion thus involves an appropriation or indeed reappropriation of our true identity, which can be framed as a rediscovery of the experience of endlessness interrupted by the reflective representation of death. When this experience is disturbed through the intrusion of a temporal perspective – one deeply steeped in the illusions of individuality – philosophy rises to a higher perspective from which it can interpret the interrupted experience and reappropriate its meaning at the level of reflection. Having come to grasp the true nature of the world, we can now *think*, and not just *feel*, that we are endless.[6] This involves shifting our viewpoint to realise that our true identity lies not in our individual consciousness but in the will of which it is a manifestation, and in the supra-individual subjectivity – no less "eternal" in kind – through which this manifestation is achieved in its purest form.[7]

The first tension structuring our account would appear on Schopenhauer's terms resolved. Yet there is a second tension lying in the wings that now demands to be more carefully addressed – a tension that leads directly to the heart of my concern. For let us attend to the philosophical process that just came before us to consider how it relates to the characterisation of Schopenhauer's philosophical standpoint offered in the previous chapter. Philosophy is called to respond to a fear; a fear that is founded on an error. It is an error, significantly, produced by an outward turn: we turn outward to look to the objective temporal course of our life, thereby disrupting our attunement with our inner nature. The moment of philosophical achievement then arrives as a (re)turn inward, to discover one's true identity and reflectively appropriate the truth that consoles. This understanding would seem to harmonise perfectly with Schopenhauer's standpoint as surveyed in the last chapter. Philosophy, we saw, commutes the knowledge of feeling into knowledge of reflection (*WWR* I:82; cf. I:271); and it undertakes its work by turning inward – a turn that characteristically brings a discovery of one's true nature.

Elsewhere, Schopenhauer explicitly deploys the terms just used – inward and outward, subjective and objective – in connection with this question,

---

[6] See also in this connection the distinction discussed by Robert Wicks between two notions of time at work in Schopenhauer's thinking, which seems directly relevant to the account just given: *Schopenhauer*, 73–75.

[7] The above has focused on what I take to be the most important strategy for addressing the fear of death, but there are others discussed by Schopenhauer. See especially essays XVII and XLI of *WWR* II, and the commentaries in note 2 above, as well as Young, *Willing and Unwilling*, 107–11.

as in the remark that if, in contrast to a "method of consideration which is directed *inwards*, we again look *outwards* and apprehend quite objectively the world that presents itself to us, then death certainly appears to be a passing into nothing" (*PP* II:275). Looking at the world "objectively" here consists of looking at it "as it appears," as a representation, that is to say: at the (illusory) level of the phenomenal that constitutes an objectification of the will. An "objective" standpoint carries clear epistemic disvalue; the privileged vantage point is rather subjective in orientation.

But if this is the main significance and epistemic valuation of these two standpoints, what are we to make of the following? For there is another usage of the term "objective" in Schopenhauer's work that contrasts sharply with this one, where an objective vantage point appears to be positively valued as the contrary – this time – of a negative notion of subjectivity. There can be no better location for taking stock of this other vantage point than the long essay titled "On Death and its Relation to the Indestructibility of our Inner Nature," appearing in the second volume of the *World as Will and Representation* and containing one of Schopenhauer's most concerted meditations on the problem of death. Here, Schopenhauer invites us to take a long empirical look at nature; or – in a metaphor already present elsewhere in Schopenhauer's work but appearing here in heightened form – to put our ear to the *language* of nature to listen closely to what it has to *say* about death. Don't assume, *look and see*, as Wittgenstein would later say: just take a look at how nature behaves. And looking closely, we see two sets of evidence – two sets of statements, or modes of speech. We see nature as it speaks through individuals: individuals shudder at the prospect of death and do their best to avoid it. Yet now we turn to look at how "the *whole* of nature" behaves towards death (*WWR* II:473); how nature speaks as a whole. And there, we see "life and death dependent on the most trifling accident," with only an ephemeral existence in between; we see "animal and plant arise today and tomorrow pass away," we see "birth and death follow in quick succession" (*WWR* II:474). We see nature declare the utter insignificance of individual beings and its indifference to their death or survival.[8]

An "objective and unprejudiced" look at this order of things will lead to the conclusion that the former region of speech must constitute only a local dialect, a conditional and one-sided region of nature's language,

---

[8] See also *WWR* II:600 for a related, illuminating juxtaposition of the two modes of nature's speech, depending on whether "she speaks from the particular or the universal, from inside or outside, from the centre or the periphery."

which achieves completion only in the vantage point afforded by the whole. And this vantage point proclaims loud and clear that the constant passing of beings in and out of existence must be an illusion, not reality but mere appearance – "a jest" (*WWR* II:474); for were it not intended as a jest, it would be an unintended absurdity. Looking at the language of phenomena in this manner, and spurred on by a catalytic sense of the absurd, one will come to perceive that what is real is not individuals, but the universals they embody. For it is on universals – on the preservation of humankind rather than particular human beings, of *leonitas* rather than individual lions – that nature lavishes her care.

A "really objective gaze" will be able to pick out that which is "at all times one and the same" instead of that which is always in flux – the endless series of individuals. If we find it difficult to think ourselves into the content of such an objective gaze, it might help to begin by imagining its subject:

> To the eye of a being who lived an incomparably longer life and took in at a single glance the human race in its whole duration, the constant alternation of birth and death would present itself merely as a continuous vibration. Accordingly, it would not occur to it at all to see in it a constantly new coming out of nothing and passing into nothing, but ... to its glance the species would appear as that which is and remains, birth and death as vibrations. (*WWR* II:481–82)

Yet if this viewpoint is here presented as one available to an idealised observer – a being, unlike any we know, capable of enjoying an "incomparably longer life," and thereby enjoying conditions of subjectivity vastly different from, and superior to, our own – in other places it appears rather more closely within our reach, for it figures in the imperative as a form of vision we may be exhorted to attempt ourselves:

> Let us now picture to ourselves that alternation of birth and death in infinitely rapid vibrations, and we have before us the persistent and enduring objectification of the will, the permanent Ideas of beings, standing firm like the rainbow on the waterfall. (*WWR* II:479)

The striking feature of these remarks is that they commend to us a mode of observation in which insight into the illusory nature of individuality and thus the nature of death is gained not by peering inward, but on the contrary, by turning sharply outward to consider the phenomena. Yet isn't this, now, an outward look that Schopenhauer had elsewhere disavowed? The idealised being who takes in the human race at a glance would seem to occupy a vantage point such as the one encapsulated in *Parerga and Paralipomena*, where, arguing the merits of a "subjective" philosophy, Schopenhauer would write: "when one looks *outwards*, where the vastness of the world and the infinitude of its beings display themselves, one's own self as a mere individual shrinks to nothing and seems to vanish. Carried away by this immensity of mass and number, one thinks further that only the *outwardly* directed, and hence *objective, philosophy* can be on the right path." It is "the *inwardly* directed philosophy," by contrast, that has found the true path (*PP* II:16–17). The ideal observer just invoked seems to be faced precisely with such an immense "infinitude of beings"; yet far from falling into the thrall of illusion, the vision makes him wise. What has happened here?

Part of what has happened is a shift in Schopenhauer's philosophical self-understanding. One of the most distinctive traits of Schopenhauer's intellectual career, it has sometimes been remarked, was the singular tenacity with which he remained attached to his core philosophical convictions throughout his lifetime. In the introduction to the second edition of his work (1844), more than a quarter of a century after the original edition in 1818, Schopenhauer would announce in clipped tones with evident satisfaction: "I find nothing to retract." (For "the truth," comments David Cartwright in his biography, "does not change."[9]) And yet that self-assessment concealed certain subtle yet significant shifts that Schopenhauer's perspective had undergone over time – shifts that directly impinged on his view of the philosophical standpoint and its "inward-looking" character.

In Schopenhauer's earlier work, the principal message had centred on the unavailability of metaphysical insight to the outward-turned gaze. Looking for the inner nature of things "from without," we are "like a man who goes round a castle, looking in vain for an entrance, and sometimes sketching the façades" (*WWR* I:99). Hence the need for a turn inward, to that self-experience where the boundary between phenomenon and thing-in-itself begins to give way, allowing one to push beyond the appearances. It is that indeed which defines the seminal moment of philosophical discovery at the opening of book 2 of the first volume of the *World as Will and Representation*. In later writings, however, a rather different emphasis appears to emerge. For while Schopenhauer continues to affirm the importance of inner experience – and the subjective standpoint – as a source of philosophical understanding, this emphasis now seems to be

---

[9] David E. Cartwright, *Schopenhauer: A Biography* (Cambridge University Press, 2010), 394; for Schopenhauer's remark, see *WWR* I:xxi.

assimilated into a more programmatic emphasis on experience more broadly. Metaphysics is described as *"the science of experience in general"* (*WWR* II:181); philosophy is "nothing but the correct and universal understanding of experience itself" (*WWR* II:183). And this means: of the *whole* of experience. It is not just the inner, but also the outer facts that are now more vocally inscribed into this whole. The inner nature of the world must be stamped upon the physiognomy of the world in its entirety, and not *only* in the pulsing of desire we find in our breast as we turn inward.

The meaning of the world, put differently, must be expressed in every part of its script. And it is indeed this metaphor – that of a system of unknown signs, a "cryptograph" (*WWR* II:182), a set of abstruse "ciphers" – that Schopenhauer now draws upon heavily to characterise the world of experience, making it the task of philosophy to unlock its meaning. This is similar to the way in which, "if we find a document the script of which is unknown, we continue trying to interpret it until we hit upon a hypothesis as to the meaning of the letters by which they form intelligible words and connected sentences" (*WWR* II:184). Philosophy must do this by seeking to connect the different parts of this unintelligible script with one another – including, crucially, the inner facts with the outer – in a way that places phenomena into the greatest possible agreement. This, *inter alia*, means that "the deciphering of the world must be completely confirmed from itself." This approach – what Rüdiger Safranski refers to as Schopenhauer's "hermeneutics of existence" – is linked with a clearer characterisation of the nature of philosophy and its aims: immanent, not transcendent; seeking to interpret, not explain.[10]

Several elements of this picture, to be sure, already had their roots in Schopenhauer's earlier work. Certainly the notion of representations as a system of mysterious signs (standing "before us like hieroglyphics that are not understood," *WWR* I:97), of nature as engaging in significant speech (every plant "says something that cannot be expressed in any other language," *WWR* I:156), and of the philosophical task as an attempt at reading or bestowing meaning.[11] The outward-looking orientation connected with this hermeneutical approach, in turn, is captured well in an anecdote Safranski records from Schopenhauer's time in Dresden, where he completed the first edition of the *World as Will and Representation*.

---

[10] For Safranski's remarks on this, see *The Wild Years of Philosophy*, particularly 203ff. and 214.

[11] Hermeneutical metaphors in fact pervade the opening of book 2; see *WWR* I:95ff. One difference would appear to be that in the later, more programmatic remarks, the emphasis is on *bestowing* meaning; in the earlier remarks the emphasis is often on accounting for the meaning that appearances *already* have for us (e.g. I:95).

"walking one day in the glasshouse in Dresden and totally engrossed in the physiognomy of the plants" he had asked himself whence these multifarious forms and colours of the plants originated. What were these plants with their curious shapes trying to tell him?[12]

The philosopher is here turned, not inward to his own soul, but outward to the world to scrutinise its appearances. Similarly, the turn outward had registered significantly in Schopenhauer's early work to the extent that it provided the content of the concluding moment of the "stepwise" unfolding of metaphysical insight. For the discovery of one's inner nature, as we may recall – accomplished by turning inward – became a discovery about the nature of the world only upon turning outward to recognise the will in all phenomena. More distinctive, in this respect, in Schopenhauer's later writings was the particular form that this engagement of outer experience would take, bringing a rapprochement with a specific kind of empirical perspective, namely that of natural science. This heightened rapprochement was visible both in the essays of the second volume of his main work, as well as in Schopenhauer's slim yet important volume *On the Will in Nature* (1836), which proposed to investigate the meeting ground of his metaphysics and the empirical sciences.[13]

Whatever the precise character of the novelty and its extent, it would seem to provide important background for approaching Schopenhauer's discussion of the fear of death in the essay we have just considered. Schopenhauer's emphasis on the "empirical standpoint" on nature, on a study of the different regions of nature's language, on an "objective" consideration of phenomena – all of this, it would seem, could be easily related to that intensified concern with the "outer facts of experience" and its more specific expression: a rapprochement with empirical science.

Or could it? My claim in fact is that it could not; and my main suggestion will be that to understand the standpoint at stake in this philosophical moment, it is not to the "objective" viewpoint of empirical science, with its outward-looking attention to the phenomena, but to that viewpoint – likewise concerned with the phenomena, but on a radically different level – constituted by a mode of attending with a far

---

[12] Safranski, *The Wild Years of Philosophy*, 216; a reference to the "physiognomies of plants" in fact appears just above the last-cited remark from *WWR* 1:156.

[13] Once again, however, this engagement of science can be traced back to earlier stages of Schopenhauer's intellectual formation. It is a striking fact, for example, as David Cartwright reports, that Schopenhauer's university education in Berlin had comprised more scientific subjects than philosophical ones (*Schopenhauer*, 170; and see generally ch. 4) – a "voracious appetite for science" that Schopenhauer would sustain throughout his life.

more central place in Schopenhauer's philosophical scheme that we need to look: the aesthetic.

For if we were seeking for a notion of objective consideration specified in epistemically positive terms, we may now recall that it was precisely in the aesthetic context that we had earlier encountered a notion of object- ivity carrying the highest epistemic credentials. In Schopenhauer's idiom, the "aesthetic" regard and the "objective" regard shaded into each other with little to divide them. And they did so in a manner that allows us to draw an important distinction between two related yet distinct senses in which the notion of "objectivity" could be understood. For on the one hand, aesthetic experience was "objective" with regard to its object, in directing itself to the purest or "most immediate objectivity of the will" – the Ideas. Yet it was also "objective" in a sense closer to our own linguistic habits, with regard to its manner, in abstracting from an object's relation- ship to one's interests. Both senses were evident in Schopenhauer's remark that "every existing thing can be observed purely *objectively and outside all relation*"; and since "the will appears in everything at some grade of its objectivity, and this thing is accordingly the expression of an Idea, every- thing is also *beautiful* … even the most insignificant thing admits of *purely objective and will-less* contemplation" (*WWR* I:210; emphasis added). The two senses were of course interdependent in so far as an Idea *was* an object abstracted from its relations to the will, and thus to other things.

The difference between the aesthetic and the scientific viewpoint, in these terms, could be understood in two ways, marking out the inferiority of the latter on both levels. For on the one hand, science takes an inferior object. While it shares the outward-looking direction to the phenomenal and indeed the universal that marks the aesthetic regard, its object is not the Idea but the concept (*WWR* II:442). Similarly, the scientific mode of attention achieves only partial independence from the operations of the will, forming a halfway house between interested and disinterested cogni- tion, where it might also potentially serve as a preparation for the latter.[14]

With this higher notion of objectivity back within our sights, we will now have no difficulty recognising all the tell-tale elements in the essay we left behind. What had been the vantage point Schopenhauer had sought to conjure, proposing it as the content of a "really objective gaze"? It was the magisterial vantage point of a being "who lived an incompar- ably longer life and took in at a single glance the human race in its whole duration." To the eye of such a being, Schopenhauer had written, "the

---

[14] See particularly the remarks in the essay "On the Knowledge of the Ideas," *WWR* II:363–66.

constant alternation of birth and death would present itself merely as a continuous vibration" (*WWR* II:481). A single glance picking up a ceaseless vibration – the nature of this act of vision is still uncertain, the implication still muted. Yet with the act transposed to the imperative, it steps clearly into the light: for "let us now picture to ourselves," Schopenhauer admonishes us, "that alternation of birth and death in infinitely rapid vibrations, and we have before us the persistent and enduring objectification of the will, the permanent Ideas of beings, standing firm like the rainbow on the waterfall" (*WWR* II:479).

Here is the tell-tale notion of the Ideas, certainly; and with it, several other telling signs. And not least among them, the crucial orientation around a focusing image in specifying the content of the objective view. The particular image just employed, the rainbow – itself a potent theme in the storehouse of Romantic imagination – would in fact recur in other contexts in explicit connection with the aesthetic standpoint, and often as a symbol of permanence within flux and unity within plurality, as when Schopenhauer would compare the Idea and the pure subject of knowing, in standing outside relations, to "the rainbow and the sun that take no part in the constant movement and succession of the falling drops" (*WWR* I:109).[15] Using different but no less evocative imagery, it is the same orientation around a magnetic image that would be exhibited elsewhere in equally telling ways. The ideal observer taking in the human race at a glance, we have been told, would no longer see "a constantly new coming out of nothing and passing out of nothing" but a mere vibration. Yet this precise spectacle is summoned even more vividly before our eyes in the words that follow using a succession of striking analogies:

> [J]ust as to our glance the rapidly turning spark appears as a continuous circle, the rapidly vibrating spring as a permanent triangle, the vibrating cord as a spindle, so to its glance the species would appear as that which is and remains, birth and death as vibrations. (*WWR* II:481–82)

A trail of geometrical signs burned into our vision by motion iterated at electric speed – a trail of fire-juggling that is nevertheless the print of

---

15 The link with the Ideas is also evident in *WWR* II:483. This symbolism is evident, for example, in *WWR* I:185 ("like the rainbow silently resting on this raging torrent"); cf. *WWR* I:278 ("The present always exists together with its content; both stand firm without wavering, like the rainbow over the waterfall"). On the broader resonance of this symbolism, see Richard Holmes' suggestive remarks on Coleridge in *The Age of Wonder* (London: HarperPress, 2008), 321, in the context of discussing a well-known debate about the antagonism between science and Romantic poetry in which the rainbow figured as a focal image.

truth. Elsewhere in the essay the giddy speed productive of vision gives way to a hypnotic sway, and the commanding image solidifies into something stabler and more imposing:

> Now if we cast a glance at the scale of beings together with the gradation of consciousness that accompanies them, from the polyp to man, we see this *wonderful pyramid* kept in ceaseless oscillation certainly by the constant death of the individuals, yet enduring in the species throughout the endlessness of time by means of the bond of generation. (*WWR* II:485; emphasis added)

Yet whether this is a triangle or a circle, a spectral rainbow or a stately pyramid, it is a set of images that we find at the heart of the act of "objective" vision that forms a central moment of Schopenhauer's discussion of the fear of death. These are images calculated to draw us away from the local language of "individuals" to the language of nature as a whole, focusing our view on "universals" as the most significant sign and absolute currency; and this means: on the "permanent Ideas of beings" that constitute them. What this suggests is that at the heart of this transition – one integral to overcoming the fear that derives from the individual standpoint with its local language, and thus integral to purging the anxiety that sets philosophy in motion – is an act of vision fundamentally aesthetic in kind.

Indeed, with the proposed act of vision characterised in these terms, the different stages of the above account can now be tied more cohesively together. For with the transcendence of nature's local dialect specified as a transcendence of individuals to the Ideas they embody, the conquest of our fear of death turns out to involve the assumption of a vantage point that will be familiar from our earlier discussion of the aesthetic moment – namely, that of the higher subjectivity that forms their correlate. If the Ideas are visible to us, it is in so far as we are considering phenomena from the perspective of our capacity as the supra-individual subject whose consciousness conditions the world. In this capacity, we lie outside the reach of these conditions, and thus outside the reach of time, as "timeless" as the "eternal Forms" (*WWR* I:179) we contemplate. The sting of death is thus removed through a reformed identity, or the reappropriation of one – an identification with what is eternal in oneself over which death has no hold. This, of course, amounts to nothing short of an act of self-transformation. With the job of philosophy done, I suggested earlier, "we can now *think*, and not just *feel*, that we are endless"; yet this thinking is itself a profoundly felt act of thought.

Don't assume; look and see, Schopenhauer had counselled. This seeing now turns out to be no ordinary act of vision.[16] Yet I would suggest that, to place this act in an even more illuminating context, it is not merely to the aesthetic standpoint, but to a more particular instance of that standpoint that we need to additionally direct our attention. For a being that could live an endless life, Schopenhauer had written, the illusions of individuality would fall away and the highest realities would be bared to view. Yet let us ask again: by what means? By a magisterial gaze launching forth – from a lofty standpoint that would appear to be located somewhere outside the world – to range over the endless expanse of time and pick out the Ideas standing stable within the flux. In Schopenhauer's description, to be sure, there was no "launching" or "ranging," only a single gaze absorbing its object in an instantaneous act of vision from a vantage point *sub specie aeternitatis*. Such verbs of motion are ones we contribute to bridge the distance between the standpoint of a superhuman being and modes of cognition closer to our own, in which movement of some kind is typically required for intellectual achievement.

And yet it may now be recalled that Schopenhauer had already sought to bridge that distance for us in the same vicinity; and he had done so in ways calculated to bring out more distinctly both the aesthetic character of this standpoint and the means for its achievement. "Now if we cast a glance at the scale of beings," he had proposed; and again: "let us now picture to ourselves that alternation of birth and death." If the nature of this invitation is still not clear in such hypothetical and hortatory formulations, it stands out even more plainly elsewhere, and perhaps nowhere more plainly than in the striking remark that appears in *Parerga and Paralipomena*, framed as a statement about the sexual impulse, yet pointing to the same familiar context:

> We can compare this impulse to the thread of a pearl necklace where those rapidly succeeding individuals would correspond to the pearls. *If in our*

---

[16] Some readers may remain unconvinced by my quick dismissal of the scientific construal of the objective standpoint; they would probably include Julian Young, given the central role science plays in his reading of Schopenhauer. Young's discussion of the "objective" viewpoint to which Schopenhauer often appeals (e.g. in the *WWR* II essay titled "Objective View of the Intellect") is indeed entirely in scientific terms, taking it to refer us to "realism with regard to that image of the world presented by natural science" (*Willing and Unwilling*, 11; and for Young's alternative construal of the "empirical" view in Schopenhauer's discussion of the fear of death and Schopenhauer's strategy for overcoming this fear, see 107–11). The issue could be debated at far greater length, but in this context I can only point to the larger body of evidence considered later in this chapter that argues for the aesthetic character of the philosophical standpoint, and in doing so supports my reading of Schopenhauer's standpoint in this particular essay.

imagination we accelerate this succession and always see in the whole series as well as in the individuals only the form permanent, but the substance or matter constantly changing, we then become aware that we have only a quasi-existence. (*PP* II:289; emphasis added)

Contributing yet another image to the gallery of visual aids already before us, Schopenhauer here articulates openly what elsewhere remains implicit. The "rapidly turning spark" that appears as a circle and the "rapidly vibrating spring" that appears as a triangle do not turn at electric speed on their own before our passive gaze, nor is the pyramid of beings that sways hypnotically before us self-moving. The movement, Schopenhauer here clarifies – a movement indispensable for minds like our own – is one effected through the use of the imagination. Equally striking, the imagination can be guided and educated to its task in methodical ways: the passage we have just read shows us how. And in doing so, it has signposted clearly the active effort required for this achievement.

This, on the one hand, brings out even more strongly the ligaments connecting this act of vision to the aesthetic context. Yet no less relevant is to notice another set of ligaments, pointing us to a rather more specific context – that of the sublime. Discussing the mathematically sublime, Schopenhauer had spoken of an experience that took its starting point in a moment when "we lose ourselves in contemplation of the infinite greatness of the universe in space and time, meditate on the past millennia and on those to come" (*WWR* I:205). This, we may recall, was an image of absorption that turned out to belie an active employment of the imagination to bring the "infinite greatness" of the world into our sights. In the mathematically sublime, the infinite world forming one's object appears without qualification; in the case of the "ideal observer," by contrast, it is the world constituted by the Ideas that forms the contemplated object. Yet if we put this apparent contrast aside, the affinities between the two moments are not hard to trace out. And these concern most notably the nature of the gaze that is constructed within them. It is a gaze, in both cases, sent out to span over a large series or expanse: one lacking in limit, infinite, unbounded. This is a vocabulary that we can in hindsight pick up in Schopenhauer's discussion of the fear of death as a pervasive motif: we are invited to picture to ourselves the succession of birth and death in "*infinitely* rapid vibrations"; to see the wonderful pyramid of beings "enduring in the species throughout the *endlessness* of time." And as in the sublime, here too it is the imagination that is charged with a central role in bringing the unbounded into view.

Earlier, I had called the vantage point of Schopenhauer's observer an "ideal" or indeed "superhuman" one, with a view to the fact that there are no such beings – ones with a longevity permitting them to survey the human race in its entire duration – among us. Yet that, it is by now fully clear, is far from true. For while this is not a viewpoint that is available to us actually, given our limited lifespan, it is certainly available to us in imagination, through an exercise of imagination not unlike the one that structures sublime experience.

There will be more to say about the importance of the infinitising view-point – what I have called the view *sub specie aeternitatis* – in what follows. But first, we need to take stock of where the above has brought us.

The aesthetic standpoint of philosophy

And on an initial estimate, it might not seem to have brought us very far at all. What had been our trajectory? Beginning from the existential concern that Schopenhauer had placed at the root of philosophical inquiry – the problem of death – we considered the solution he proposed for overcoming it. It was a solution that threw us straight into an apparent tension between the avowed inward-looking (or subjective) standpoint of Schopenhauer's philosophy and another, this time outward-looking (or objective) standpoint that Schopenhauer invoked in articulating his solution. A conflict? we asked; and looked first towards Schopenhauer's increased later engagement of outer experience and scientific empiricism, and then towards a more familiar perspective in which a privileged notion of objectivity was already at home: the aesthetic. It was a notion of objectivity whose appearance might seem unsurprising given its special significance within Schopenhauer's scheme. And the supposed conflict could be dismissed by reaffirming the general relation between the two standpoints to hold as follows. Philosophy first looks inward to discover metaphysical truth – that is a view concerning how philosophy should be done. But with the task of philosophy complete, the world is revealed to be a place inescapably filled with suffering. Aesthetic contemplation offers itself as a respite, providing temporary appeasement by turning our gaze outward to the world's aesthetic spectacles. On this account, the "inward" and "outward" standpoints reflect different stages of engagement, prior to posterior, within inquiry and outside it.

Yet what should now be remarked is a fact that may seem so self-evident that it risks escaping attention altogether: and this is that the act of vision examined above appears, not *outside* philosophy and once its task has been completed, but within philosophy itself. And it appears indeed within philosophy as one of the methods by which its insight stands to be achieved, helping us see beyond the epistemically conditioned level of individual phenomena to the Ideas that form the highest representable reality. The aesthetic vision Schopenhauer encourages us to adopt does not form a stage posterior to philosophical inquiry, but a procedure contained within it.

What importance should we attach to this fact? And should we be surprised by it? Whether we stand to be surprised by it, I will suggest, depends on which direction we face, and which resources we draw on in constructing our understanding. Yet my main argument – one that forms the heart of my reading, to unfold over this chapter and the next – will be that, having faced in the direction that brings the full gamut of evidence into view, the simple fact just remarked is indeed a significant one, and points to something broader with immediate relevance for the way we understand Schopenhauer's philosophy. Considered more carefully, the aesthetic standpoint turns out to be, not posterior to philosophy, nor merely an isolated episode within it, but an element that demands to be acknowledged as a seminal aspect of Schopenhauer's philosophical standpoint and philosophical self-understanding.

What has hampered this recognition, in great part, has been Schopenhauer's own singular reticence on the topic. For on the one hand, a comparison of Schopenhauer's characterisation of the philosophical and the aesthetic viewpoints in his main work immediately throws up revealing affinities. We may recall Schopenhauer's evocative first account of the moment of aesthetic contemplation: "we no longer consider the where, the when, the why, and the whither in things, but simply and solely the *what*" (*WWR* I:179). Compare this with the philosophical moment, described by Schopenhauer as one in which one "does not ask about the whence, whither, and why of the world, but always and everywhere about the *what* alone" (*WWR* I:274). And if both moments share the parsing of their object – a "what" abstracted from relations – it is not surprising that they should share the transcendence of the will this reflects. Speaking of aesthetic experience, Schopenhauer would rehearse a familiar motif in declaring that the state of subordination in which knowledge ordinarily stands to the will can be transcended, so that "knowledge can withdraw from this subjection, throw off its yoke and ... exist purely for itself" (*WWR* I:152).

Elsewhere, Schopenhauer would characterise philosophical reflection in terms that directly resume the ones just heard, referring to the philosopher's intellect as "detaching itself … from the totality of things" and "existing by itself" (*WWR* II:161).

A withdrawal from the world; a moment of self-subsistence to contemplate the essential – these similarities seem more than superficial, and are already richly suggestive. Yet despite these promissory notes, closer inspection reveals a dearth of explicit remarks that would connect philosophy to aesthetic perception. One seeks for them in vain, for example, in the locations where the character of philosophy comes up for direct discussion, and where one would have naturally expected to receive some orienting cues. Indeed, what Schopenhauer *does* say about the task of philosophy in such locations seems calculated to make doubt deepen. For prominent in Schopenhauer's characterisation of philosophy is a notion of "articulation" that we have seen, and that seems to be closely associated with the rational, the conceptual, and the abstract. The task of philosophy is ultimately to offer what Schopenhauer describes as a "universal survey of life as a whole," which is an advantage human beings have over animals through the faculty of their reason (*Vernunft*) (*WWR* I:85). Philosophy constitutes "the most universal rational knowledge" (*Wissen*), which must be "a sum of very universal judgments" that would deliver "a statement in the abstract of the nature of the whole world … *a complete recapitulation, so to speak, a reflection of the world in abstract concepts*" (*WWR* I:82–83). Reason or rational thought (*vernünftiges Denken*) is closely linked, indeed at times identified, with the capacity to form abstract concepts (e.g. *WWR* I:39, 151, 233).

Yet if we think we have any grip on Schopenhauer's understanding of epistemic privilege and the divide that constitutes it, abstract concepts would appear to fall squarely on the wrong side of this divide. They are associated with science (*WWR* I:233), which is confined to asking *why* questions that presuppose the principle of sufficient reason – certainly not *what* questions like those that define the philosophical standpoint, for which even the principle of sufficient reason must be open to question. They are associated with temporal perception (*WWR* I:151) – time belonging to the forms of the phenomenon that aesthetic perception transcends. And there are clear statements to the effect that abstract thought is still governed by the will (*WWR* II:369: "In all abstract employment of the mind, the will is also the ruler"). Conceptual or rational knowledge is sharply contrasted with perceptual or intuitive knowledge (*anschauliche*

Erkenntniß), such as the perception of the Ideas involves (*WWR* 1:186), and there is no doubt which of the two possesses epistemic privilege.[17]

All in all, Schopenhauer seems to exhibit little interest in locating his own philosophical activity in explicit relation to the aesthetic ideal that occupies the highest epistemic pedestal within his scheme. Given these facts, it is little wonder that the relationship between the aesthetic viewpoint and the viewpoint of philosophy should not have figured positively in many of the readings of Schopenhauer's philosophy responsible for our prevailing understanding of him.[18]

It would be a mistake, however, to succumb to these appearances too quickly. And perhaps the strongest initial hint to that effect, in this case, is the one offered by considerations of a biographical kind. For how, given Schopenhauer's adulation of the artist-genius with a gift for the objective gaze, given the formidable place assigned to him at the apex of Schopenhauer's intellectual aristocracy – "the elect," he calls them, "the truly beautiful and the men of genius" (*WWR* 11:396) – and given the pervasive contempt that marks Schopenhauer's attitude towards ordinary minds that remain shackled to self-interest, can it be conceived that he could have drafted his role such as to exclude himself from the upper echelons? That he has not, however, is already implicit in the sprawling discussions of genius that recur in all of Schopenhauer's works, which expound on the topic in minute and dilatory detail that bears all the air of intimate and first-hand expertise. We hear how geniuses think, how they feel, how they act and how they look, down to the weight and size of their brain from the inside: Schopenhauer seems to know genius inside out.[19] Yet it is in the reflections contained in his private diary, *Eis Eauton*, that this self-identification perhaps achieves its most explicit form, as signalled in Schopenhauer's remark about the "importance of the intellectual immortal man in me" that is "infinitely great compared with that of the individual," or the importance of "the ideas left behind by beings like me."[20] These words – which embody Schopenhauer's awareness of his

---

[17] There have been many doubts, by contrast, concerning the defensibility of this distinction; for more on this distinction, see Janaway, *Self and World in Schopenhauer's Philosophy*, 160–66, and also Young, *Willing and Unwilling*, 18–22 (and see the account of conceptual knowledge that follows, 22–25). Cf. Gardiner, *Schopenhauer*, 110–22.

[18] "Positively," as against negatively; see Chapter 5.

[19] See particularly the essay XXXI, "On Genius," in *WWR* II, and ch. III, "Ideas Concerning the Intellect Generally and in All Respects," in *PP* II.

[20] Arthur Schopenhauer, "Eis Eauton," in *Manuscript Remains*, ed. A. Hübscher, trans. E. F. J. Payne (Oxford: Berg, 1990), vol. IV, 486–87. And note the explicit "we, the salt of the earth" in *PP* II:275. Cf. Hübscher's relevant remarks in *The Philosophy of Schopenhauer in its Intellectual Context*, 142.

extraordinary intellectual standing – point us clearly to his characterisation of the artist-genius and the supra-individual subjectivity he brings to
bear on his encounter with the world.

Yet if this kind of evidence already prepares us to look beyond immediate appearances, perhaps the most direct key for gaining access to what
lies past them – what Schopenhauer himself would have called the "subterranean route" – is the very notion of articulation mentioned moments
ago as the heart of Schopenhauer's view of the philosophical task. For if
philosophy articulates, what it articulates into rational form, as may be
recalled from the last chapter, is something that originally constitutes a
knowledge of perception or feeling. Indeed, the emphasis on immediate
experience, and on a direct confrontation with the perceived world as the
genetic source of insight, forms a central element in Schopenhauer's philosophical self-understanding – and the understanding of where his own
philosophical distinction lies. For "the entire neglect of knowledge of perception," Schopenhauer writes, "has at all times been the main source of
the errors of dogmatic philosophising" (*WWR* II:85). And Schopenhauer's
view of the uniqueness of his own philosophy is then summed up in the
contrasting claim that "each one of [its doctrines] has been thought out in
the presence of perceived reality and none has its root in abstract concepts
alone" (*WWR* II:184). In this respect, it shares precisely the orientation
of the arts, as made clear in the telling remark that "to enrich the concept from perception is the constant endeavour of poetry *and* philosophy"
(*WWR* II:74; emphasis added).[21]

The open connection forged in this remark between art and philosophy
is laid even barer elsewhere, where the long-awaited cues – still spartan,
yet sufficiently clear – are finally received. For it is not *any* kind of intuition or perception, but the specific intuition that forms the object of the
aesthetic regard – "that purely objective intuitive perception ... wherein
the (Platonic) Ideas of things are apprehended" – that, in *Parerga and
Paralipomena*, is explicitly named as the material and kernel, not only of
works of art, but indeed of "a real philosophical argument" (*PP* II:418). And
driving more directly into the revelatory moment providing his own philosophy with its spine, Schopenhauer would elsewhere state: "whenever the
inner nature of mankind is disclosed to us in history or in our own experience, we have apprehended this experience poetically" (*WWR* I:244). The
suggestive analogies traced above between Schopenhauer's characterisation

---

[21] Cf. *PP* II:9: "Like art and poetry, [philosophy] must have its source in an apprehension of the world
through intuitive perception."

of the aesthetic and philosophical standpoints, in turn, prove to be far from incidental, and what was merely suggested there is stated explicitly when Schopenhauer remarks that both "philosophy but also the fine arts work at bottom towards the solution of the problem of existence," to satisfy the desire to "comprehend the true nature of things, of life, and of existence" and give "an answer to the question, 'What is life?'" (*WWR* II:406).[22] What is also worth noting in this context is that in specifying the "what" that philosophy takes as its question – a question answered through a statement of the inner nature of the world – Schopenhauer can often be seen alternating between two different formulations. For the correct answer to the question "what *is* the world?" is strictly speaking "will"; and this indeed is the specification Schopenhauer often invokes. At other times, however, it is the Ideas that figure as the primary reference, as attested by Schopenhauer's remark that

> the genuine method of considering the world philosophically, in other words, that consideration which acquaints us with the inner nature of the world and thus takes us beyond the phenomenon, is precisely the method that does not ask about the whence, whither, and why of the world, but always and everywhere about the *what* alone ... thus it is the inner nature of the world ... *in other words the Ideas of the world*, that forms the object of our method of philosophy. (*WWR* I:274; last emphasis added)[23]

Turning back, in fact, to the observation concerning Schopenhauer's characterisation of philosophy in rational or conceptual terms, it would seem that the soundest way of understanding this is by taking the conceptual to constitute, not the starting point, but the form in which the starting point that gives philosophy its material – what is essentially a feeling, intuition, or perception – comes to be expressed. Philosophy, to put

[22] In some of Schopenhauer's pre-*WWR* reflections, as Hübscher notes, the link between art and philosophy was made even more strongly and went as far as identifying the two, as in the bald statement: "philosophy is art" (*The Philosophy of Schopenhauer in its Intellectual Context*, 49). Hübscher stresses the continuity between these views and those expressed in Schopenhauer's main work. Another note found in Schopenhauer's *Nachlaß*, cited by Alexis Philonenko (*Schopenhauer* [Paris: Vrin, 1980], 177), is more significant in turning this statement on his own philosophy: "My philosophy must be distinguished from all preceding ones, with the exception of Plato's, in that it is not a science but an art."

[23] The same thing is implied in a remark already quoted – "everyone knows without further help what the world is, for he himself is the subject of knowing of which the world is representation": *WWR* I:82 – in so far as the subject of knowing forms the correlate of the Ideas. Yet note in this connection Sandra Shapsay's argument that the "strict" answer in terms of the will also bears a poetic character, one attesting the proximity of art and philosophy and Schopenhauer's status as a "poetic metaphysician": "Poetic intuition and the bounds of sense: metaphor and metonymy in Schopenhauer's philosophy," in A. Neill and C. Janaway, eds., *Better Consciousness: Schopenhauer's Philosophy of Value* (Oxford: Wiley-Blackwell, 2009). See also the next section.

it plainly, "is not supposed to work *out of* concepts, but *into* them, in other words, to deposit its results in them, but not to start from them as that which is given" (*WWR* II:83).[24] To give abstract or rational form to experience merely means to render it communicable – and to *that* extent Schopenhauer would avow his philosophy to be rationalistic (*PP* II:10).

Philosophy then aims to commute an intuition into a communicable thought. And to the extent that this intuition is aesthetic – to the extent that philosophy takes its material from an intuition identified in certain locations with the aesthetic object *par excellence*, the Idea – the aesthetic character of philosophy is already manifested in its starting point.[25] That, however, only still forms half of the story. To place the full story before us, it is a typically Schopenhauerian move that we need to perform, turning inward to take stock of our own responses. Because to many readers, the encounter with Schopenhauer's work would seem impossible to characterise fully in terms that fail to make reference to the aesthetic character of one's response to it. And it has been Schopenhauer's dazzling flair for the winning image that has often stood at the foreground of this encounter, imparting to the reading experience many of its climactic moments.

Schopenhauer can never resist an image – a simile, an analogy – to illustrate his philosophical positions; time and time again, he reformulates his points anew in vivid comparisons, as if perpetually on the look-out for better-fitting bezels to bring out the sparkle of precious gems. Wittgenstein once complained of being unable to shake off a disposition to think in pictorial ways; Schopenhauer positively revels in it.[26] We have already had the chance to witness this in considering Schopenhauer's resolution of the fear of death, where the use of image emerged as a central motif. Yet a few additional examples can help bring this pervasive bent more fully alive in this context. We may thus consider the analogy Schopenhauer offers on the same theme – the fear of death – in a bid to win us over to his view of our eternal nature: "Just as on the globe everywhere is above, so the form of all life is the *present*; and to fear death because it robs us

---

[24] Cf. Hübscher, *The Philosophy of Schopenhauer in its Intellectual Context*, 183 (see also 184).

[25] My view thus agrees with James D. Chansky's as framed in "Schopenhauer and Platonic Ideas: a groundwork for an aesthetic metaphysics," in von der Luft, ed., *Schopenhauer: New Essays in Honor of His 200th Birthday*, 81, n.14. See also in the same volume Jerry S. Clegg's "Schopenhauer and Wittgenstein on lonely languages and criterialess claims," for some interesting remarks about the "extraordinary, private language of the genius" (with whom Schopenhauer is classed) relevant to this context.

[26] I have in mind the remark relayed by Ray Monk in *Wittgenstein: The Duty of Genius* (London: Vintage, 1991), 379.

of the present is no wiser than to fear that we can slip down from the round globe on the top of which we are now fortunately standing" (*WWR* I:280). Or again: "Death … is like the setting of the sun, which is only apparently engulfed by the night, but actually, itself the source of all light, burns without intermission, brings new days to new worlds, and is always rising and always setting" (*WWR* I:366). Discussing the priority of the will over the mind: "the intellect strikes up the tune, and the will must dance to it; in fact, the intellect causes it to play the part of the child whom its nurse at her pleasure puts into the most different moods by chatter and tales alternating between pleasant and melancholy things" (*WWR* II:208). Discussing the renunciation of the saint: "If we compare life to a circular path of red-hot coals having a few cool places, a path that we have to run over incessantly, then the man entangled in delusion is comforted by the cool place on which he is just now standing … and sets out to run over the path. But the man who sees through the *principium individuationis* … is no longer susceptible of such consolation; he sees himself in all places simultaneously, and withdraws" (*WWR* I:380).

Such examples could be multiplied indefinitely, and for many readers, what they would illustrate is a point made expressly by Bryan Magee when he wrote about Schopenhauer's use of images that they "demand from the reader an imaginative response which is almost poetic."[27] And the accent, I believe, should indeed be placed on the notion of a "demand" just invoked, and on the question this invites concerning the status of such literary elements in Schopenhauer's understanding of philosophy. It has sometimes been asked, in the ongoing debates about the relationship between philosophy and literature, what importance we should attach to the form or style of a piece of philosophical writing in approaching it. In Arthur Danto's view, the key question concerns the relationship between the concept of philosophical truth and the form of philosophical expression as this should be understood. Analytical philosophers, in this respect, have often been accused of a cavalier disregard of form – of the dialogue (in Plato), the meditation (in Descartes) – in seeking to engage the philosophical past on their own terms. Yet in doing so, Danto suggests, they run the risk of ignoring what the form of the text may be telling us about the notion of truth at stake, and the kind of relationship to which the text seeks to summon the reader: for it is possible that

---

[27] Magee, *The Philosophy of Schopenhauer*, 47–48, in the context of the observation that "all through his writings [Schopenhauer] tries to relate his formulations to concrete perceptions," some of which "enter permanently into one's way of seeing things."

"something is intended to happen to the reader other than or in addition to being informed."[28]

One might raise a similar (if not identical) question concerning the philosophical importance, and methodological status, attaching to the poetic elements of Schopenhauer's writing. And I would suggest that there is a strong argument to be made for deeming the presence of these elements far from incidental, reflecting something deeper about Schopenhauer's epistemic ideal – about the notion of truth-making involved, and what must "happen to the reader" in making contact with it. For central to this ideal is an emphasis on perception and immediate experience that we have already seen, and that Schopenhauer expresses again clearly in the apophthegmatic remark that "all truth and all wisdom ultimately lie in *perception*" (*WWR* II:74). Yet Schopenhauer contributes something more to his specification of this ideal when in *Parerga and Paralipomena* he states: "To understand anything really and truly, it is necessary for us to grasp it *in intuitive perception*, to receive a clear picture [*ein deutliches Bild*] of it, if possible from reality itself, but otherwise by means of the imagination" (*PP* II:48). What this remark betrays is a governing equation between perceptual representations and images, which Schopenhauer reinforces more explicitly elsewhere.[29] It is this equation, combined with the privilege assigned to perceptual knowledge, that seems to underlie the special status carried by the image in Schopenhauer's epistemology.[30] Truth takes place in perception, and perceptual representations are pictures.

Given this view, Schopenhauer's embrace of poetic image may seem unsurprising; and Schopenhauer makes the connections clear when, having identified "genuine comprehension" with perception and the grasp of image, he relates this to the use of figurative expressions, whose aim is precisely to "reduce everything abstract to something intuitively perceptual" (*PP* II:48) and thus secure the object of understanding. It is indeed the broader capacity to discern patterns, analogies, and similarities – a capacity of which the use of figurative language would seem to constitute a more particular manifestation – that Schopenhauer elsewhere marks out as the special appanage of people with exceptional intellectual powers

---

[28] Arthur C. Danto, "Philosophy and/as/of literature," in G. L. Hagberg and W. Jost, eds., *A Companion to the Philosophy of Literature* (Oxford: Wiley-Blackwell, 2010), 55.

[29] See for example *WWR* I:95; II:67 (*Bilder* is the recurring word); this assumption is also expressed in Schopenhauer's comparison of consciousness to a "lantern" at *WWR* II:138.

[30] What is in question here is the special status of images as perceptual representations in general, as contrasted with conceptual or abstract representations. Those particular perceptual representations that take Ideas as their object – aesthetic representations – carry an additional though related privilege.

(*WWR* II:29).[31] This is the larger epistemological context that must be taken to situate Schopenhauer's own heavy employment of images and the pronounced literary features of his writing. It has been suggested that in Plato's works, "the use of images ... to convey philosophical insights demonstrates something philosophical about modes of human knowing."[32] Something similar could be said of Schopenhauer.

Yet it is now important to consider how the epistemic ideal just outlined stands to be related to the different forms of art as Schopenhauer understands these. For there is one particular form of art that this ideal would seem to stand in an especially intimate relation to; and that is poetry. To see this, all we need to do is to briefly bring into view how Schopenhauer characterises the task of poetry in his main work. For poets, as for other artists, what underpins artistic activity is a prior encounter with the Ideas through direct experience of the world. Having come into contact with the Ideas, the poet's task is to establish this contact for the reader using his special medium – abstract concepts. In the *World as Will and Representation*, Schopenhauer reaches for the telling language of chemistry to describe the transformation involved: "Just as the chemist obtains solid precipitates by combining perfectly clear and transparent fluids, so does the poet know how to precipitate, as it were, the concrete ... the representation of perception, out of the abstract, transparent universality of ... concepts" (*WWR* I:243). This activity, it will be readily seen, arrives as a direct fulfilment of the epistemic ideal articulated above. Yet it is important to place the chemical process in full display before proceeding further, and this involves attending, not only to the agency of the artist, but also to the activity exacted from the reader. For if the poet is to succeed in communicating the Ideas to the reader through the use of abstract concepts, Schopenhauer explains, "this can take place only by the assistance of his own imagination" (*WWR* I:243; cf. *WWR* II:424ff.). This is an assistance that Schopenhauer elsewhere stipulates as "a condition of aesthetic effect," extending to all fine arts as their "fundamental law" (*WWR* II:407–8).

The task of poetry thus turns out to involve two kinds of commutation. On the one hand – and resuming the terms we had earlier used to describe the philosophical task – it seeks to commute the intuition of an Idea into communicable form, performing a movement away from immediate experience to the shared world of language. Yet this movement

---

[31] Cf. *WWR* II:72: "All original thinking is done in pictures or images."
[32] Jill Gordon, *Turning toward Philosophy: Literary Device and Dramatic Structure in Plato's Dialogues* (University Park, PA: Pennsylvania State University Press, 1999), 13.

then finds its complement in another – a commutation working in the opposite direction, designed to return us to the immediacy of experience. For the next step, taking place within the reader, must be to return the concept to its origin, placing the reader in contact with the intuitions that formed its living source, and mobilising the reader's imagination for this achievement.

If we were looking for a paradigm within Schopenhauer's analysis of artistic forms in which his own writing could best be situated, it is indeed poetry that would seem to present the most hospitable terms, allowing us to locate both Schopenhauer's reliance on imagery and the explicit appeal to the imagination to which this is tied. It seems to be no accident, in this respect, that in several places Schopenhauer draws poetry and philosophy into special connection, as we saw earlier (*WWR* I:244; II:74). As with poetry, the aesthetic character of philosophy turns out to be realised on two closely related levels: with regard to its origin, in taking its beginning (at least in part) from an objective apprehension, and with regard to its expressive form, in using imagery to place the reader in contact with its genetic fount.[33]

Indeed, even without the inward look – to our own responses – that gave us our foothold for bringing the aesthetic character of Schopenhauer's work to clearer articulation, the striking manner in which Schopenhauer insists on characterising his own work might have served us equally well as an initial compass. "A single thought," Schopenhauer would assert in introducing the first edition, is in reality all that finds itself expressed in the lengthy discursive journey extending between these two covers (*WWR* I:xii–xiii; cf. 285–86). Not a system of thought – whose parts stand connected in chainlike relations of dependence, of prior and posterior; in which one stone supports another, and should one give way, *a fortiori* should the founding stone do so, the supervening edifice collapses – but a single thought constituting an organic unity, whose parts

---

[33] To locate philosophy within a poetic paradigm is not to collapse the two. Schopenhauer himself offers a suggestive handle on the differences in *WWR* II:382 when he contrasts the philosopher's guiding question ("What is all this?") with the artist's ("*How* is it really constituted?"), and again in some remarks in *WWR* II:406–7, which Julian Young glosses as offering a distinction between saying and showing: "while a great and successful philosophy *says* what life is like, art *shows* what it is like" (*Schopenhauer* [London and New York: Routledge, 2005], 137, and generally 137–42). Yet of course different arts have different ways of drawing the balance between showing and saying, and poetry in particular shows *through* saying, in Schopenhauer's view. See also Young's interesting earlier discussion in *Willing and Unwilling*, 97–99, focused by the question whether Schopenhauer's account has not indeed reduced art to philosophy; Young similarly concludes that the standpoint of the genius is common to both artist and philosopher. And see also Schaeffer's relevant (though harsh) discussion in *Art of the Modern Age*, 201–6.

might be dispersed for the purpose of communicating them to another's understanding, but all the while retain the most cohesive internal bonds.

A perfect unity diffusing itself spatio-temporally through the prism of understanding – yet these, of course, are terms that immediately evoke the ones Schopenhauer uses to describe the Ideas as they enter the filters of individual representation.[34] As such, they point powerfully towards the aesthetic notions governing Schopenhauer's philosophical self-understanding. And they do so, it may be noticed, in ways that provoke a telling echo of Schopenhauer's description of the philosophical task as we have elsewhere seen it. Not to demonstrate – not to move forward from one claim to another in a linear progression typical of argument, of "philosophy as system" – but to articulate a single intuition into its prismatic conceptual form.[35]

Inward, outward – forward through rational argument? The "argument from analogy" revisited

I have been arguing that the participation of Schopenhauer's philosophy in the standpoint identified on his own terms as aesthetic enters into Schopenhauer's self-understanding in important ways, and should do so equally in the way we characterise his philosophical standpoint. In this context, the discussion surveyed earlier – Schopenhauer's response to the fear of death, with its focus on images, its conscription of the imagination, and references to the archetypal aesthetic objects, the Ideas – becomes easier to place, and read in its entire significance.

There is still a final step to be taken before the above account is complete – a step that will enable us to extend it to its full reach, and in doing so, to tie our evidence more tightly together. Yet it will be helpful here to briefly pause to survey the distance covered, placing in full profile the understanding of Schopenhauer's philosophical method that has emerged from this investigation. Our point of departure was an apparent conflict between two standpoints or methods exhibited in Schopenhauer's work – the subjective or inward-looking standpoint avowed by Schopenhauer, and a different objective or outward-looking standpoint invoked in his discussion of the fear of death. A closer examination of the latter pointed us towards its aesthetic character, and a broader sweep of the evidence

---

[34] Compare Hübscher's suggestive remarks in *The Philosophy of Schopenhauer in its Intellectual Context*, 113–14.
[35] Cf. Atwell, *Schopenhauer on the Character of the World*, 2.

suggested that it stands to be aligned with a more wide-ranging specification of the philosophical standpoint in aesthetic terms. With the apparent
conflict resolved, both turns – inward and outward – thus demand to be
recognised as occupying an integral place in Schopenhauer's philosophy.

I have been speaking of two turns distinct enough to be placed in conflict; yet having argued for the presence of both in Schopenhauer's scheme,
it is important to attend to what unites rather than divides them. For
the facts of self-consciousness that provide one's inner gateway to what
lies beyond the phenomenal clearly stand to be distinguished from the
objects of aesthetic vision, which are located firmly within the phenomenal boundary. As John Atwell points out (echoing Schopenhauer), the
awareness of the will cannot be a matter of intuition (*Anschauung*) – as are
the Ideas – because all intuition is spatial and the willing subject is not in
space.[36] Yet the identity of one's will and one's body that constitutes the
metaphysical insight produced by this inward look, we may note, is one
that Schopenhauer describes as a knowledge in the concrete (*Erkenntniß
in concreto*), and a knowledge one normally possesses as feeling (*Gefühl*)
(*WWR* I:102, 109).[37] As Schopenhauer explains elsewhere (*WWR* I:51–53),
"feeling" is a broad category that includes every modification of consciousness that does not constitute an abstract knowledge of reason; thus,
it is essentially a negative concept. As such, the perception of the Ideas
must also be presumed to be included within its scope. It is this general
epistemic category therefore under which both turns – inward and outward – allow themselves to be jointly ranged, providing Schopenhauer's
method with its formal unity. Not reason, but feeling: this is the soil from
which philosophy takes its beginning and its material. And this, after all,
was a point that Schopenhauer had already openly proclaimed when he
had written, "everyone knows without further help what the world is"; the
task of philosophy is simply to "reproduce this in the abstract," providing
rational articulation to "successive, variable perceptions, and generally all
that the wide concept of *feeling* embraces" (*WWR* I:82).

Yet this statement of methodological unity, it must now be remarked, is
not entirely free from difficulties – difficulties once again stemming from a
scrupulous comparison of different regions of Schopenhauer's philosophy,

---

[36] *Ibid.*, 121; cf. *WWR* II:196.

[37] As Moira Nicholls argues, the use of the language of manifestation to speak of the relationship
between these ostensibly separate things makes it clear that what is in question – the access to
which consists in feeling – is the will as thing-in-itself. See Nicholls, "Schopenhauer, feeling and
the noumenon," *Schopenhauer-Jahrbuch*, 76 (1995), 64–65; and see generally 53–71 for a helpful
account of the centrality of feeling in Schopenhauer's thought.

and this time the testimony of his theoretical remarks with the evidence of his practice. It is in fact the formulation employed in closing the last section that here offers us the best point of entry into one of the most important difficulties. The task of philosophy, it was said, is not to move forward from one claim to another, in the style of systematic philosophy; philosophy indeed does away with proof and rational argument altogether. It is a description of the philosophical task, of course, that will be familiar from the previous chapter, which the above remarks concerning the status of feeling directly resumed. If the notion of "movement" is to be applied to philosophical inquiry at all, I suggested in Chapter 1, the most appropriate way of characterising this would be as a movement, not *forward*, but *upward* – a movement upward from knowledge of perception or feeling to its rational articulation.

And yet it may not have passed unnoticed that it was precisely the vocabulary of a rectilinear progression "forward" that had infiltrated that earlier discussion (Chapter 1) at a key juncture. For Schopenhauer's philosophical discovery, indeed, appeared to bear the character of a sequential unfolding from the start: *first* there was the experiment of imagining one's body from an objective vantage point (one's will estranged); *then* the surprised recovery of one's body from the inside (one's will remarked); *then* the realisation – intuitive and indemonstrable – that one's body *is* one's will. Yet this sequential character appeared to deepen as soon as that first indemonstrable insight was achieved, and having turned inward to discover the will as one's own inner nature, one turned outward to recognise it as the inner nature of all phenomena. One went on to extend that first insight to other human beings, via a rejection of solipsism; then to all other beings, via a rejection of the uniqueness of the human phenomenon; and then to the entire world. "Moving forward in this manner," I had suggested, one gradually came to recognise the will in all natural phenomena. Yet how now, given Schopenhauer's own view of the philosophical task, could one make sense of this sequential movement?

It is a question that commentators have not ceased to press; and given the position of high architectonic importance this moment occupies in Schopenhauer's philosophical process, it is no accident that it should have come up for special – and often incisive – scrutiny. If our attention was earlier focused on the tense relation between "outward" and "inward" in Schopenhauer's method, it is the "forward" that has seemed particularly troubling in this part of his account. The visible ambivalence displayed by readers over the most appropriate term for characterising the moment at stake is in itself revealing of the interpretative difficulties involved.

And these, above all, are difficulties concerning how to engage the strong emphasis on argument or demonstration – the very notions whose applicability in philosophy Schopenhauer had elsewhere called into question – that appears to govern it, imparting to this movement forward all the inevitability of a logical drive. We find it referred to as a process of "projection" or "transfer" (Schopenhauer's own locution); yet we also find it referred to as "an argument" – an "argument from analogy" that, Arthur Hübscher notes, has long been deemed to hold Schopenhauer's thought together.[38]

And the last characterisation, it must be admitted, would seem to find significant grounds for support in Schopenhauer's discussion. How to deny, indeed, the logical transitions that appear to form the hinges of the movement by which philosophical insight flows outward from self, to other human beings, to world? *If* the key to my own phenomenon is the will, *then* the same must be the case for other human beings. *If* it is the case with other human beings, it *must* be the case with all other beings and phenomena in this world. *Otherwise*, my only discovery would be a personal truth applicable to none other than myself.[39]

Yet if this is an argument, as several commentators have suggested, it seems to be an awkward one in many ways. As Robert Wicks has interestingly observed, for example, the analogy seems to move entirely in the wrong direction. "If we have a large set of items that are identical in many key respects," he points out, "and if we are sure that a newly encountered item has all those key respects, except for one, about which there remains some uncertainty, then it is reasonable to suppose that it has the remaining aspect."[40] In this case, by contrast, we are not trying to subsume the one into the many, but the reverse. Julian Young, on his part, has suggested that the transfer of the metaphysical insight to organic nature is more strongly motivated by rational grounds than the transfer to inorganic nature. The former is grounded in Schopenhauer's understanding of teleology, but "in contrast to the *demand* for the extension of will to organic nature, we have a certain choice about extending it any further." Schopenhauer, however, offers us two reasons for completing the transfer, in Young's view: the law of homogeneity (which seeks to subsume all species under the highest genus, and methodologically demands that if we

[38] Hübscher, *The Philosopher of Schopenhauer in its Intellectual Context*, 70. Hübscher's reference to this as a "so-called" argument is suggestive of his own view of the matter.
[39] The key passages are to be found in section 19 of *WWR* I.
[40] Wicks, *Schopenhauer*, 55.

can extend it, we *must*); and the fact that failure to do so would condemn our understanding of the natural world to irredeemable obscurity.[41]

Writing in a similar context, John Atwell initially calls upon the language of argument and inference in discussing this philosophical moment, yet he goes on to suggest that, on closer inspection, the argument fails due to a problematic premise, namely, that we represent other bodies in the same way as we represent our own. He then proposes an alternative construal that centres on Schopenhauer's analysis of human action and takes Schopenhauer's main insight to concern the duplicity of human action – as a bodily movement and as an act of will, or as a manifestation of character and an act of character. Yet this proposal, significantly, is accompanied by an outright dismissal of the language of argument and inference. Schopenhauer, Atwell states, "does not think … that logic or reasoning (certainly not reasoning by way of an argument by analogy) demands an extension of what we recognise about ourselves to outer objects." And like Young, Atwell stresses Schopenhauer's reliance on the unwelcome consequences of failure to perform this extension: the acceptance of the mad, but also evil, belief in theoretical egoism (what was referred to as "solipsism" above), and the failure to arrive at a satisfactory understanding of the world.[42]

What these readings suggest is that if there is an argument, it is only an argument in part, or it is an argument that fails its purpose; and on one interpretation, there is no argument at all. Yet if we set aside the merits of the argument itself, it is important, in approaching the issue, to be clear about the consequences that would arise for Schopenhauer's own philosophy from granting the mere existence of argument in this context. And the central consequence, as already stated, would be to reveal a grave stress fracture within his philosophy, bringing Schopenhauer's philosophical practice and his philosophical theory – where the disavowal of argument had been expressed in clarion terms – into direct collision, and into a collision taking place right within its heart. Given the problems of internal

---

[41] See Young, *Willing and Unwilling*, 68–70; Young's view is embedded in his controversial naturalistic interpretation of Schopenhauer: what would thus fail to be completed is a *scientific* account of the world; his invocation of teleology is grounded in a similar framework.

[42] See Atwell, *Schopenhauer on the Character of the World*, ch. 4, for Atwell's discussion of the discovery of the will and argument from analogy; 94 quoted. Cf. the remarks on 102, which rehearse the claim concerning the absence of argument in seemingly stronger yet also seemingly question-begging terms ("there is no, and can be no, transference of what I find as my essence to other things; for to find the essence of anything is to find the essence of everything"). Matthew A. Ray criticises Atwell's view in his *Subjectivity and Irreligion: Atheism and Agnosticism in Kant, Schopenhauer and Nietzsche* (Aldershot: Ashgate, 2003), 44; but Ray seems to confuse the general deployment of a notion of analogy; and the more specific use of an *argument* from analogy.

coherence this would pose, not to mention the problems attaching to the argument itself, this ought to serve as a *prima facie* ground for conferring on the last-mentioned interpretation – one doubting the presence of argument – the default privilege.

It is then as a way of redeeming this privilege that one might suggest returning to Schopenhauer's account to consider in greater detail one of its climactic moments – the moment in section 21 of *WWR* I, where Schopenhauer turns to recapitulate the first step of the discovery: my nature is will. The passage that follows is one that we have already seen in part in Chapter 1, and can now place before us in full to appraise its significance. "The reader who with me has gained this conviction" – the conviction concerning his own nature – Schopenhauer writes, "will find that of itself it will become the key to the knowledge of the innermost being of the whole of nature." He continues:

> He will recognize that same will not only in those phenomena that are quite similar to his own, in men and animals, as their innermost nature, but continued reflection will lead him to recognize the force that shoots and vegetates in the plant, indeed the force by which the crystal is formed, the force that turns the magnet to the North Pole, the force whose shock he encounters from the contact of metals of different kinds, the force that appears in the elective affinities of matter as repulsion and attraction, separation and union, and finally even gravitation, which acts so powerfully in all matter, pulling the stone to the earth and the earth to the sun; all these he will recognize as different only in the phenomenon, but the same according to their inner nature. He will recognize them all as that which is immediately known to him so intimately and better than everything else, and where it appears most distinctly is called *will*. It is only this application of reflection which ... leads us on to the *thing-in-itself*. (*WWR* I:109–10)

Now how are we to understand the epistemic process placed on display in this marvellously suggestive passage? We may notice that Schopenhauer speaks of "continued reflection" (*Reflexion*). Atwell glosses: "hence" what is at stake is "a function or operation of human reason." For one of the capacities and functions of reason, as Schopenhauer himself has suggested, is to survey the world as a whole (recall: "the universal survey of life as a whole [is] an advantage which man has over the animal through the faculty of reason," *WWR* I:85). And it is such an act of holistic surveying that Atwell takes this passage to be representing. This, in turn, appears to provide the grounds for Atwell's view – which seems to sit awkwardly with the non-rationalistic bent of his account of Schopenhauer's metaphysical insight as we just heard it – that philosophical knowledge is gained through reason.[43]

And yet is this indeed the most plausible interpretation? For on the one hand, it must be readily conceded that in the overwhelming majority of contexts in which the term "reflection" appears, it seems to be strongly linked with rational and abstract knowledge. We see this, for example, in the remark with which Schopenhauer introduces the notion of abstract reason in *WWR* I:36, writing: "yet another faculty has appeared in man alone of all the inhabitants of the earth; an entirely new consciousness has arisen, which with very appropriate and significant accuracy is called *reflection [Reflexion]*." We see it again in a remark that contains a quintessential expression of Schopenhauer's view of philosophical inquiry: "intuitively ... every man is really conscious of all philosophical truths; but to bring them into his abstract knowledge, into *reflection*, is the business of the philosopher" (*WWR* I:383; emphasis added). On the other hand, it may be noted that there is a certain slippage between two separate terms indifferently translated as "reflection" in Payne's English text – namely, *Reflexion* and *Besonnenheit* – and there are contexts in which the latter is associated, not with the abstract knowledge of reason, but with the objective perceptual knowledge of genius.[44]

Such considerations might seem to lend force to Atwell's remark that the internal evidence is too slender, and Schopenhauer too reticent on the topic, to fix the usage of this term and give it a firm and technical place within Schopenhauer's epistemology.[45] And in the light of such evidential shortage, the main basis for Atwell's interpretation would seem to lie in the assumption – apparently supported by Schopenhauer's own testimony – that a more holistic way of regarding the world forms the epistemic preserve of reason. Now on the one hand, the foregoing discussion should already have done some work to loosen the grip of this kind of assumption, in bringing into view an encounter with a boundless ("holistic") object that turned out to be aligned with an aesthetic rather than rational regard.[46] Yet

---

[43] Atwell, *Schopenhauer on the Character of the World*, 102; cf. 179: "the abstract, philosophical knowledge (gained through the 'faculty of reason')."

[44] For example, *WWR* II:382: "in this sense [the genius] is reflective [*besonnen*]"; cf. *WWR* I:518, where reflection is again linked with reason, yet this time indicated by *Besonnenheit*: "deliberation and reflection [*Besonnenheit*] have arisen in man through the gift of reason" (and cf. *WWR* II:571, where the relevant term is *Besinnung*). The former passage (II:382) is picked up by Cheryl Foster when she aligns reflection with the extra-ordinary (and supra-rational) perception of the genius: "Ideas and imagination," 225–27.

[45] Atwell, *Schopenhauer on the Character of the World*, 204, n.45.

[46] And see Chapter 3 for a more direct attempt to dislodge this assumption.

to loosen it further, it is to the above passage itself that we need to turn back to discover the resources that best serve to interpret it.

For Schopenhauer indeed has spoken of the application of "reflection" as what "leads" a person who has gained the primary insight into his own nature to discern the same nature in everything around him. Yet it is a rather different emphasis – an emphasis not on compulsive logical progression, but on freely self-disposing movement – that has been sounded in the remark just preceding, where the initial conviction is described as one that "of itself" becomes a key for the understanding of nature. The reader "*will* find" – not the reader "*must*." Whatever view we take of these delicate markers, however, it is clear that there is little in the act of reflection presented in this passage to suggest a progression mimicking an argument in form – a progression from one claim to another, from premises to conclusion. Instead, it is a different kind of affinity that this passage evokes. For we may recall, in this context, one of the ways in which Schopenhauer elsewhere speaks of the philosophical task. Faced with a world of unknown "ciphers" and "signs," philosophy strives to decipher them; the mark of a successful deciphering is the way it places phenomena in the greatest agreement. It is to this picture that the above passage unobtrusively returns us – with its suspenseful notion of a "key," suggestive of closed doors and unsolved mysteries – and likewise to its conception of epistemic achievement, one that lies in the discovery of agreement, of harmonious connections, of recurrent pattern. The keyword here is "recognition"; it is a matter of coming to recognise that everything around one exhibits a common pattern or signature, so that one sees everything *as* something or sees something *in* everything. The act of reflection registers as a moment of perceptual synthesis, of synthesising disparate phenomena under a single sign – the sign that represents what is essential in them.

Yet these, of course, are terms that directly evoke the ways in which we have heard Schopenhauer describe aesthetic contemplation. The cognitive act through which one succeeds in beholding the will in particulars – and the will, Schopenhauer writes, "is indivisible and is wholly present in every phenomenon"[47] – and that act through which one succeeds in beholding the Ideas both involve a transcendence of the particular towards its

---

[47] *WWR* I:155 (cf. I:332); there is some awkwardness here given that, as Hilde Hein notes, the will can no more be "in" the phenomenon than can the Ideas, given that the distinction between the will, the Ideas, and particulars is epistemological and not ontological in kind ("Schopenhauer and Platonic Ideas," 135–36).

essential reality. Already, the link to the aesthetic context seems plainly carved out. It stands out even more plainly elsewhere, and nowhere more so than in a remark that appears only shortly after the passage we have been considering, to resume and re-express its standpoint. There, leaving behind the descriptive tones he had earlier employed to characterise the transition by which the will is read into the entire world ("he will recognise," "continued reflection will lead"), Schopenhauer turns to issue us with an invitation – an invitation whose protreptic undertone may make our memory stir.[48] "Let us consider attentively [*mit forschendem Blicke betrachten*] and observe," he suggests to us there,

> the powerful, irresistible impulse with which masses of water rush downwards, the persistence and determination with which the magnet always turns back to the North Pole, the keen desire with which iron flies to the magnet, the vehemence with which the poles of the electric current strive for reunion, and which, like the vehemence of human desires, is increased by obstacles. Let us *look* at the crystal being rapidly and suddenly formed with such regularity of configuration; it is obvious that this is only a perfectly definite and precisely determined striving in different directions constrained and held firm by coagulation. Let us *observe* the choice with which bodies repel and attract one another, unite and separate, when set free in the fluid state and released from the bonds of rigidity ... If we *observe* all this, it will not cost us a great effort of the *imagination* [*Einbildungskraft*] to recognise once more our own inner nature, even at so great a distance. (*WWR* I:117–18; emphasis added)

With the last remark, the penny finally drops – yet in a way that only makes explicit something that the visual language pervasive throughout the text had already richly signalled. And this is that the effort of recognition to which it is appealing is one distinctly aesthetic in kind. To see the will in all things, we need to *look* – and to look with the eyes of the imagination.[49] It was an exercise of the imagination, as we have already had occasion to discover, that Schopenhauer would not be urging upon his readers for the last time.

If the above is correct, Schopenhauer's philosophical practice in this central moment turns out to be in full harmony with his theory, preserving its commitment to excluding rational argument from the sphere

---

[48] I speak of an "undertone" and not a "tone" given that, unlike Payne's openly protreptic "Let us ...," in the German this invitation is issued more indirectly through a conditional: "*Wenn wir ...*"

[49] Hübscher picks up on this aesthetic appeal from a different yet related perspective when he comments on Schopenhauer's figurative use of language in this connection: *The Philosophy of Schopenhauer in its Intellectual Context*, 75.

of philosophical method.[50] What takes its place is seen to be a way of
engaging the phenomena that bears a strongly aesthetic aspect. Unified
in this manner, Schopenhauer's method exhibits the double character of
an inward and outward turn that share their opposition to the methods
of rational thought. Yet I would argue that, even with this richer account
in place, the character – and more specifically the aesthetic character – of
Schopenhauer's philosophical standpoint has still not stepped fully into
the light. For this to happen, the picture requires an additional touch of
depth; or what, in keeping with Schopenhauer's own diction and philosophical spirit, we might aptly call its "height." Let us turn to address it.

---

[50] To deflect the appearance of argument from this central moment is certainly not to expunge it
from Schopenhauer's works. Thus, we elsewhere hear Schopenhauer speak of "inferring" the identity of inner and outer (*PP* II:93), or of having "fully discussed and demonstrated" that the inward
turn reveals the will as the ultimate reality (*WWR* II:494; cf. *WWR* I:128: "as I believe I have sufficiently proved and made clear"). Yet it is perhaps in Schopenhauer's engagement of natural science
that the accent on demonstration is most startlingly sounded: Schopenhauer speaks of his dogma
as obtaining "more detailed and special proofs" through the results of the empirical sciences; of the
concordance between these results and a philosophical system as offering "so firm and satisfactory
external proof of its truth and correctness that none greater is possible" (*On the Will in Nature*,
trans. E. F. J. Payne, ed. D. E. Cartwright [New York and Oxford: Berg, 1992], 3, 22). In this context, however, there is much to suggest that a recognition of metaphysical truth is presupposed
for the evidence of science to be recognised *as* a proof of that truth. Similarly, there is evidence
that even scientific experience ultimately rests on a moment of perception strongly aesthetic in
kind. Discussing William Herschel's reference to gravity as a form of "will" (*On the Will in Nature*,
85), for example, Schopenhauer advises us, in order to "share in [Herschel's] *aperçu*," to "carefully
observe the violent fall of a stream over masses of rock, and ask ourselves whether so decided an
effort, such raging, can occur without an exertion of strength, and whether any exertion is conceivable without will" (87). Talk of "conceiving" and "conceivability" suggests a rational examination
of intellectual options. Yet the first step in this "examination" ("can effort occur without exertion?",
"is exertion conceivable without will?") is a description (the stream makes *effort*, it *rages*) that is not
argued, but rather a figurative form of seeing like the one found in related passages of *WWR* and
referred to by Hübscher above.

CHAPTER 3

Philosophy as: *sublime*

Sub specie aeternitatis: philosophy as a practice of the sublime

In the last chapter, I gave several reasons for reading Schopenhauer's philosophical standpoint as aesthetic in character, arguing that both the starting point and the expressive form of Schopenhauer's philosophy invite us to engage them in aesthetic terms. Yet if that is the standpoint of philosophy, then we might have to wonder how to find our feet in the glorious passage that opens the second volume of Schopenhauer's *World as Will and Representation*:

> In endless space countless luminous spheres, round each of which some dozen smaller illuminated ones revolve, hot at the core and covered over with a hard cold crust; on this crust a mouldy film has produced living and knowing beings: this is empirical truth, the real, the world. Yet for a being who thinks, it is a precarious position to stand on one of those numberless spheres freely floating in boundless space, without knowing whence or whither, and to be only one of innumerable similar beings that throng, press, and toil, restlessly and rapidly arising and passing away in beginningless and endless time. (*WWR* II:3)

Where *is* it that we are standing as we speak (or hear) these words? Endless space extending before us; astronomical bodies spinning; we zoom in to see ourselves spinning with them. Our own head begins to spin. From what position is it that this extraordinary spectacle presents itself to our gaze? We are in the world we survey, rotating with the sphere on which we are cast; yet if we can survey our position we must also be standing outside it. So, to ask again: where do we stand? And – are we still doing philosophy? Or again: who is "we"?

It is a set of questions that Schopenhauer gives us several occasions for asking and asking again throughout his work. For this episode is not isolated; it belongs to a larger family of instances present in his writings. Connecting these instances to one another – with sometimes more weakly and sometimes more strongly visible physiognomic traits – is a standpoint that, looking towards the passage that has just given us our initial exemplar, we may call: a cosmic viewpoint, a viewpoint *sub specie aeternitatis*; or again, adopting an expression of Thomas Nagel's: a view from nowhere. For while the object available to this standpoint has the character of a sweeping cosmic vista, there is a real question to be asked as to where we stand within it.

At its weakest, the physiognomy in which this family resemblance is expressed is given in a fact so simple that it is easy for it to pass unnoticed, and this is the sheer pervasiveness with which the large notions of "life" and, even more so, "the world" appear in Schopenhauer's writings. The question that the philosopher confronts, as we have already seen, is "What is life?"; the philosopher's quest, more widely formulated, is to "comprehend the true nature of things, of life, and of existence" (*WWR* II:406). From the start, the object to which the philosopher directs his gaze is understood in spectacularly sweeping terms. In his essay "On Man's Need for Metaphysics," Schopenhauer discovers the philosopher in an act of stepping back – from nothing less than everything: detaching himself, "so to speak, from the totality of things, facing this whole" (*WWR* II:161). Yet it is often the "world" that serves as the central term in some of Schopenhauer's most important ruminations: it is the riddle of the *world* that philosophy seeks to solve; it is the inner nature of the *world – what the world is* – that preoccupies it; it is the *world* that appears on the cover as a mystery solved: it is will and representation.

"Life," "existence," and above all "world" constitute one of the salient conceptual woofs of Schopenhauer's philosophical writings, images of a whole that philosophy is responsible for addressing. And this should no more pass unnoticed than, as Martha Nussbaum has suggested, the cry "oh human being!" that Plato puts in the mouth of Sophocles near the opening of the *Republic* (329c), where what is worthwhile in human life and what is the true standpoint for value judgements of this kind has come into question. For this lofty cry, Nussbaum writes, implies clearly that "the problem lies with our distinctively human nature; that correct perception would come from a standpoint that is more than human, one that can look on the human from the outside."[1] The utterance of "human" implies an overcoming of the human, a standpoint outside it. Something

---

[1] Martha Nussbaum, *The Fragility of Goodness: Luck and Ethics in Greek Tragedy and Philosophy*, rev. edn. (Cambridge University Press, 2001), 138.

similar could be said here: the utterance of "world" implies a standpoint from which one can look on the world from outside it.

This telling if delicate conceptual signature, however, elsewhere gives way to a more strongly pronounced set of traits. It is a set of traits, in fact, that we already had occasion to bring into view in the previous chapter when discussing the fear of death. For certainly, several elements within Schopenhauer's response to this question pointed us to an aesthetic context – the vivid use of visual imagery, the recruitment of the imagination, the reference to the Ideas. Yet what needs to be registered more strongly – rehearsing a point already made in that context – is the specific nature of this imagery and of the exercise of the imagination involved in conjuring it. For the imaginative gaze invited to pick out the enduring images within the stream of time was summoned to an object marked by lack of limit, by infinite progression: to an endless series, a succession of birth and death seen in "infinitely rapid vibrations," a pyramid of beings "enduring in the species throughout the endlessness of time." The ideal philosophical observer was a being of non-human longevity who could master an infinite vista with a single magisterial gaze that launched forth – from a standpoint seemingly located outside this expanse – to pick out the Ideas standing stable within the flux.

Yet the distinctive traits that constitute this viewpoint stand out even more clearly in the flourish of breathtaking hauteur that opens one of the sections in book 4 of the first volume of the *World as Will and Representation*.

> At every stage illuminated by knowledge, the will appears as individual. The human individual finds himself in endless space and time as finite, and consequently as a vanishing quantity [*verschwindende Größe*] compared with these. He is projected into them, and on account of their boundlessness has always only a relative, never an absolute, *when* and *where* of his existence; for his place and duration are finite parts of what is infinite and boundless. (*WWR* I:311)

The vivid visual elements of the passage that opened this chapter are absent; so is its rotating motion – the vista is still, not moving. Yet we will recognise many of its other ingredients: summoned before us is a sweeping vista; an individual is then called up to be located within it. The vertiginous effect is the same; for even though the vista itself is not in motion, the individual is: he is sent flying into its endless expanse. His position seems as dangerous as it did in the first passage, when he was rooted to a limited spot. Indeed, the sense of motion intensifies in the words that

immediately follow; and with it, the seasickness. Even though we are projected into a boundless scene, Schopenhauer continues, our "real existence
is only in the present." Yet the present turns out to provide no anchor in
this cosmic scene, no solid ground in this flux; it too is melting:

> [Our] real existence is only in the present, whose unimpeded flight into
> the past is a constant transition into death, a constant dying ... a con-
> tinual rushing of the present into the dead past ... just as we know our
> walking to be only a constantly prevented falling, so is the life of our body
> only a constantly prevented dying ... Every breath we draw wards off the
> death that constantly impinges on us. In this way, we struggle with it every
> second, and again at longer intervals through every meal we eat, every sleep
> we take, every time we warm ourselves, and so on. Ultimately death must
> triumph ... and it plays with its prey only for a while before swallowing it
> up. (*WWR* I:311)

We find the same vertiginous motion in another significant passage,
which opens the essay "On the Vanity and Suffering of Life" in the second
volume:

> Awakened to life out of the night of unconsciousness, the will finds itself
> as an individual in an endless and boundless world, among innumerable
> individuals, all striving, suffering and erring; and, as if through a troubled
> dream, it hurries back to the old unconsciousness. Yet till then its desires
> are unlimited, its claims inexhaustible, and every satisfied desire gives birth
> to a new one. No possible satisfaction in the world could suffice to still its
> craving, set a final goal to its demands, and fill the bottomless pit of its
> heart. (*WWR* II:573)

In the last quoted passage, the motion had been produced by the relentless passage of time; here, the motion is imparted by the infinity of desire.
It is an infinity that notably mirrors that of the spatio-temporal world in
which the individual is displaced. Yet this other infinite is now within us,
not outside us. And whether the motion is that of time or desire, in both
cases it is linked with an image of struggle and compulsion – a compulsive
struggle with conditions that constitute inexorable necessities. For death
"*must* triumph"; and "no *possible* satisfaction *could* suffice."

It is these kinds of examples – several of them drawn, significantly,
from curtain-raising moments within Schopenhauer's writing: the beginning of an essay, of an entire book – that offer the strongest expression of
the type of physiognomy I referred to above as the "cosmic viewpoint."
The examples of the imaginative act of vision discussed in the last chapter – which I had described there as a magisterial vantage point *sub specie
aeternitatis* – turn out to be far from isolated.

That, however – it may be pointed out – was a vantage point that Schopenhauer had summoned in that context with a purpose (it had seemed) to console, resolving a profound existential anguish that gave philosophy its beginning. This vantage point, by contrast, seems markedly different in spirit, as evidenced in the vocabulary used above to speak of its effect: not pacifying, but vertiginous. It locates us without securing us: it comes with a distinct sense of danger.

Now it could be questioned, on the one hand, to what extent the viewpoint Schopenhauer had urged in his discussion of the fear of death carried a wholly consolatory character. For if it was consolatory, its consolation could hardly be dissociated from its desolating effect: the hard-won liberation from the fear of death was achieved only through a reformation that rid one of one's fear by ridding one of the individual identity that underpinned it. And that, for many, would be one valuable too many to leave behind without demur. Equally importantly, the cost of Schopenhauer's solution to the fear of death would have to be deemed as light – or as heavy – as the price to be paid for the larger solution to the riddle of the world in which this more particular solution was embedded. And this larger solution was a grim one indeed.

Yet with the grimness of this solution freshly in mind, one might now turn back to the vantage point expressed in the above passages to let oneself be struck by an obvious feature. For on the most immediate reading, central to the content of this vantage point – central, above all, to the aspects of its content that occasion our vertiginous response – would seem to be a set of messages that do no more than restate the core of Schopenhauer's metaphysics. This is plainer than daylight in the last passage, as the lightest of glosses shows. "Awakened to life out of the night of unconsciousness" – the basic condition of the will – "the will finds itself as an individual in an endless and boundless world, among innumerable individuals, all striving, suffering and erring" – as they are fated to do, given their fundamental nature – "and, as if through a troubled dream" – the world is only our representation – "it hurries back to the old unconsciousness. Yet till then its desires are unlimited, its claims inexhaustible, and every satisfied desire gives birth to a new one" – for the world is will. Troubled by finitude, harassed by desire – these are the essential adjuncts of a being whose form of representation includes time, and whose inner being consists of desire. It is such facts that show suffering to be essential to life, and reveal life in its vanity.

It is terrible; but it is true. Before us we have nothing but the terrible truth of the world as philosophy has revealed it. And in these images it seeks to do so again with implacable imaginative power. See yourself in this mirror: this is who you are. "For a being who thinks, it is a precarious position to stand on one of those numberless spheres freely floating in boundless space" – be a thinking being, and see where you stand; you stand where you think. And where you stand is in the middle of a boundless world; and that is to say: you are adrift.

The image of the individual dwarfed by the infinite world is an image of compounded meaninglessness. And it is, as I have just suggested, an image that on one level does little more than retransmit the core message of Schopenhauer's philosophy, showing us differently what Schopenhauer has already told us in other words and in more discursive forms. Yet what I want to call attention to here is something more specific. For this image of the individual dwarfed by the world – standing before its boundless expanse with all the exposure of extreme vulnerability – is one that will certainly make our memory stir. Where was it that we had seen this image before – that we had heard these selfsame words? "The human individual finds himself in endless space and time as finite," "as a vanishing quantity [*verschwindende Größe*]." It should take only a moment's reflection for remembrance to dawn. And when it does, the immediate effect of these words will be to catapult us straight into Schopenhauer's aesthetics; and more specifically, to that occasion of high moment that had marked the encounter with the sublime. It was an encounter whose trigger had been given when the human observer cast his eyes upward to the starry sky – to the infinite greatness of the universe in space and time, in its physical immensity and its innumerable worlds – or cast his thoughts towards the millennia lying behind and ahead. This vision produced a sudden contraction: "we feel ourselves reduced to nothing," Schopenhauer had written, "transient phenomena of will, like drops in the ocean, dwindling and dissolving into nothing" (*WWR* I:205). Schopenhauer had spoken of the sense of our "insignificance" (*Unbedeutsamkeit*); of our "nothingness" (*Nichtigkeit*); of our experiencing ourselves as a "vanishing nothing" (*ein verschwindendes Nichts*) before this great whole.

With this moment (the mathematically sublime in Schopenhauer's division) again firmly within in our sights, it will take little effort to recognise in the turns of phrase deployed within the body of what I have termed the "cosmic viewpoint" or the view *sub specie aeternitatis* a direct rehearsal of its core: the discovery of one's nullity before the spectacle of an infinite world. The recurrence of its characteristic vocabulary clearly lighted the way. Yet it is also important to notice another set of lights that pointed us in the same direction, this time through the material of our own responses.

Examining Schopenhauer's account of aesthetics in Chapter 1, I noted that the sublime presented the sharpest challenge to Schopenhauer's insistence on excluding emotion from aesthetic experience. The experience of the sublime could hardly be comprehended without reference to its affective content. And it was the dialectic of pride and vulnerability providing the sublime with its spine, I suggested – a dialectic thematising the notion of self-esteem – that gave this experience its distinctive and constitutive affective tenor.

The responses the above passages are calculated to provoke are pervaded by an affective tone of similar richness, as my way of articulating them will have suggested; and it is a tone that we may recognise as mirroring the one at the heart of the sublime, and pointing to the same grounding dialectic. The vertiginous effect of these passages – in which we watch with swimming eyes as we are projected into a boundless world – would not be imaginable without it. It is our sense of dignity that is repeatedly engaged in the characterisation of our condition placed on display in these passages. And if an affront to dignity was expressed clearly in the confrontation with the boundless world, it is carried with equal force by other elements. It was an affront implicit in our first passage, which set before us a vision of human beings rising to awareness out of a mouldy film topping a hard crust topping a hot core: so much for the glory of conscious awareness. This gesture to our ignominious origins was then replicated in the notion of "awakening" that opened another of our passages ("awakened to life out of the night of unconsciousness"), which resumed Schopenhauer's view of the will as unconscious and unminded, and implicitly resumed its affront to a sense of dignity articulated in terms of our capacity as rational beings.

It is the ligament just brought to the open that stands at the heart of my reading of Schopenhauer's philosophy. At an earlier moment of my discussion (Chapter 2) I had argued that the viewpoint of the "ideal observer" pointed us more narrowly to the aesthetics of sublime experience; it is a proposal I now wish to situate more broadly. What I would like to suggest at this stage is that it is the aesthetics of the sublime that offers itself as the most illuminating context in which to locate the "cosmic" viewpoint appearing in different forms and varying degrees of physiognomic strength in Schopenhauer's work, and more broadly as the context that provides the richest resources for approaching Schopenhauer's philosophical standpoint. It is a standpoint, as I will argue, that participates in the structure of the sublime in its most important defining features: in its composite dramatic sequence, constituted by a double movement of tension and release; and no less significantly, in the dialectic that under-pins it, and forms the source of its dramatic power.

And it is indeed that dramatic sequence – a sequence whose constitutive second moment of release has not yet come into our view – that we must first turn to consider more closely. For where – to repeat a familiar ques-tion – do we now stand? We stand, as stated above, where Schopenhauer's philosophy has discovered us: infinitesimal beings on a mouldy crust sur-rounded by an infinite world; riven internally be desire; fractured by time. This is the moment of contraction: the moment of philosophical truth. The terrible that gives the sublime its base tone is simply: *the world in its reality*.

And yet. It is an "and yet," as I will argue, that unfolds on two lev-els; and on both levels it marks a turning point in the dramatic structure of philosophy, in which the tension that constitutes its first moment – a mortified systole before the spectacle beheld, a movement downward – is followed by a second moment – an expansive movement upward – that metabolises and supersedes it. To locate this superseding moment on its first level, all we need to do is turn back to the curtain-raising passage that gave us our initial impetus: "in endless space countless luminous spheres"; "for a being who thinks, it is a precarious position to stand on one of those numberless spheres freely floating in boundless space." "For a being who thinks": I proposed above that we hear these words as an invitation: think and you will see the precarious position in which you stand. It is our thinking that reveals our dangerous perch in the world. Yet Schopenhauer's continuation in this essay, it must now be remarked, suggests that a rather different face could be placed on these same words, reading the act of thinking not as what puts us – what puts us by revealing us – in danger, but on the very contrary: as what releases us from it.

For only a few lines down Schopenhauer is enunciating the statement that is the headline and main topic of this essay, running under the title "On the Fundamental View of Idealism." This statement will not surprise us; it reads: "The world is my representation." Yet with the utterance of this familiar line, everything has abruptly shifted. The sweeping cosmic vista that had been summoned only moments ago, placing or displacing human beings within it – the scenery of floating spheres, of dizzying motion, of mouldy crusts – suddenly goes *poof!* and disappears. For the camera has now turned back to the camera; the camera snaps shut and the world goes dark. The objective has been swallowed up into the subjective. We have seen the human eye.

It is not in fact *we* who are standing precariously, Schopenhauer's next statement goes on to suggest, but the infinite world: for "however immeasurable and massive it may be, its existence hangs nevertheless on a single thread; and this thread is the actual consciousness in which it exists" (*WWR* II:3–4).[2] The world on which we had spun with vertiginous sensations now hangs from the end of a spun yarn. The world that formerly terrified us has been trampled underfoot. If the triumphal tone of this discovery is not clear in the words I have just quoted, it rings out with almost venomous intensity – only thinly disguised by and thereby all the more clearly betrayed in its academic tones – elsewhere in the same volume: "we are justified in asserting that the whole of the objective world, so boundless in space, so infinite in time, so unfathomable in its perfection, is really only a certain movement or affection of the pulpy mass in the skull" (*WWR* II:273). We thought *we* were humbled by our lowly biological origins ("a mouldy film," a "cold crust," a "hot core"). Yet this insult now appears to be discharged, having been deflected to the world. The whole world, it turns out, is nothing but an epiphenomenon of our biological nature.[3]

We do not thus depend on the world, but the world rather depends on us. Yet this, of course, mirrors precisely the structure of sublime experience as we had seen it. Turning outward we are humbled by the world's immensity; turning inward we realise that this "ghost of our nothingness" is a "lying impossibility," and "there arises the immediate consciousness that all these worlds exist only in our representation, only as modifications of the eternal subject of pure knowing. The vastness of the world … now rests within us; our dependence on it is now annulled by its dependence on us" (*WWR* I:205).

The first "and yet" that obtains our release from the moment of the terrible thus rehearses the truth of transcendental idealism, replacing mortification with mastery by revealing the world in its dependence. You don't stand in the middle of a boundless world; the boundless world stands

---

[2] A direct shift has taken place here in the subject of the notion of "precariousness." The word recurs in the first and second paragraphs of the essay; yet in the first it is predicated of conscious beings ("for a *being who thinks*, it is a precarious position to stand ..."); in the second it is predicated of the world ("among the many things that make the *world* so puzzling and precarious, the first and foremost is that ... its existence hangs ... on a single thread").

[3] This formulation though points to a tension between Schopenhauer's naturalistic view of the mind and his transcendental idealism that has sometimes been brought explicitly to his door. See David E. Cooper, *The Measure of Things: Humanism, Humility, and Mystery* (Oxford University Press, 2002), 86, for a statement of the problem.

within you. But this form of release, now, needs to be read in an add-itional context – on an additional level closely connected to yet distinct from this one. For let us again go back to one of the statements that gave us our leverage. "For a being who thinks," Schopenhauer had written, "it is a precarious position to stand on one of those numberless spheres freely floating in boundless space." My initial suggestion for reading this was: be a thinking being, and see where you stand; or again: you stand where you think. The above discussion has suggested a different way of under-standing the importance of "thinking" in this connection. Yet there was a separate insight available in that first response that it is important to appropriate.

For certainly, "you stand where you think" would seem to be true in the simplest sense that, for self-aware beings, their position cannot be sepa-rated from their understanding of their position. But the question is now whether, if *thinking* makes for *standing*, it might not also make it come loose; or, to put it differently: whether indeed it is not also true to say that where you *think* is precisely where you do *not* stand. Bringing this closer to the present context we might say: if you are thinking of yourself standing, or seeing yourself standing, you are not where you see yourself, but where you see yourself *from*. The natural question to ask then will be: where are you seeing yourself from? And this, of course, is simply to resume our starting question: where *is* it we are standing as we speak (or hear) these words? Or again: who is "we"?

The short answer to both questions would seem to be: we are stand-ing at the vantage point from which philosophy is done; and the "we" is the capacity in which we do philosophy. Yet the meaning of this answer will remain unavailable to us unless we begin from lower down. And lower down, the most evident answer to the foregoing question will at first register as a platitude: we are standing at that position from which we can survey our own position. Or again: we are standing where we can see ourselves stand from. Have we made any progress? All that this answer – in all its perplexing banality – perhaps brings out more dis-tinctly, with its pointed terminological repetition, is the simple fact that there are two notions of "standing" or "position" in question. Yet the most important facts in this connection are indeed the simplest ones. And what this formulation allows us to remark more clearly is that one of these two standpoints is located within the content of our vision or representation; and the other is constituted by that act of vision itself. We relate to the position that forms the content of this representa-tion as the subject that represents it. And making a leap that may seem

unjustifiable to some and tautological to others, let us give the shortest
yet most significant answer to the questions we have been asking and
say: to occupy the second standpoint is to unseat yourself from the first;
to survey your own position is to stand outside it. Or let us restate this
again more meaningfully still: to survey your own position is to overcome it. I suggested earlier that we hear Schopenhauer's opening words
in the second volume of the *World as Will and Representation* as an invitation: "See yourself in this mirror: this is who you are." And yet if you
can see yourself, we may say, this is not *only* who you are. Your seeing
has overcome this being, and defined a new one.

It is the notion of overcoming just brought out, I would now like to
suggest, that provides the content of the second movement I have been
looking to track, by which the contraction produced by the terrible that
philosophy places before us comes to be purged. And it is this construal of
the movement, I would argue, to which the character of Schopenhauer's
philosophy is most deeply bound, and which provides us with the most
illuminating reading of its subtext. The world is (nothing but) my
representation: this is transcendental idealism. The terrible aspect of the
world – mortifying to the human observer – is overcome by recognising
the world in its dependence on the human observer. Yet it is overcome
even more potently by an act of cognition that mirrors the structure of
the former and that can be parsed as its philosophical counterpart. The
world is my representation: I have fathomed the world. The world is my
representation: I have made the world the object of (philosophical) understanding. And in doing so, I have overcome it. I have overcome being by
seeing. The terrible has been metabolised into the sublime by the very fact
of cognising it. The gaze now turns inward and the breath is caught in
thrill: we have beheld the power of the human mind.

Yet to allow the structure of this particular sublime – one that unfolds
within the heart of philosophy itself – to stand out before us with full
clarity, we need to attend more closely to its constituents. For indeed, as
suggested above, we stand at the vantage point from which philosophy
is done; and the "we" is the capacity in which this is possible. The question must now be: just what capacity is that? Put differently: if where we
stand is at the position from which we can survey our own position, what
is the force of the "can" that appears in this proposition, and indeed registers as its least platitudinous element? And the most pertinent way of
parsing this question will be the following: if the representation we have
seen – a view of the human predicament *sub specie aeternitatis* that acts as a
"precipitate" of Schopenhauer's broader philosophical outlook – provides

a true characterisation of the human predicament, how does the possibility of this representation enter into its content?

On the most immediate reading, the unequivocal answer would simply seem to be: it does not. For part of the content of this picture – a part central, indeed, to its terrible aspect – had been given in a very specific understanding of the mind and its powers. The human head might physically tower above the rest of the human body; yet this architectonic position, in Schopenhauer's view, should not lead us to be deceived as to the true nature of the mind and its destiny. The mind is not a master of the will but its servant, constructed by the metaphysical will as a dim lantern to light its path as it pursues its satisfaction, and destined to remain subservient to its origin. It is an understanding Schopenhauer had expressed in strong words when writing:

> [The will is] the root of the tree of which consciousness is the fruit ... It is the will that holds all ideas and representations together as means to its ends, tinges them with the colour of its character, its mood, and its interest, commands the attention, and holds the thread of motives in its hand. (*WWR* II:139–40)

And with the mind made out a mere puppet to the will, what chance could a philosophical understanding of the world – an understanding of the order of reality as it is in itself – truly stand? Little chance indeed, as Schopenhauer appears to state plainly in another passage: for "a consciousness subject to such great limitations is little fitted to explore and fathom the riddle of the world" (*WWR* II:139). This sceptical note – sounding the death knell, it would seem, for the prospects of philosophy – is sounded again elsewhere in terms that bind it even more closely to our own context. To reach out to reality itself, Schopenhauer suggests, would involve an ability to grasp our own preconditions that we do not possess. "That which precedes knowledge as its condition ... cannot be immediately grasped by knowledge, just as the eye cannot see itself." And again: "knowledge presupposes the existence of the world, and for this reason the origin of the world's existence does not lie within the province of knowledge" (*WWR* II:287).

Yet statements like these must strike us as astounding. For if "the eye cannot see itself," what *were* we doing when we said: "the world is my representation," and turned the camera back to the camera? As such, they have often provoked readers to remark with some impatience the blatant contradiction holding between Schopenhauer's philosophical representation of the world and the commitments implicit in his own act of representing – between his theory and the presuppositions of his own practice. For a philosopher who prided himself on solving the riddle of the world, Schopenhauer would seem to be singularly short-sighted when it came to locating himself within it. If "reason is no more than a clumsy calculative device for the realization of desires," Terry Eagleton points out in trenchant tones, then Schopenhauer's "own work would be strictly speaking impossible. If he really credited his own doctrines, Schopenhauer would be unable to write. If his theory is able to dissect the insidious workings of the will, then reason must be to that extent capable of curving back on itself, scrutinizing the drives of which it proclaims itself the obedient servant."[4]

The happening of philosophy, such criticism suggests, ought to strike us as a paradox. Yet why not rather say: "a miracle"? Because it is the difference between the paradoxical and the miraculous that might here light the way towards a resolution of this problem, once this has been cast as a conflict (yet again) between Schopenhauer's theory and his practice. For certainly, the mind is ordinarily shackled to the will, and an act of understanding as grand as that of fathoming the mystery of existence ought to lie beyond its proper powers. Yet as we have seen, the mind's ordinary state can be transcended in exceptional conditions. And this is when, shedding the habitual way of considering things, one abstracts from their relationship to the will and rises to behold them in their highest objectivity. Ordinary consciousness is transcended in the aesthetic regard. If my proposal in the previous chapter is correct, it is in this aesthetic kind of regard that Schopenhauer's own philosophical standpoint must be understood as participating; and it will be its characteristic mode of transcendence that it will similarly share. Philosophy, if it is happening, *is* a miracle: a "wholly abnormal occurrence" (*PP* II:68), something "foreign to human nature, something unnatural, properly speaking supernatural" (*WWR* II:384–85) – like every transcendence of instrumental awareness that involves a departure from our natural condition.[5]

But to resume our thread, it is this precise resistance that our natural condition presents to the act of understanding that renders the latter, not

---

[4] Eagleton, *The Ideology of the Aesthetic*, 167.

[5] This answer, of course, will not appease critics unhappy with miracles, such as Schaeffer, who takes aesthetic no less than philosophical understanding to be outlandishly improbable given that, on Schopenhauer's terms, "ontological knowledge is possible only through an ecstatic use of faculties that are otherwise heterotelic" (*Art of the Modern Age*, 190). For a response to this kind of criticism and a proposal for locating this miracle more firmly within Schopenhauer's scheme, see Alex Neill, "Aesthetic experience in Schopenhauer's metaphysics of will," in Neill and Janaway, eds., *Better Consciousness*.

only miraculous, but wondrous in the more specific register belonging to the sublime. For it emerges against the background, not of a "because," but a "despite." That an individual "awakened to life out of the night of unconsciousness" for a brief moment of daylight should be able to overcome its origins and its daily subjection to the will's domination to "marvel at its own works, and ask itself what it itself is" (*WWR* I:160), finally rising to "the universal survey of life as a whole" (*WWR* I:85), is what provides this self-marvelling with the darker exultation that typifies the sublime. "A consciousness subject to such great limitations is little fitted to explore and fathom the riddle of the world" – yet it has fathomed it despite itself. The answer lies between the covers of the two volumes you hold in your hands.

If the happening of philosophy is miraculous, to locate it within the structure of the sublime is to foreground the fact that this is a miracle that requires conquest to occur. It requires conquest, on the one hand, in the way that all aesthetic contemplation does, in demanding the transcendence of interested awareness to a disinterested form of apprehension; and this, indeed, is a conquest that is simultaneously a self-conquest. Yet in the aesthetic regard constituted by the view *sub specie aeternitatis*, there is a more exacting type of conquest to be considered. For our ordinary condition, as we saw in the last chapter, is to be immersed in the present, to live as though we were destined to live for ever – a condition that provides a direct phenomenological expression of our inner nature as will. The state of absorption and self-absorption in which we act out our lives is evoked dramatically by Schopenhauer in a remarkable passage:

> Just as the boatman sits in his small boat, trusting his frail craft in a stormy sea that is boundless in every direction, rising and falling with the howling, mountainous waves, so in the midst of a world full of suffering and misery the individual man calmly sits, supported by and trusting the *principium individuationis*, or the way in which the individual knows things as phenomenon. The boundless world, everywhere full of suffering in the infinite past, in the infinite future, is strange to him, is indeed a fiction. His vanishing person, his extensionless present, his momentary gratification, these alone have reality for him. (*WWR* I:353)

Our natural bent, Schopenhauer here suggests, is to keep our eyes fastened within the spatio-temporal confines of our own lives, and trained on what is immediately present. Our vision is the tunnel vision we need in order to walk our narrow path. To bring the boundless world into our field of vision and summon its viewpoint on our lives will thus be an achievement whose difficulty the oceanic metaphor governing this passage fully anticipates in terms that resume those of my discussion above, suggesting we characterise it as an experience of long-delayed seasickness. Turning outward, we now catch sight of the howling sea around us that, with our eyes chained to the inside of our creaking boat, we had hitherto been able to ignore. The vertiginous effect of the cosmic viewpoint could hardly have stood out more palpably before us. Nor could the deep nerves connecting this viewpoint to the sublime, which this passage once again lays bare by linking the cosmic viewpoint to an image – the crashing waves and stormy seas – that had served as a key exemplar in Schopenhauer's sublime aesthetics.

And with these connections in sight, the heightened conquest and indeed self-conquest at stake stands out with equal clarity, in ways that allow it to be anchored more firmly within the structure of the sublime as we had earlier approached it. For on the one hand, if an act of self-conquest is required, that is because this viewpoint confronts us with a spectacle that we would rather turn away from. The vision of human life it affords – one that, in keeping with Schopenhauer's parlance, we may call a vision of the Ideas of the world, the *what* of the world, but also more narrowly the Idea of human being, or the *what* of human life – is one that is "terrible to the will," and as such demands that one "forcibly tear oneself from his will and its relations" to behold it (*WWR* I:201). On the other hand, confronting this spectacle is not merely a matter of lifting the gaze to a present object to maintain it. For contrary to the experience of stormy seas in the above passage – aligned with the dynamically sublime in Schopenhauer's division – and similar to the experience of the mathematically sublime with which the viewpoint *sub specie aeternitatis* is most strongly linked, the aesthetic object is one that we ourselves must work to place before us, through an active effort registering as a separate moment of conquest. The viewpoint from which the spectacle of human life fully confronts us is one that we must actively reach out to occupy and appropriate. The activity through which we do so will be nothing less than the practice of philosophy with its peculiar range of techniques, and its characteristic appeal to the imagination.

With this background, we can return to an earlier question to provide it with a more substantive answer. "Who is 'we'?" I asked, when first calling up the view *sub specie aeternitatis*. The capacity in which we do philosophy, I later suggested. This answer can now be specified more fully. For certainly, having brought the "mountainous waves" of a world "full of suffering and misery" into view, the anticipated texture of our experience ought to have been churning seasickness or blind panic. Yet if, looking out to this spectacle from the pages of philosophy, the calm of the individual journeying perilously through stormy seas does not give way to such sensations once the environing world has come into view, the reason for this will be clear. And this is that, in beholding it, we have transformed it into an aesthetic spectacle that implicates us in a related self-transformation, raising us to that capacity of our being that aesthetic contemplation involves as its adjunct. This capacity, in Schopenhauer's terms, consists in the higher subjectivity through which one transcends one's identity as an individual being, constituting one as the "eternal, serene subject of knowing, who as the condition of every object is the supporter of this whole world." In this capacity, "the fearful struggle of nature [is] only his mental picture or representation; he himself is free from, and foreign to, all willing and all needs, in the quiet comprehension of the Ideas" (*WWR* I:205). We have ascended to an impassible subjectivity whose only passion is to experience the exaltation of a cognitive conquest that, by relating us to this picture as its representing subject, has placed us outside it.

Writing in a vein not far removed from this one, the Italian poet and pessimist writer Giacomo Leopardi would proclaim the abdication of "every childish consolation and deception," the "courage to bear the privation of every hope, to gaze intrepidly on the desert of life, not to conceal … any part of human unhappiness, and to accept all the consequences of a philosophy that is grievous, but true." Staring into the abyss yet thereby rising above it in defiant hauteur: for Schopenhauer, this defiance would have the tone of a "transcendental pride" typifying, it has been said in the past, the world-creating subject.[6]

I have been focusing on the importance of the act of cognition in constituting the expansive movement upward that succeeds the contraction before the terrible truth that philosophy brings into view. This is an act of cognition through which a consciousness emerging out of a force dark to reason can nevertheless turn a brilliant light upon life as a whole to survey it from a position of magisterial remove, in doing so mastering suffering through understanding. It is this possibility – a possibility that forms the exclusive preserve of human beings, the reflective apex of a pyramid whose larger body remains steeped in darkness – that grounds the special status of human beings within the world of nature, and constitutes their claim to

---

[6] The expression is Hans Blumenberg's, quoted in this context by Bart Vandenabeele in "Schopenhauer, Nietzsche and the aesthetically sublime," *Journal of Aesthetic Education*, 37 (2003), 94. Leopardi's remark comes from *Operette Morali*, as quoted in Joshua F. Dienstag, *Pessimism: Philosophy, Ethic, Spirit* (Princeton University Press, 2006), 81.

grandeur. The dialectic of vulnerability and mastery enacted in this philosophical development, however, will remain incompletely expressed unless we attend to the moment that succeeds the act of cognition and arrives as its consummation.

For the grand act of understanding just outlined – in which the entire world in its enormity is summoned before the human mind to be freely surveyed – is complemented by a second act no less magisterial in kind and expressive of the same unbounded inner freedom. Having been dragged to the witness box to disrobe before the dilating yet unblinking human eye, the whole of existence now confronts an eye hardening with the implacable resolve of a magistrate, who, with all the *gravitas* that befits one who knows himself to be pronouncing his judgement in the name of the whole of creation, shakes his head slowly and utters a categorical "No" upon the naked spectacle that dismisses that boundless world with all its suns and galaxies (*WWR* I:412) in all its sublimity and cruelty, power and grandeur. Having considered the whole of life, "the willing or not willing of which is the great question" (*WWR* I:308), the judgement comes: it "ought not to be" (*WWR* II:170).[7] Let the matter-of-fact tones again not deceive us: compounded in this act of judgement is all the truculent intensity of a suffering being that has overthrown its tormentor in a coup of triumphant hauteur.

In our person, the whole of existence comes up, not only for self-knowledge, but for self-judgement; and the "Yes" or "No" we pronounce is correlatively one we utter in the name of the whole of creation. In the last chapter, I suggested that poetry offers itself as the most instructive aesthetic context in which to situate Schopenhauer's philosophy and appreciate its features. Yet it is more particularly tragedy, it may now be remarked, that would appear to form the most natural paradigm for attuning ourselves to its specific character, for reasons that Schopenhauer himself indicates clearly when he designates it as "the summit of poetic art." For the task of tragedy, in Schopenhauer's view, is to place before us the terrible side of life; and in doing so, to yield a knowledge of the world that may lead us to the denial of the will to life.[8] In the structure of this double task, we will have no difficulty recognising the twofold act of cognition and judgement described above precisely mirrored.

---

[7] In its original context, the quoted phrase appears indirectly and apostrophised; yet the doctrine of the denial of the will represents nothing but a longer and more direct restatement of this very phrase.

[8] See the discussion in *WWR* I:252–55.

An "intoxicating vision": the philosophical sublime in its context and phenomenology

It is in this double act of cognition and judgement that the full sublimity of human beings must thus be taken to lie, giving content to the moment of exaltation through which the terrible is metabolised into the sublime. And it is philosophy that provides the stage for both acts. It is no accident, I would therefore suggest, that the vantage point *sub specie aeternitatis* set out above should appear at curtain-raising moments of Schopenhauer's work – the start of an essay, of an entire book – when philosophy first seeks to position itself on the stage. For this reflects something important about the position from which philosophy is being written.

The above account might elicit a response of recognition from those commentators who have seen in the sublime the linchpin of Schopenhauer's aesthetics, or indeed of Schopenhauer's philosophy as a whole.[9] Yet it will elicit equal recognition from all those readers of Schopenhauer's works who have attuned themselves to the profound importance carried by the notions of "altitude" and "ascent" in his epistemic ideal. These are notions that we may recall having seen pervasively expressed within Schopenhauer's understanding of the aesthetic regard, where the notion of "rising" registered as a recurrent conceptual hinge. "Raised by the power of the mind" we abandon the ordinary way of regarding things and come to see the Ideas they embody. We "soar aloft" in aesthetic contemplation and "rise" from individual awareness to supra-individual subjectivity. The mark of the genius is precisely his capacity to soar above the realities actually present to his gaze – not to remain "as the mussel fastened to its rock, compelled to wait for what chance brings it," but to move freely about as though he were "winged." The task of philosophy, similarly, is to "raise" feeling to reflection, its ascent mirroring the ascending movement of the aesthetic regard in which it participates.[10]

---

[9] Several commentators have claimed a central place for the sublime in Schopenhauer's thought. Robert Wicks, for example, makes the sublime the basic category of Schopenhauer's aesthetics (with the beautiful as its species: *Schopenhauer*, 105–6), and considers all modes of transcendence described by Schopenhauer – aesthetic, moral and ascetic – to be strongly linked with it (102, and generally chs. 8–10). This structure has elements in common with Julian Young's discussion of the "eternal standpoint" in *Willing and Unwilling*: the feeling of exultation that characterises the sublime is linked with the eternal standpoint (99) and the latter is said to yield the right practical stance towards the world. Terry Eagleton's interesting discussion has already been cited; see especially *The Ideology of the Aesthetic*, 163–64.

[10] See Chapter 1 for all this.

The truth only fully reveals itself to the distant viewer, Schopenhauer elsewhere suggests, as in a remark that contrasts the pre-philosophical state of absorption with the vantage point from which the true significance of things becomes available. For

> the normal person is immersed in the whirl and tumult of life ... his intellect is filled with the things and events of life, but he does not in the least become aware of these things and of life in their objective significance; just as the merchant on the Amsterdam exchange hears and understands perfectly what his neighbour says, but does not hear at all the continual humming of the whole exchange, which is like the roaring of the sea, and which astonishes the distant observer. (*WWR* II:381–82)

At other moments, Schopenhauer reaches for the more potent language of mountainous ascent in conveying the privilege that attaches to the distant viewpoint within philosophical activity. The task of the philosopher, Schopenhauer writes in his late work *Parerga and Paralipomena*, is to lead his reader upward – to "take [his reader] firmly by the hand and see how high above the clouds he can reach, step by step on the mountain path" (*PP* II:6). This was a conception of philosophical ascent that had captured Schopenhauer's imagination from the days of his earliest philosophical reflections, as indicated by the youthful note penned in 1811 several years before the publication of his main work, which frames the same notion in rather more striking terms, this time as a solitary journey:

> Philosophy is a high-altitude Alpine road; it can be reached only by a steep path over sharp stones and prickly thorns. It is lonely and ever more deserted the higher you climb, and whoever takes it must be immune to terror ... Often he will stand over an abyss, seeing the green valley below. Vertigo draws him powerfully down; but he must hold on ... But in exchange he will soon see the world below him ... He himself always stands in pure cool Alpine air and sees the sun when below black night still lingers.[11]

It is an image rich in philosophical resonance. For in this moment of brilliant emergence into daylight, we will have no difficulty recognising an echo of the ascent solemnised by Plato's allegory of the cave, in which the prisoners escape their chains to climb out into the open air and behold the sun – the vision of the Good. Yet it is another type of resonance that seems even more telling in this context. For Plato's prisoners emerged from a realm of illusion conceived as a subterranean location to a realm of truth

---

[11] Quoted in Safranski, *The Wild Years of Philosophy*, 105.

located on ground level.[12] In Schopenhauer's image, by contrast, ground
level serves as the baseline, and the truest reality dwells higher, on mountainous terrain. In doing so, it expresses a sensibility that had been central
to the development of the sublime in eighteenth- and nineteenth-century
philosophy and literature, in which the discovery of mountains as an aesthetic object, and the analysis of the exalting emotional response provoked by them, had occupied a cardinal place. Schopenhauer himself had
participated directly in this aesthetic sensibility when confronting Mont
Blanc during his long European tour of 1803–4, reacting with an exhilaration in which many other travellers of his time would have recognised
their own experience.[13] Yet even if that resonance had failed to come alive
through the mountainous imagery, the tell-tale notions of a "terror" and
"vertigo" occasioned by the glimpse of the abyss would have sufficed to
trace out the key ligament. It is an abyss into which, even as early as 1811,
Schopenhauer already knew philosophy to be staring.

In the sublime, of course, it was the mind to which the gaze ultimately
turned back to behold it in wonder, turning away from the spectacle of
nature that had provoked the initial wondering response. It is this precise inversion that Schopenhauer would elsewhere place on display, in the
context of discussing the disposition of genius, in a spectacular comparison in which the mind became mountain before the awestruck gaze:

> The gloomy disposition of highly gifted minds, so frequently observed, has
> its emblem in Mont Blanc, whose summit is often hidden in the clouds.
> But when on occasion, especially in the early morning, the veil of clouds
> is rent, and the mountain, red in the sunlight, looks down on Chamonix
> from its celestial height above the clouds, it is then a sight at which the heart
> of everyone is most deeply stirred. So also does the genius, who is often
> melancholy, display at times that characteristic serenity already described,
> which is possible in him alone, and springs from the most perfect objectiv-
> ity of the mind. It floats like a radiant gleam of light on his lofty brow; *in
> tristitia hilaris, in hilaritate tristis.* (*WWR* II:383)

The mind itself has become the object of contemplation, stirring our
hearts as we behold it sending down its gaze from its Olympian heights.
In doing so, the soul (to use an unSchopenhauerian locution) has been

---

[12] This contrast needs to be placed in perspective, however, as there is more to unite Schopenhauer
and Plato than to divide them here; see the discussion in Chapter 5.

[13] See Cartwright, *Schopenhauer*, 80. The classic discussion of the transformed view of mountains
involved in the development of the natural sublime is Nicolson's *Mountain Gloom, Mountain
Glory*. Nicolson identifies Thomas Burnet's *The Sacred Theory of the Earth* (Latin 1681/English 1684)
as a turning point in this transformation; interestingly, Schopenhauer seems to gesture to the background of these developments at *WWR* I:426.

split into spectacle and spectator. For if we stand at the foot, trembling with awe, yet we stand also at the summit, an awe-inspiring object. No sharper image of the inner hierarchy presupposed by this ascent could have been found.

The proposal to locate Schopenhauer's philosophical standpoint in the aesthetics of the sublime, I have been suggesting, ties in with an epistemic ideal – privileging notions of distance and ascent – that receives wide expression in Schopenhauer's work, and provides us with a richer framework for appreciating the significance of this ideal. Yet it is time to finally perform a long-awaited turn inward to consider another aspect of the philosophical *phainomena* that this proposal would seem to bring into agreement. Readers have sometimes responded to Schopenhauer's philosophical pessimism with a peculiar brand of suspicion to which philosophies would not normally appear to be exposed: the suspicion of an insincere philosophical profession. To many, Schopenhauer's grim message of pessimism has seemed almost too theatrical, too flamboyantly flaunted, to be believable – to be believed, that is, as a belief truly held. It is one of many moments in which the content of Schopenhauer's philosophy invites us to engage its author in personal terms; and a profusion of colourful biographical details duly come pouring into this newly opened space, detailing Schopenhauer's epicurean tastes and overall unmistakably world-embracing lifestyle as evidence to contradict his world-denying professions.

Schopenhauer, of course, had never claimed that the attitude of resignation in which metaphysical insight achieved its most appropriate climax was an easily accessible ideal, and had on the contrary signalled that it was rarely to be attained in practice. And to stipulate, indeed, that one may only enunciate as theory what one can definitely execute in practice is a demand that brooks its own dangers, as Schopenhauer's biographer Rüdiger Safranski suggests. For there are "truths that can be lived and others than cannot"; and to insist that action should be true to thought is a "call for consistency [that would] ultimately lead to self-censorship," for then "one only dares to think what one believes one can also live."[14]

Yet I would suggest that it is not as a mismatch – and yet another charge of disharmony – between Schopenhauer's theory and Schopenhauer's practice, or his philosophy and his biography, that we do best to approach the question. For to do so is to ignore something internal to Schopenhauer's

---

[14] Safranski, *The Wild Years of Philosophy*, 338.

work from which the reactions of incredulity noted above take their
point of departure, and if not their departure, their fuel. And this is a
certain kind of exuberance – a ferocious zest and boundless *élan* – that
pervades his writings from one end to the other. It is an *élan* that comes
to more than what Nietzsche, in the *Genealogy of Morals*, described as a
relish for battle, a love of "grim, green, galling words," or as a happiness
found in "rage for the sake of raging," which for Nietzsche gave the lie to
Schopenhauer's pessimism.[15] Bryan Magee was giving voice to this aspect
when he wrote: "There is an all-pervading relish in the writing that gives
the lie to any notion of unrelieved pessimism." In his formulation, this
registered as a conflict between the form of Schopenhauer's work, and its
content: there seems to have been "a lifelong disparity between the content of what Schopenhauer said … and the way he said it. The content
was so often negative – corrosive, sarcastic … pessimistic, sometimes
almost despairing – yet the manner was always positive, indeed exhilar-
ating. Its gusto and verve both express and impart a *joie de vivre* which is
almost gargantuan." Iris Murdoch seemed to partly echo this judgement
when she stated that "Schopenhauer's irrepressible empiricist gaiety is in
tension with his nihilistic hatred of the ordinary world."[16]

Now in talking of a specifically *empiricist* gaiety – of Schopenhauer's
"worldly" relish, of his "omnivorous *interest* in the world," his "innocent
love of the world," which is "an endless source of the 'value' which is so
formally excluded" – Murdoch would appear to be calling our attention
to one particular aspect of Schopenhauer's philosophical procedure. For as
we saw in the previous chapter when considering the different meanings of
Schopenhauer's "objective" viewpoint, philosophy engages experience on
two levels, inner and outer; and one of the ways in which Schopenhauer
articulated the imperative of engaging outer experience was as an engagement of empirical science and the data provided by a study of the natural world. Schopenhauer would express disdain for the "childish" way in
which theologians approached nature, exclaiming over its wonders and
acclaiming them as a testimony to divine design. Yet what is noticeable is
that the same affective tone would be preserved in his own philosophical
responses. The works of nature "can never be sufficiently admired," we
hear (*WWR* II:321); the order and harmony of the world are such that "the

---

[15] Friedrich Nietzsche, *On the Genealogy of Morals*, trans. D. Smith (Oxford University Press, 1996),
   essay 3, §7, 85.
[16] Magee, *The Philosophy of Schopenhauer*, 260 (where Schopenhauer's epicurean lifestyle is
   held up for attention), 25; Murdoch, *Metaphysics as a Guide to Morals*, 70. See here David E.
   Cartwright's relevant discussion in "Schopenhauerian optimism and an alternative to resignation?"
   Schopenhauer-Jahrbuch, 66 (1985), esp. 153–58.

more distinctly and accurately we learn to understand it, the more are we astonished" (*WWR* II:323). "If we give ourselves up to the contemplation of the inexpressibly and infinitely ingenious structure of any animal, be it only the commonest insect," we "lose ourselves in admiration" (*WWR* II:328).[17] And again: "It is a world so rich in content that not even the profoundest investigation of which the human mind is capable could exhaust it" (*WWR* I:273).

The affective tone manifested in these statements provides ample testimony to the kind of relish that Murdoch remarks. Yet it seems to me that to focus on this aspect of Schopenhauer's procedure – on this interpretation of Schopenhauer's "objective" viewpoint – would be to disregard another aspect, and another interpretation, vested with deeper significance, and carrying a rather different affective tone – we may still call it a kind of wonder, yet now a wonder that has altered its affective charge. It is indeed that different tone that would appear to be reflected in the ways in which several readers have in the past expressed their reaction to Schopenhauer's work, and which converge (almost uncannily) on a striking emphasis – not on the childlike innocence of wonder – but on a more dangerous and adult experience of drunken inebriation. Nietzsche would speak giddily of Schopenhauer's "intoxicating vision," which threatens to turn our heads by its "loftiness and dignity." The Romanian pessimist writer Emile Cioran would communicate his reactions in equally rapturous tones in his early *Tears and Saints*: "After reading Schopenhauer, I always feel like a bridegroom on his wedding night." These expressions reverberate in those of several other readers reporting on their discovery of Schopenhauer's work. Tolstoy would speak of the "continuous ecstasy" he had felt on reading Schopenhauer and of a "series of mental pleasures ... never before experienced"; Thomas Mann would refer to the "intoxication" he had experienced "after drinking that metaphysical magic potion" (of Schopenhauer's philosophy) for the first time as a young man.[18]

---

[17] These are expressions of wonder that would have been familiar to many practitioners of seventeenth- and eighteenth-century science, for whom theological and scientific concerns were tightly intertwined. See Claude-Olivier Doron, "The microscopic glance: spiritual exercises, the microscope and the practice of wonder in early modern science," in Vasalou, ed., *Practices of Wonder*, for a discussion that provides an illuminating context for Schopenhauer's remarks.

[18] Respectively: Friedrich Nietzsche, "Schopenhauer as educator," in *Untimely Meditations*, trans. R. J. Hollingdale (Cambridge University Press, 1997), §5, 156; Emile M. Cioran, *Tears and Saints*, trans. I. Zarifopol-Johnston (University of Chicago Press, 1995), 101; Sigrid McLaughlin, "Some aspects of Tolstoy's intellectual development: Tolstoy and Schopenhauer," *California Slavic Studies*, 5 (1970), 188 (though as this study shows, Tolstoy would later join several other readers in adopting a far more critical attitude to Schopenhauer); and Thomas Mann, "Schopenhauer," in *Essays of Three Decades*, trans. H. T. Lowe-Porter (London: Secker & Warburg, 1947), 396.

The kind of thrill expressed in these reactions to Schopenhauer's philosophy might at first sight appear unintelligible, in light of the grimly pessimistic message that lies at its heart. Yet if my foregoing proposal is accepted, here we might instead read, not contradiction, but harmony. For the content of the message does not survive its own production untouched, but undergoes a dramatic transformation in ways that the structure of the sublime allows us to appreciate fully. The darkness of the message is commuted into exultation in the very act of its formation and through its very possibility. Magee was right, it might be said, to point to a discrepancy between content and form; yet the "form" at issue is the basic fact that philosophical representation is occurring. It is the thrill inseparable from the utterance of the terrible that the responses of these readers would seem to be appropriating or reflecting. It is not, as Murdoch suggests, the empirical relish of someone standing within the world that provides the most significant tone of Schopenhauer's writing, but the relish of one capable of standing outside it.

It is no part of my proposal, of course, that something like the structure of the sublime can in all cases be relied upon to account for the phenomenology of Schopenhauer's readers, even for that particular phenomenology expressed in the language of "thrill" and "exhilaration" that would seem to point us in that direction. Nor, indeed, does it render dispensable the need to study such thrilling reactions more closely in order to appreciate their specific context and significance. Similarly, however, to accept that the sublime provides us with an illuminating framework for considering these responses does not obligate us to assent to Schopenhauer's analysis of the transformation that, as readers, these responses reveal us to be undergoing.

Writing in the context of a question about the relationship between philosophy and literature, Arthur Danto has suggested that literature is universal in the sense that it is "about each reader who experiences it." Literary reference is universal in that it "is about each individual that reads the text at the moment that individual reads it, and it contains an implied indexical. Each work is about the 'I' that reads the text, identifying himself not with the implied reader for whom the implied narrator writes but with the actual subject of the text." Yet this relationship of "aboutness," he argues, is one not so much passive as transfigurative in kind: it shows us, not what we are, but what it makes of us. Literature is "a mirror less in passively returning an image than in transforming the self-consciousness of the reader who in virtue of identifying with the image recognizes what he is." It is in this sense, he has argued, that "philosophy is literature in that among its truth conditions are those connected with being read, and reading those texts is supposed then to reveal us for what we are in virtue of our reading."[19] Using these terms, we may say that the "I" to which Schopenhauer's philosophy appeals – the subject with which we identify through the act of reading, and which this act reveals us to be as it transforms us into it – is the supra-individual consciousness or "subject of knowing" identified as the subject of the aesthetic regard. Yet even when we step away from this philosophical mirror, we need not accept its interpretation of our identity in order to assent to the thought that our phenomenology has taken an experience of transcendence – one produced by participating in its characteristic mode of regard – as its heart.

These remarks finally allow me to return to the frame of questioning with which I prefaced my discussion and sought to articulate my task. Is there anything to interest us, I asked, in the type of astonishment that moves a particular philosopher to his undertaking? Can a concern with the specific character of a thinker's astonishment – whether the genuine astonishment he departs from and seeks to produce, or the false wonder he seeks to eliminate through philosophical effort – function as a meaningful category for investigation?

I hope the above discussion – extending over this chapter and the last – has given sufficient grounds for justifying an interest in approaching Schopenhauer in these terms, suggesting several reasons why Schopenhauer's philosophy stands to be illuminated by reading it under the sign of a response that the above formulation glided unobtrusively between calling one of "astonishment" or "wonder." There is a family of concepts here, no doubt, and we should be careful about trying to mark the boundaries between them too cleanly. Yet if these concepts are to serve as a meaningful backbone for the unfolding of Schopenhauer's philosophy, it is important to retain some heuristic sense of the boundaries that divide them. For some of the most important hinges of Schopenhauer's philosophical movement would indeed seem to be supplied by a response whose broadest (most neutral, almost categorial) instance we might call "astonishment"; and it is in part as a transition from one strain of astonishment to another that the story of this movement could then most instructively be told.

For philosophy, as I suggested in the last chapter, opens with a surprise: "I am!" followed by (or perhaps simultaneous with; or indeed conditioned by) another: "Soon I will not be!" We might call the first response

---

[19] Danto, "Philosophy and/as/of literature," 63, 64, 67.

"wonder," in so far as it is governed by a keen sense of the value of its object; we might call the second "horror," in so far as it is governed by a shocked awareness of the value of an object now exposed to loss.[20] It is this combination of wonder and horror that leads one to philosophy in search of a therapeutic. Philosophy offers a remedy; yet that involves turning a critical spotlight on the assumptions that underlie one's reactions, and above all the conception of one's identity that underpins it. For the horrified wonder or wondering horror that gives philosophy its beginning turns out to be false, in the sense that it is founded on a notion of one's identity that stands in need of revision. The true "I" is not the individual "I" that can pass in and out of existence, setting off emotional shocks in its wake that track the seams of becoming and unbecoming. One's true identity lies in the "I" that survives such events and lies outside their seismic reach. This identity, in the deepest sense, is one's inner nature as will. Yet it is rather one's identity as the supra-individual subject of knowing – as a conscious being *simpliciter* – on which the most significant resolution turns out to rest. It is a resolution, indeed, that appears to offer itself as a transcendence of that first and deepest identity; and it is with this resolution, as this chapter has suggested, that the identity of philosophy itself is bound up. This reformation of identity, crucially, is accompanied by a corresponding shift in the type of astonishment to which one's relationship to the self is coded. The wonder and horror tied to the post of individual identity are swept away by a sense of the sublime that directs itself to one's status as a conscious being, one capable of overcoming the domain of suffering through the very act of cognising it. It is a form of wonder whose tinge is darker for containing the terrible as its strain, yet all the more resplendent for transcending it.

The unfolding of philosophical understanding can thus be narrated as a transformation of identity simultaneously expressed as a progression from one strain of astonishment to another. And given the notion of the self that stands at the heart of these emotional responses, this is a progression that, as I suggested at an earlier juncture, must also be drafted as a drama of self-esteem at every stage. For if the beginning of philosophy lies in a strain of astonishment that registers as horror, one may also describe this as an experience of affront to a sense of self-worth implicit in one's emotional response. Philosophy offers to medicate this insult through a remedy that seems at best homeopathic, confronting one with a ruthless

---

[20] For a closer exploration of the notion of wonder, see my "Wonder: toward a grammar," in Vasalou, ed., *Practices of Wonder*, and several other essays in the same volume.

spectacle of life as a whole — surveyed from a universal or cosmic vantage point — calculated to make injury deepen. Yet this upward movement turns out to mark the unveiling of an identity vested with higher dignity, in which humiliation is purged through the discovery of new pride. Writing about Schopenhauer's philosophy in deeply appreciative tones, Thomas Mann would suggest that it is this sense of human dignity — of a pride that reaches the point of reverence for "the crown of creation" — that reveals the profound humanism watering the roots of Schopenhauer's philosophical vision.[21]

Poised at the summit of being with the world at our feet — we stand where Schopenhauer's philosophy has proposed to bring us. It is the right moment to ask: where to?

---

[21] Mann, "Schopenhauer," 402.

CHAPTER 4

Reading Schopenhauer

Why read Schopenhauer? Philosophical approaches and appraisals

It is a question that has been asked before of Schopenhauer's philosophy, though perhaps not as often as it should; and when it has, it has been posed, not at the apex of this steep acclivity, but looking up to this philosophical prospect from its very foot. And it has taken the form of a basic query: why read Schopenhauer? It is a question that remained in the shadows in the foregoing discussion, which was governed by a concern largely interpretative in kind. After an introduction to the broad outlines of Schopenhauer's philosophy and a first characterisation of his standpoint in Chapter 1, I considered Schopenhauer's response to the fear of death and used this as leverage for making a claim concerning the aesthetic character of Schopenhauer's standpoint in Chapter 2. Chapter 3 developed this characterisation further, tying Schopenhauer's philosophical standpoint to the aesthetics of the sublime. The perspective of this discussion has been pitched overwhelmingly as one "on Schopenhauer's terms" – a phrase that recurred at several junctures. Difficulties with Schopenhauer's positions have briefly come into view only to be shelved as largely incidental to the task. And while achieving an understanding of any given viewpoint may carry intrinsic importance – one might even call it, somewhat sententiously, a *moral* importance – one may still ask what should motivate us to methodically strive to understand one viewpoint as against another. One might rephrase this to read: among the many philosophical mountains available to be climbed, why climb this one?

It is a kind of question, of course, that anyone taking decisions about the allocation of finite resources will be compelled to confront. Yet for philosophers examining these topographic possibilities with a more programmatic eye, it is a need for justification that has often been felt to be particularly pressing when faced with works belonging to the history of philosophy as against its present. "Why read Schopenhauer?" takes its place next to "Why read Boethius or Aquinas?" and "Why read Leibniz or Voltaire, Descartes or Kant?" This question about *who* to read, in turn, has often been linked to a question about *how* to read, which has been dominated by a dilemma concerning how to balance the desire for philosophical relevance with the need for historical sensitivity. As Alasdair MacIntyre has reformulated this dilemma as often perceived: "*Either* we read the philosophies of the past so as to make them relevant to our contemporary problems and enterprises, transmuting them as far as possible into what they would have been if they were part of present-day philosophy ... *or* instead we take great care to read them in their own terms." The first approach – which we might follow Richard Rorty in referring to as "rational reconstruction" – has often been exposed to accusations of anachronism. Yet it has seemed better equipped to justify an engagement with the past than the second ("historical reconstruction"), which seems to preserve the "idiosyncratic and specific character" of philosophies at the cost of converting them to "museum pieces" to which our only philosophical response can be a politely curious stare.[1]

The pairs just mentioned – "Boethius or Aquinas, Descartes or Kant?" – already point to the fact that the request for justification will be more easily satisfied, and less frequently posed, for some philosophers than for others. Writing in this context, thus, Charles Taylor has argued that the imperative of engaging the history of philosophy is connected, not merely to its historical role in constructing the present, but indeed to its enduring presence within it. For genetic origins have a way of worming themselves into our presuppositions, as Descartes' formulations have been assimilated into our epistemological models, or Locke's and Kant's into the basic assumptions of our ethical and political thinking. Having done so, they ossify into a sense of self-evidence from which we cannot release ourselves without understanding the process of its formation. Foundations then have to be dug up in order to reopen them to reason-giving, whether to reject them or reappropriate them more fully. This is why "philosophy is inescapably historical."[2]

---

[1] The quotations are from Alasdair MacIntyre, "The relationship of philosophy to its past," in R. Rorty, J. B. Schneewind, and Q. Skinner, eds., *Philosophy in History: Essays on the Historiography of Philosophy* (Cambridge University Press, 1984), 31; and see Rorty's essay in the same volume, "The historiography of philosophy: four genres."

[2] See the discussion in Charles Taylor, "Philosophy and its history," in Rorty, Schneewind, and Skinner, eds., *Philosophy in History*.

As will be clear, however, this argument will be as strong in a given case as the genetic links that tie a particular thinker to the philosophical present from whose perspective it is being considered – as strong as the silent presence of this philosophical "other" in the unexamined self. This is something that Richard Rorty brings out with equal force in the same context when discussing the "canon" of "great dead philosophers" and commenting on the way we experience its relevance in engaging the past. "Rational reconstructors," he points out, "do not really want to bother reconstructing, and arguing with, minor philosophers. Historical reconstructors would like to reconstruct people who were 'significant' in the development of something – if not philosophy, then perhaps 'European thought' or 'the modern'."[3] In determining which philosophical mountain to climb, we ask exacting questions about the value of our alternatives.

Our enthusiasm about engaging past philosophers, in fact, would seem to be most strongly affected by two main considerations: on the one hand, their historical importance and perceived role in crafting the contours of the philosophical present; and on the other, their capacity to be drafted as "conversational partners" (Rorty) with resources for treating the problems and questions that form the subject of current preoccupation. And with these considerations in view, it will not be difficult to see why the question "Why read Schopenhauer?" would resist easy answer. For to be sure, Schopenhauer's philosophy has not been without influence, and a large number of writers and artists – Thomas Mann, Leo Tolstoy, Thomas Hardy, Richard Wagner, Marcel Proust, to mention but a few – are known to have been exposed to it. Schopenhauer's influence on the course of *philosophical* history, however, has been more maverick and uncertain in kind. The most prominent philosophers with whom his name has been linked are no doubt Nietzsche and the early Wittgenstein; yet especially writing from the perspective of anglophone philosophical tradition, it would be hard to include him in a story of philosophical descent like the one Taylor has in mind. And if he cannot figure significantly in such a story, he has figured even less so in any specification of the philosophical "canon."[4]

Yet it is relative to the second consideration that one can appreciate more materially the challenges with which Schopenhauer's philosophy

[3] Rorty, "The historiography of philosophy," 60.
[4] Notably, Schopenhauer's name appears only twice, and tangentially, in the above-cited volume of essays; one of these occasions is in Rorty's list of philosophers who have not made the canon of great dead philosophers but could be helpfully studied within the broader genre of "intellectual history": *ibid.*, 69.

confronts its would-be modern-day readers. For if one's engagement of the past is to be governed, at least in part, by a search for relevance, and an effort to place the past in meaningful conversation with the present – and as Rorty argues, this needn't be conceived as a sharp dilemma between *either* addressing past philosophers on our own terms *or* understanding them on theirs, but an ecumenical aspiration to do *both* – the philosophical practice of the present, especially in the English-speaking world, has been dominated by a particular understanding of its proper excellence. And this is an understanding in which logical argument and analytical rigour have been assigned a central role. Against this conception of philosophical excellence, Schopenhauer – the philosopher of pessimism with the saturnine world-view sung in baritone – has been a person with whom it has often been difficult to decide how to do business. It will in fact be helpful at this point to offer a brief critical overview of some of the most important efforts philosophers writing for an English-speaking audience – to which I here confine my focus – have made to engage Schopenhauer's work and to respond to its peculiar challenges.

The necessity of determining how Schopenhauer stands to be engaged was already clearly attested in one of the earliest works that stimulated what might modestly be called a tradition of Schopenhauer studies, Frederick Copleston's *Arthur Schopenhauer, Philosopher of Pessimism* (1946, rev. 1975). Copleston proposed himself the task of assessing the strength of Schopenhauer's philosophical position and the arguments on which it was based; yet this was a project he notably felt obliged to defend. Most readers, he evidently assumed, were not interested in Schopenhauer's arguments, but rather in the "lyrical" or practical aspects of his philosophy – in what Copleston called its "impressionistic vision" or overall world-view – and had little time for "small-minded" fastidious objections about the methods employed to arrive at this vision. In Copleston's view, however, this need not be a dilemma: *either* we believe that philosophy is all about examining arguments, *or* we claim that "all that counts is impressionistic vision." Thus, "unless we propose to treat metaphysical systems simply as though they were analogous to pictures or poems or symphonies, we can examine and assess the argument by which a given philosopher claims to establish his views."[5]

This remark, interestingly, evokes a characterisation of Schopenhauer's work originally coined by Thomas Mann, who likened it to a

[5] Frederick Copleston, *Arthur Schopenhauer, Philosopher of Pessimism*, rev. edn. (London: Search Press; New York: Barnes & Noble Books, 1975), x–xi, in preface to 2nd edition.

symphony in four movements – a metaphor in turn picked up by some
of Schopenhauer's most appreciative readers.[6] The comparison is instructive in its contrast, however, for at the hands of these readers, the aesthetic
metaphor had positive and not reductive connotations, and certainly did
not stand for "what is left over once rational argument fails." These connotations would seem even more palpable in Copleston's negative conclusions, which the above remark indeed prefigured. For having examined
Schopenhauer's arguments and pronounced them to be riddled with flaws,
he would conclude that Schopenhauer's system might not be true, yet it
might instead "be profitably viewed as an aesthetic whole, a work of the
creative imagination."[7]

The self-conscious air surrounding Copleston's project to engage
Schopenhauer in argument has not clung to later commentators, who
have been unabashed about their interest in investigating Schopenhauer's
philosophy with exacting analytical rigour. Yet Schopenhauer's philosophical credentials have not often emerged from this crucible in a
correspondingly brilliant light. Patrick Gardiner's *Schopenhauer* (1963),
one of the first works to follow Copleston's, seemed to shed Copleston's
embarrassment yet retain his conclusions, and more particularly
his view concerning the difficulties and inconsistencies adhering to
Schopenhauer's thought. Whatever his other merits, Gardiner would
conclude, Schopenhauer was "not a rigorous thinker" and his work
lacked integrated structure; and like Copleston, Gardiner would fall
back on artistic terms in referring to Schopenhauer's "fantastic and in
many ways repellent picture of the world."[8]

Later works have continued to battle with this negative assessment.
D. W. Hamlyn (1980), thus, concluded that Schopenhauer's principal philosophical arguments were deeply flawed and that his system was
not a real candidate for philosophical acceptance in our times, even as
he offered restitution by insisting that there is "much to admire in the
sweeping grandeur of the argument as a whole," which forms "a magnifi-
cent intellectual construction."[9] Efforts to reverse this negative assessment,
however, have gathered greater pace in recent times. And while the step
taken in this direction by Bryan Magee (1983, rev. 1997) might still appear
too hesitant to many – the division of his discussion into a long uncritical

---

[6] Mann, "Schopenhauer," 394; cf. Hübscher, *The Philosophy of Schopenhauer in its Intellectual Context*,
113–14.

[7] Copleston, *Philosopher of Pessimism*, 77.   [8] Gardiner, *Schopenhauer*, 301, 183.

[9] D. W. Hamlyn, *Schopenhauer: The Arguments of the Philosophers* (London: Routledge & Kegan Paul,
1980), 164, 170.

exposition and a brief appendage of critical remarks self-described as "severe" leaves one with an uncertain impression of Schopenhauer's merits and demerits – recent work by Julian Young, Christopher Janaway, and John Atwell has striven for a more decisive stance.

The works of the latter – particularly his *Schopenhauer on the Character of the World: The Metaphysics of Will* (1995) – offer a sharp contrast to earlier studies in that, while Atwell is strongly oriented by an awareness of the charges of inconsistency levelled against Schopenhauer, he does not take these blemishes to render his philosophy irredeemable, and his overall approach is sympathetic though not uncritical. Atwell's approach, however, introduces a new scruple, one that problematises one's mode of engagement on a different level. For if a philosophical system that had been proved incapable of disarming charges of profound incoherence might be led to its demise, the ability to deflect rational charges would not necessarily constitute a sign of philosophical vitality. And Atwell's account – executed with the organising objective of examining Schopenhauer's metaphysics in isolation – would seem to bear the appearance of a scrupulously accomplished exegetical exercise that has offered negative defence against attack without providing positive justification and evidence of living pulse, and above all without persuading us that this is a viewpoint with a claim to philosophical truth, which we might truly consider accepting as our own.[10]

That this vitiated philosophical pulse is tied to the specificities of Atwell's approach, and more narrowly to his occupation of a predominantly exegetical standpoint that remains internal to Schopenhauer's work, is suggested by the rather different readings offered by Janaway and Young, both driven by more ambitious aims. In his *Self and World in Schopenhauer's Philosophy*

---

[10] A modified version of these remarks could be applied to another recent work, G. Steven Neeley's *Schopenhauer: A Consistent Reading* (Lewiston, NY: Edwin Mellen Press, 2003), which undertakes to defend Schopenhauer against critics who argue he is "painfully, and perhaps even fatally, inconsistent," and to demonstrate that despite occasional "roughweld" in the machinery, "the engine nevertheless functions well" (187). One of the ways in which Neeley proposes to accomplish this is by dispelling the difficulties attaching to Schopenhauer's claim to knowledge of the thing-in-itself – an attempt that does not prove as convincing as might have been hoped. More importantly, while Neeley sometimes suggests that he has the intention of claiming for Schopenhauer's philosophy, not merely the negative ability to escape contradiction, but the positive status of philosophical truth – we hear that "Schopenhauer has correctly identified the thing-in-itself as will," that "Schopenhauer has unearthed a 'subterranean passage' which leads ... to the thing-in-itself," that "Schopenhauer has indeed gained access to the noumenon" (25, 12, 37) – this exercise ultimately seems to retain an exegetical character and remains internal to Schopenhauer's terms. The numerous evocations of the courtroom that refer us to Neeley's legal background – "charges" are "quashed" and "indictments" are levied – also tempt one to consider that this might be a case in which a sincere belief in the client's account of the truth is not a precondition for undertaking his defence.

(1989), Janaway offers a statement of his own aims that locates his project squarely within the horizon of the more programmatic kind of engagement referred to above as a "rational reconstruction" of the past. His hope is to persuade a philosophical audience educated in the traditions of analytical philosophy of the interest of Schopenhauer's work, suggesting more specifically that "a reading of Schopenhauer greatly and happily broadens our understanding of the questions that should be debated by philosophers with an interest in 'the self'." And his reading, he makes clear, is one concerned not merely to inquire into coherence, but also to develop arguments in positive terms.[11]

Janaway is sensitive to the difficulties analytical philosophers would find both with Schopenhauer's questions and with the methods he employs in answering them. And he is no doubt right to resist the restrictive view that only philosophers whose questions and methods overlap with those that currently engage us are worthy of interest, and in thus proposing that *both* parties undertake to question their perspectives in order to meet on the common ground of a philosophical conversation.[12] At the same time, and without taking this as a summary pronouncement on Janaway's reconstructive project as a whole, one cannot help wondering whether Schopenhauer's philosophical merits emerge from this process of mutual adjustment looking sufficiently compelling. In many locations, Schopenhauer's arguments turn out to be poor or question-begging, and it is indicative that, in one of the most central aspects of his view of the self – the relation between the willing subject and the knowing subject, or the "I will" and the "I think," which Schopenhauer claims "flow together into the consciousness of one 'I'" – Janaway should comment that "in his philosophy if they do 'flow together' in this way, it still has to be by way of a miracle."[13] It is not incidental, indeed, that Janaway's discussion ends with an acknowledgement of philosophical disappointment, and with an invitation, not to deny inconsistency, but to seek to read it in more positive terms, connecting it to the "dynamic" or "dramatic" unfolding of Schopenhauer's work.[14]

---

[11] Janaway, *Self and World in Schopenhauer's Philosophy*, 4, 15.

[12] *Ibid.*, 12–15.

[13] *Ibid.*, 266. This resumes Schopenhauer's remark in *The Fourfold Root of the Principle of Sufficient Reason*, speaking about the identity between the willing and knowing subject: "Anyone who properly makes present to himself the inexplicability of this identity will call it with me the miracle *kat' exochēn* [*par excellence*]" (194).

[14] See Janaway, *Self and World in Schopenhauer's Philosophy*, 285–88.

Young's engagement of Schopenhauer in his *Willing and Unwilling* (1987) differs from Janaway's in significant respects, not only in having a broader reach – it seeks to address all major aspects of Schopenhauer's philosophy – but also in not being as clearly signposted in its intentions. The intention, in one sense, could hardly be clearer: to engage Schopenhauer philosophically; and without a shred of doubt, the Schopenhauer that emerges from Young's pen is a vibrant philosophical voice with animated pulse. If he is flawed – and Young brings difficulties and inconsistencies into view without hesitation – his flaws are not such as to place him outside the bounds of philosophical conversation, but rather the foibles of an interlocutor whose language one ultimately shares. Yet it is this experience of a shared language – a language in which contemporary philosophers will discover themselves to be already fluent – that most strongly signals the reconstructive effort that has been under way, which seems to have admitted Schopenhauer into our conversation by getting him to leave his more "idiosyncratic or specific character" at the door.

There is no moral scruple of course to be registered against reconstructive conversations of this kind – ones that, in Rorty's words, "impose enough of our problems and vocabulary on the dead to make them conversational partners" – however liberal in spirit; conversations with the dead can be drawn up on any terms one wishes. It is only taken as an interpretative undertaking (or a "historical reconstruction") that they open themselves to objections, becoming answerable to the kind of constraint articulated by Quentin Skinner: "No agent can eventually be said to have meant or done something which he could never be brought to accept as a correct description of what he had meant or done."[15] And in this case, given the uneasy way in which Young's account straddles the boundary between reconstruction and interpretation, the problems attaching to Young's interpretative approach cannot be brushed aside. This approach, it must be said, takes its place in a debate almost as old as Schopenhauer's work, centring on the question: was it Schopenhauer's serious belief that he had gained an insight into the thing-in-itself? Young's flat denial that it was forms the linchpin of his naturalistic interpretation. With this stroke, followed by several others, the most fantastical elements of Schopenhauer's metaphysics fall away one by one – the thing-in-itself, the Platonic Ideas, the transcendental subject of knowing, among others – purging Schopenhauer of his most outlandish concepts-in-trade and assimilating him into a vocabulary

---

[15] Rorty, "The historiography of philosophy," 49, 50.

more familiar to our philosophical ears.[16] This is Schopenhauer sanitised of his flamboyant visionary metaphysics, of his illuminationist bursts, of the "miracles" that uphold his philosophy at key points – from the burst of illumination from which it departs (Nietzsche would call the discovery of the will "a poetic intuition") to the burst of illumination at which it ends (Schopenhauer would gesture towards the "ecstasy" and "rapture" of the mystics for a more positive specification of the denial of the will).[17]

About the particular debate just referred to, there will be more to say at a later juncture. Yet if this account of Schopenhauer is opened to question, then it is again the not-so-naturalist Schopenhauer with his not-so-sedate tones that we are forced to place again across the table. And with him, all those miracles that litter his philosophical scheme at countless junctures. The miracle *par excellence* that he saw in the confluence of the willing and knowing subject; the mystery he saw in the act of freedom by which the will abolishes itself, grandly rehearsing Malebranche's remark, "la liberté est un mystère" (*WWR* 1:404) – which, in the words of one commentator, really "tells us nothing more than that it happens because it happens."[18] To this miracle one could add a host of other extraordinary occurrences, such as the "inexplicable," "astonishing," or "mysterious" fact of aesthetic perception,[19] though no occurrence more extraordinary than the initial subterranean discovery of the thing-in-itself.

And if we admit there is no room for miracles in philosophy, then we return to the vexing language of inconsistency and contradiction and to the many difficulties commentators have found in Schopenhauer's philosophical scheme. His account of the discovery of the thing-in-itself has left readers incredulous; his very use of the word "will" has struck commentators as problematic; his account of the Platonic Ideas has been thought gratuitous and inexplicable on his own terms, his account of the seminal distinction between concept and Idea vague, and his explanation

---

[16] Some of the difficulties attaching to Young's interpretative approach have already been discussed; see e.g. Chapter 1, note 6. And see also Chapter 6, where the question concerning the knowledge of the thing-in-itself comes up for direct discussion.

[17] *WWR* 1:410; and for Nietzsche's remark, "On Schopenhauer," translated in C. Janaway, ed., *Willing and Nothingness: Schopenhauer as Nietzsche's Educator* (Oxford: Clarendon Press, 1998), 260: "the thing [Schopenhauer] puts in place of the Kantian X – the will – is created only with the aid of a poetic intuition. The attempted logical proofs, meanwhile, can satisfy neither Schopenhauer nor us."

[18] Fox, "Schopenhauer on death, suicide and self-renunciation," 166.

[19] The first two characterisations are Atwell's, grounded in Schopenhauer's own: *Schopenhauer on the Character of the World*, 141–43 (Atwell notes Hübscher's correction that the preceding remark is not Malebranche's, but Helvetius' [213, n.37]). The third is Schaeffer's, and unlike Atwell's, decidedly unsympathetic in tone: *Art of the Modern Age*, 190.

of aesthetic perception elliptic. Central claims in his epistemology – such as his belief in conceptless intuitions – have not escaped censure, nor has his statement and justification of idealism. His view about the possibility of denying the will has seemed to contradict everything he had said about phenomena; and his claim that this denial does not itself constitute an act of will has been declared a patent absurdity by Nietzsche as by many others.[20]

Nietzsche, in fact, had reserved scathing words for Schopenhauer's philosophy even before his formal break with it, wondering "how on earth someone with a system so full of holes could arrive at such pretensions." He had singled out as deeply suspect Schopenhauer's central claim to have identified the thing-in-itself (that "totally obscure, inconceivable X"), remarking that all the predicates used to name it – such as its unity, eternity or freedom – were drawn from the phenomenal world, and complaining that Schopenhauer requires one to think objectively of something that can never be an object.[21] And what is important in this context is that the same criticism – here addressing the opening movement of Schopenhauer's philosophy – would seem to address itself no less forcefully to the movement in which it achieves closure, and on one reading, grounds its claim to success – namely, its resolution of the fear of death. For if "eternity" cannot be properly asserted of the will that lies beyond phenomena, it has no more title to be applied to our own inner nature, whose discovery in ourselves, as suggested in Chapter 2 – and whose more specific discovery as an "eternal" element that "survives" the destruction of our individuality – was supposed to medicate our fear.[22]

---

[20] Some of the major criticisms against Schopenhauer are discussed by Hübscher in *The Philosophy of Schopenhauer in its Intellectual Context*, ch. 11. Hübscher himself appears to regard such criticisms dismissively, averring that "the search for inconsistencies and contradictions" fails to "reach the totality of [Schopenhauer's] doctrinal edifice" (387). The inconsistencies at stake are certainly central enough to affect the doctrinal totality. Underlying Hübscher's understanding of and respect for this totality, however, seems to be a larger view of philosophy expressed in the remark: "Let a philosophical thought be ever so much the source of argumentation, it remains true and valid, as long as it embodies an essential form of humanity" (413). It is not incidental that Simmel would voice a similar reverence for the "total structure," for the "organic" connection between part and whole, for the "structured spiritual unity" of a work (*Schopenhauer and Nietzsche*, 13) and display a similar understanding of the nature of philosophy. See the discussion below.

[21] Nietzsche, "On Schopenhauer," 260 and 262; cf. his later assertion that this involves a contradiction in terms: *Beyond Good and Evil*, trans. M. Faber (Oxford University Press, 1998), §16. This kind of criticism had in fact already turned up in some of the earliest reviews of Schopenhauer's work; see Cartwright, *Schopenhauer*, 380ff. On this point, see also Copleston, *Philosopher of Pessimism*, 63–69; Gardiner, *Schopenhauer*, 172–74; Janaway, *Self and World in Schopenhauer's Philosophy*, 197 (and generally ch. 7).

[22] Schopenhauer seems to make an effort to address this difficulty at *WWR* II:493ff., though it could be debated with what degree of success.

These represent some of the numerous difficulties readers have found
to adhere to Schopenhauer's philosophy, and for many commentators, it
has been a question, not of denying them, but of seeking to explain them.
One of the explanations that have been around since at least the time of
Gardiner's work locates Schopenhauer's principal liability in his commitment to Kantian metaphysics, which hamstrung his efforts to express his
unique philosophical vision.[23] Another, formulated by Moira Nicholls in
connection with Schopenhauer's seven-veil dance around the knowabil-
ity of the thing-in-itself, has the merit of attributing development to that
philosopher whom Nietzsche declared wholly lacking in it, suggesting that
these contradictions may reflect different stages of Schopenhauer's philosophical thinking.[24] To this Nicholls adds a further suggestion, namely
that it was Schopenhauer's practice of beginning from the phenomena –
from the "real world" of experience – that was responsible for the instability of his philosophy, so that his "acknowledged tendency to investigate
particular problems independently of each other resulted in a metaphysical system with inherent tensions and inconsistencies."[25]

These explanations are instructive, but they all involve acknowledging
the inherent conflicts and inconsistencies that pervade Schopenhauer's
scheme. In doing so, they rehearse the terms of the dilemma about how
to do business with Schopenhauer without resolving it. In briefly outlining these different styles of engagement, I have tried to show that they
all evince an awareness of this dilemma and embody different attempts
to address it.[26] Yet my own view is that while these efforts indeed deepen

[23] Gardiner, *Schopenhauer*, 301–3; cf. Nicholls, "Schopenhauer, Young, and the Will," 154, and Atwell,
Schopenhauer on the Character of the World, 74. Atwell's reading here parallels a suggestion offered
by Dale E. Snow and James J. Snow in "Was Schopenhauer an Idealist?" *Journal of the History of
Philosophy*, 29 (1991), where an "essentialist" description of Schopenhauer's view is proposed.

[24] See "Schopenhauer, Young, and the Will," 154–55, for Nicholls' more specific proposal, which
focuses on Schopenhauer's growing interest in mysticism.

[25] *Ibid.*, 152; compare Gardiner's earlier remarks in *Schopenhauer*, 190. Nicholls' suggestion points
to another brand of difficulty that Schopenhauer's engagement of the "real world" – particularly
the natural world as investigated by science – creates for modern readers. For in drawing scientific facts so deeply into his philosophy, Schopenhauer has rendered his philosophy vulnerable to
their peculiar possibilities of obsolescence. Discussing head injuries that result in the loss of brain
matter, for example, Schopenhauer states: "we never read that, after an accident of this kind the
character has undergone a change" – only the intellect; for "the will does not have its seat in the
brain ... as the metaphysical, it is the *prius* of the brain" (*WWR* II:246); one dreads to think how
Schopenhauer would have reacted to the case of Phineas Gage. One has similar thoughts concerning Schopenhauer's claim that the brain pauses in deep sleep or that emotion does not affect the
brain, or his denial that the brain is responsible for the full range of the body's organic functions
(see *WWR* II:241, 499, and generally essay XX in *WWR* II) – all claims that demote the significance
of the brain and thus the intellect, uniformly rendered suspect by modern science.

[26] The above has offered an indicative and not exhaustive survey of the literature, notably (yet not
solely) leaving out of view several introductions to Schopenhauer, such as Janaway's (*Schopenhauer*,

our understanding of Schopenhauer's thought through the methodical philosophical attention they train on it, their cumulative record does not entirely remove one's scepticism about the fruitfulness of engaging Schopenhauer – or engaging him predominantly, let alone exclusively – in these terms. And these, as noted earlier, are terms that strongly privilege argument, and place the burden of attention on the character and force of Schopenhauer's rational arguments in approaching his work.

Argument and expression in Schopenhauer's philosophy

The terms of this engagement, as just suggested, may render it "unfruitful"; yet it is now important to connect this external judgement of fruitfulness or utility to a perspective rather more indigenous to Schopenhauer's philosophy, and to the terms of its self-understanding. An avid follower of the reception of his work, Schopenhauer had been keenly aware from early on of the charges of incoherence reviewers levelled against it. With regard to such charges, there were times when he seemed to adopt an attitude of dismissive hauteur. "I was never concerned," he would write grandly on one occasion, "about the harmony and agreement of my propositions ... not even when some of them seemed to me to be inconsistent." At other times, he would respond with rather more visible pique to those who presumed "that the spirit of my thought did not observe the simplest of all logical laws, the law of contradiction."[27] The law of contradiction would already appear to be placed under palpable strain by such remarks; yet it is important for our own context to consider – or indeed, reconsider, given the earlier discussion in Chapter 2 – how this particular contradiction would most plausibly resolve.

For Schopenhauer might here vacillate about what tone to strike – the hauteur of one who defies, or the hauteur of one who perfectly conforms – towards the laws of thought invoked by his detractors. The prestige attaching to logical argument, and to more traditional forms of philosophical persuasion, could scarcely be shaken off with ease. The same ambivalence would sometimes be exhibited within the body of his philosophy, in which the language of argument would appear and disappear like an unsteady weave.[28] Yet Schopenhauer's programmatic view of philosophical

Oxford University Press, 1994), Young's (*Schopenhauer*, 2005), Jacquette's (*The Philosophy of Schopenhauer*, Montreal: McGill-Queen's University Press, 2005), and Wicks' (*Schopenhauer*, 2008).
[27] Cartwright, *Schopenhauer*, respectively 394 and 538; the first remark was made in 1851, the second in 1856.
[28] See Chapter 2, note 50.

excellence and procedure contained no such vacillation. Within this procedure, rational argumentation had been displaced by a method that "rose" above it. The method of philosophy, as we saw in Chapter 2, was not to argue, but to "raise" feeling to reflective form; the fundamental insight of Schopenhauer's philosophy – which took us beyond representation and its laws, including the laws of thought, to discover the inner nature of the world – was itself immune to demonstration. If place for proof still existed, this was to be, not at the beginning of philosophy, where philosophy received its light, but demoted to its very end, as Schopenhauer would indicate when stating that "in the case of every original insight, conviction exists prior to the proof, which is only subsequently thought out."[29]

Philosophy seeks not to prove but to interpret, to "decipher" experience in a way that brings the phenomena into agreement. This is an agreement that in Chapter 2 I suggested we understand in aesthetic terms, connecting it to the broader aesthetic character of Schopenhauer's standpoint. To emphasise this character was in fact precisely to call away from the relevance of argument, and to place the accent on the non-rational character of Schopenhauer's philosophy. It is a non-rational character that Schopenhauer would foreground distinctly in his late *Parerga and Paralipomena*, where he would look back to the intellectual life of his youth to wistfully remark: "When in the heyday of my intellect at the height of its powers the hour came through favourable circumstances in which the brain was at its highest tension, my eye would encounter any object it liked, and this spoke revelations to me" (*PP* II:53–54). Here, the irrationalist notion of "revelation" appears to be aligned with the aesthetic posture as characterised earlier: the philosopher stands before the phenomena and, goaded by their metaphysically significant beauty, seeks to probe the meaning of their speech. Elsewhere, however, Schopenhauer would charge this notion with a more audacious, quasi-religious meaning, in what David Cartwright describes as a "half-playful and half-serious appropriation of religious terms to refer to his philosophy and its reception." Some of the sections of the fourth book of the *World as Will and Representation*, Schopenhauer states, "could be regarded as inspired by the *Holy Ghost*"; the source of some of his most profound insights "can be called a *revelation*."[30] Little wonder that the truth given through such ecstatic throes

---

[29] Schopenhauer, *On the Will in Nature*, 87.

[30] Cartwright, *Schopenhauer*, 540, 541. It is also interesting to note the quasi-religious, visionary terms in which Schopenhauer describes his realisation of the suffering of the world: "In my seventeenth year, without any learned school education, I was affected by the *wretchedness of life*, as was the Buddha when in his youth he caught sight of sickness, old age, pain, and death" (*ibid.*, 78).

should then startle our rational mind at the hour of its wakefulness; for the truth may be outlandish – fantastic to behold. This emphasis on the non-rational indeed seems to be linked to an open acknowledgement of the fantastic nature of his philosophy, as conveyed in a comparison that few could equal in dramatic effect. His claim that the world is will and representation, Schopenhauer writes, is as wild as the central moment in the *Bhagavad-Gita*, "when Krishna appeared to Arjuna in his true divine form with his hundred thousand arms, eyes, mouths, and so on."[31]

The acknowledgement of the fantastic just expressed seems exuberant, almost gleeful. And it is a sense of glee, it has to be said, that Schopenhauer's writing does not exude at every step in this connection. The appeal of traditional forms of rational persuasion, as already mentioned, was hard to surrender; and that is surely because in doing so one would seem to run the risk of surrendering wholesale the notion of "persuasion" as such. One may thus pick up on the remarkable note of defeat that Schopenhauer would elsewhere strike when struggling to communicate particular philosophical insights, as for example when presenting an account we might call the "genealogy" of the Platonic Ideas, discussing the process of conflict through which higher objectifications of the will arise by subduing lower Ideas. "I wish it had been possible for me," Schopenhauer remarks with an almost audible sigh, "by clearness of explanation to dispel the obscurity that clings to the subject-matter of these thoughts. But I see quite well that the reader's own observation must help me a great deal, if I am not to remain uncomprehended or misunderstood" (*WWR* 1:145). These are tones of vulnerability and defeat that evoke the travails of the artist seeking to give birth to an idea already seen in the eye of the imagination: it is a failure to express, not to argue. To make up for the shortcomings of his own expressive efforts, Schopenhauer refers the reader to his own experience – the fount from which Schopenhauer draws, and to which his reader has equal access, so that both can face it independently to verify their insights.

Yet this element of vulnerability, and Schopenhauer's struggle to negotiate it, comes even more sharply into view in another context, which is worth considering with closer attention given its significance. This is in Schopenhauer's discussion of the aesthetics of music, where he offers an account of the inner nature of music whose paradoxical character he is aware of from the first breath, proposing that we understand music as

---

[31] *Ibid.*, 441. Cf. his remarks concerning the "paradoxical" character of his philosophy in *On the Will in Nature*, 19 and 21.

an analogy or copy of the entire world, the ascending tones of the octave mirroring the ascent of the will through the grades of objectification. "I recognise," writes Schopenhauer,

> in the deepest tones of harmony, in the ground-bass, the lowest grades of the will's objectification, inorganic nature, the mass of the planet … Further, in the whole of the ripienos that produce the harmony, between the bass and the leading voice singing the melody, I recognise the whole gradation of the Ideas in which the will objectifies itself. Those nearer to the bass are the lower of those grades, namely the still inorganic bodies manifesting themselves, however, in many ways. Those that are higher represent to me the plant and animal worlds. The definite intervals of the scale are parallel to the definite grades of the will's objectification, the definite species in nature … Finally, in the *melody*, in the high, singing, principal voice, leading the whole and progressing with unrestrained freedom, in the uninterrupted significant connexion of *one* thought from beginning to end, and expressing a whole, I recognise the highest grade of the will's objectification, the intellectual life and endeavour of man. (*WWR* I:258–59)

The first-person pronoun that holds up this sequence of thinking at every joint – "*I* recognise," "they represent *to me*" – is not incidental. It is a personal cadence that recurs in this discussion, along with some of the strongest autobiographical references that we hear in the entire work: "I have devoted my mind entirely to the impression of music in its many different forms; and then I have returned again to reflection and to the train of my thought expounded in the present work" (*WWR* I:256–57). Such remarks historicise Schopenhauer's act of reflection in a way that calls attention to its personal character. And in doing so, they compound an air of vulnerability that clings to Schopenhauer's discussion of music throughout.

Schopenhauer sounds apologetic about the limitations of his powers to persuade, yet fundamentally resigned to them: "it is essentially impossible to demonstrate this explanation"; "this explanation is quite sufficient *for me*." Only the converted – "whoever has followed me and has entered into my way of thinking" – might be accessible to this preaching. For the rest, one must stand helpless before the response of every reader, incapable of controlling it directly: "I must leave the acceptance or denial of my view to the effect that both music and the whole thought communicated in this work have on each reader" (*WWR* I:257). Either one feels this truth, or one does not – it is all a matter of how it affects us. Can one blame Schopenhauer for this retreat? The poetic character of his philosophical reflections had never seemed more starkly in evidence. It is hard not to acknowledge the appearance of a merely poetic "as if" that Schopenhauer's analogy carries; and it is not incidental that this analogy should remind us of another, with a more central role in Schopenhauer's philosophical progression, whose poetic character earlier came up for comment (Chapter 2). The limitations of persuasion, correspondingly – a persuasion that publicly available argument might have been able to secure – had never seemed clearer.

If there is defeat, however, there is immediately defensive retrenchment: Schopenhauer chafes at this surrender; he cannot accept the retreat to a sphere of merely private experience, abandoning the aspiration to a claim that carries universal validity. He cannot tolerate the vulnerability of depending on the vagaries of personal impression and arbitrary judgement; he needs objective defence. He prescribes criteria for what will count as true conviction: "I regard it as necessary," he now states in sterner tones, "in order that a man may assent with genuine conviction to the explanation of the significance of music here to be given, that he should often listen to music with constant reflection on this; and this again requires that he should be already very familiar with the whole thought which I expound" (*WWR* I:257). Notably yet characteristically, Schopenhauer's requirements stipulate what we might call homework of an experiential kind – exposing ourselves to the experience of music and listening to it with an intensity comparable to Schopenhauer's, keeping Schopenhauer's account in mind as we shuttle between our experience and Schopenhauer's interpretation of our experience. Only once our personal response has been regulated through such normative safeguards can it be entitled to a hearing; and then the likelihood is that we will have entered into Schopenhauer's insight and acknowledged its truth.

It is thus important to note that it is an act of sympathy – in the double sense of an act of feeling (in connecting us to our own experience) and fellow-feeling (in doing justice to another's experiential intuition) – that is required at the moment when philosophical intuition attains its greatest profundity, enabling us to be transported into a viewpoint that had initially struck us as uncompelling. In doing so, it brings out the complex appeal to experience that provides the hinges of some of Schopenhauer's most critical philosophical moments, lending to them a non-rational character that registers gleefully at times and more vulnerably at others.[32]

---

[32] It is a struggle with vulnerability that would continue to be waged even after these remarks: later referring back to this discussion, Schopenhauer would astonishingly describe its accomplishment as that of having "*demonstrated*" the parallelism between music and nature (*WWR* II:447).

It is not incidental to note in this connection that, while tragedy might offer the most natural artistic paradigm for Schopenhauer's philosophy in one sense (as suggested in Chapter 3), it is to music that Schopenhauer himself connects philosophy most strongly. Music and philosophy share the same task – to "repeat" or "express" the inner being of the world, the one in tones, the other in concepts (*WWR* I:264). In seeking to express the "what" of the world, and in seeking to express the way in which *music* expresses this same object, philosophy would seem to be confronted by similar difficulties and appeal to similar epistemological resources.

Commentators on Schopenhauer's philosophy have often picked up on the weakness of his arguments; I have been suggesting that this weakness needs to be located more self-consciously against an understanding of philosophical activity and its proper excellence that Schopenhauer openly embraces, in which argument is assigned a drastically diminished role. And yet it must now be acknowledged that to place the accent exclusively on the notion of "excellence," and on the corresponding notion of an intentional "embrace," would be to ignore a rather different way of approaching these philosophical phenomena. This is a route, indeed, that mobilises a characteristic turn inward to achieve its insight. It is an inward turn unlike any we had seen in our earlier discussion, yet one that in many ways stood in the shadows – and in the above discussion of music already partially stepped out of them – as the most natural denouement of this philosophical rotation.

Nietzsche would seem to have been inviting a turn of just this kind when he wrote in his early reflections: "If anyone wishes to refute Schopenhauer for me with reasons, I murmur in his ear: 'But, my dear man, world-views are neither created nor destroyed by logic.'"[33] Yet if world-views are not created by logic, by what instead? It is perhaps Georg Simmel – a sensitive reader of both Schopenhauer's and Nietzsche's works – who would offer the most limpid answer to this question in discussing Schopenhauer, when he would caution against speaking about "errors" in connection with "decisions based on ultimate sentiments about world and value." For such decisions, he would suggest, "are the expression of a specific being, of a specific attitude of a soul towards the world." The notion of "truth" and "falsehood" that we bring to bear on them should undergo correspondingly radical revision: "their 'truth' consists in an adequate and honest expression of the reality such that it can be imitated from within."[34]

---

[33] Quoted in Christopher Janaway, "Schopenhauer as Nietzsche's educator," in Janaway, ed., *Willing and Nothingness*, 18.

[34] Simmel, *Schopenhauer and Nietzsche*, 58.

Simmel would put the same point elsewhere in lapidary terms offering an even stronger grip for our context:

> The very image of the *whole*, which seems to imply the fullest and purest objectivity, reflects the peculiarity of its possessor much more than the objective image of any *particular* thing usually reflects it. If art is, as it is said to be, an image of the world seen through a temperament, then philosophy is a temperament seen through an image of the world ... [Thus] in philosophical assertions there is no question of correspondence (however understood) with an "object"; the question is whether the assertions are an adequate expression of the being of the philosopher himself or of the human type that lives within him.[35]

If this remark illuminates, it does so by resuming the precise vocabulary that Schopenhauer makes heavy use of in articulating his epistemic ideals and describing the philosophical task – the orientation to the "whole," the celebration of "objectivity" as the highest ideal, of the mind as a "mirror" reflecting back the "image" of the world. Yet in Simmel's resumption, they involve an unmistakable subversion. It is not simply that the image no longer reflects the world but rather the mind that represents it; this is a formulation to which Schopenhauer himself would not have withheld his assent. Yet he would have accepted it, significantly, on a particular understanding of how the "mind" at stake should be specified: as the supra-individual mind or "subject of knowing," the world-supporting "I" of transcendental idealism, which, in its philosophical exercise, sees the Ideas of the world and fathoms its nature. Simmel, by contrast, has something visibly different in mind when he speaks of a "specific being" or specific "temperament"; and whether, as in the last lines of the extract quoted above, we choose to speak more narrowly of "the being of the philosopher himself" or more broadly of "the human type that lives within him," Schopenhauer would have recognised here a change of register that, rejecting the philosopher's own aspiration to an objective standpoint from which the "in-itself" of being is revealed, has pronounced his philosophical vision a representation of what-the-world-is-relative-to-him. What he has seen is merely the world as it appears to him, in his full-blooded particularity as an individual with a specific character.

It is a move, of course, that Schopenhauer's philosophy would seem to have prepared for so well that it is hard to credit the thought that it should itself be taken by surprise by it. "The world is my representation" is

---

[35] Simmel, "On the nature of philosophy," quoted in Simmel, *Schopenhauer and Nietzsche*, translators' introduction, xxiii.

a formula that Schopenhauer himself has taught us to always keep before our eyes; and if, in its deployment to express the truth of transcendental idealism, the "I" that appears in this proposition should refer us to our higher subjectivity, Schopenhauer has also articulated this same truth on another level, in which the "I" at stake is rather more visceral in kind. It was this more visceral truth he had expressed when stating that "it is the will that holds all ideas and representations together as means to its ends, tinges them with the colour of its character, its mood, and its interest" (*WWR* II:140). A representation of the world that is not suffused with the colour of the individual "I" – the individual subject deeply enmeshed in the world, filtering everything through the prism of self-interest and its passionate nature – is by and large unavailable to us. Schopenhauer had described its availability as "abnormal," "unnatural," indeed "supernatural" (*PP* II:68; *WWR* II:384–85). In *Parerga and Paralipomena* he goes further: "an absolutely objective and thus perfectly pure intellect is … impossible"; the "tainting and infection of knowledge through individuality" is inescapable (*PP* II:65).

In the last chapter, I suggested that the happening of philosophy would have to count as a miracle – a miraculous transcendence of individual awareness to a purer subjectivity. That miracle, Simmel's remark suggests, has not taken place. And it suggests it by giving voice to an inarticulate suspicion that Simmel will not be alone in having been exposed to in the course of his reading. For one's reading of Schopenhauer's philosophy is haunted throughout, and at many of its most strategic philosophical moments, by a recurring question whether, if it is experience in general that serves as its avowed ground, it is nevertheless not a very specific experience that achieves expression within it.

It is a suspicion that is distinctly aroused, for example, by the "empirical proof" Schopenhauer offers as a confirmation of his claim that the will is determined, which involves the description of a certain experience we have of ourselves – we might call it the phenomenology of decision-making – when "some difficult and important choice lies before us, yet only under a condition that has not yet appeared but is merely awaited, so that for the time being we can do nothing." In such circumstances, our conscious mind diligently strives to place the possible courses of action in the clearest view, yet it awaits "the real decision as passively and with the same excited curiosity *as it would that of a foreign will*" (*WWR* I:291; emphasis added). A similar notion is expressed when Schopenhauer considers those occasions on which the mind labours to weigh the merits of complex alternative courses of action. While this is happening, Schopenhauer writes, "the will has been idly resting; after the result is reached, it enters, as the sultan does on the divan, merely to express again its monotonous approval or disapproval" (*WWR* II:207). Or again, characterising the way in which the knowledge of our own will becomes available to us:

> In self-consciousness ... the subject of knowing stands facing the will as a spectator, and although it has sprung from the will, *it knows that will as ... something foreign to it*, and thus only empirically, in time, piecemeal, in the successive agitations and acts of the will; only *a posteriori* and very indirectly does it come to know the will's decisions. (*WWR* II:499; emphasis added)

Embodied in these characterisations are some of Schopenhauer's basic philosophical claims concerning the will and its relationship to the mind, reinforcing a picture of the mind's subservience. Yet if one was to temporarily bracket their status as philosophical claims, one would be inclined to react by saying: what these formulations describe is a particular experience, a particular relationship to the self – a particular pathology. What they describe is a person with a disturbed relationship to desire; with an alienated experience of his own desires. The repeated appearance of the term "foreign" (*fremd*) in the above is more than suggestive in this regard. The will is experienced as a stranger, its movements and actions as brute as those of the oriental sultan constituting a textbook image of autocracy. Equally diagnostic would seem to be the pervasive elements that present "our" relationship to "our" will in terms we might have used to describe a natural event lying outside our control. The will is something we "await," that we anticipate "passively" with emotions of curiosity and excitement; the will is something we "discover" *a posteriori* with emotions of surprise or regret, complacence or horror; the will is something we confront as spectators.[36]

The spectatorial stance, of course, was closely linked to the standpoint of philosophical investigation. And indeed the last-quoted remark (*WWR* II:499) may provoke more than a passing reminiscence of that moment in Schopenhauer's philosophical execution where this standpoint had first found its grip. How had that grip been achieved? By means of a thought

---

[36] Cf. the descriptive characterisation of our intentions as "calculations of the relative strength of the different opposing motives" or predictions carrying different degrees of "probability" that can be proven true or false (*WWR* II:248). Note that this disfiguring account of the notion of intending is connected to Schopenhauer's interest in narrowing down what counts as a "real act of will" so as to facilitate his claim concerning the identity of inner and outer, act of will and bodily movement. See also Eagleton's powerful remarks about the image of alienation presented by Schopenhauer's philosophy in *The Ideology of the Aesthetic*, 161.

experiment that had first compelled us to lose it, by inviting us to consider our own body and its actions from an objective vantage point. Viewed in this manner, our body is merely "a representation like any other, an object among objects"; its movements and actions appear to us as "strange and incomprehensible" as those of all other perceptual objects, our conduct "follow[ing] on presented motives with the constancy of a law of nature, just as the changes of other objects follow upon causes, stimuli and motives" (*WWR* I:99). This thought experiment was counterfactual, of course. For Schopenhauer went on to assert that our actions are *not* strange, they *are* unravelled to us, though "in an entirely different way" – namely, as will. We turn inward to recover our relationship to our body. The objective regard is purged by the subjective turn.

Yet one may here raise the question whether there are not certain philosophical starting points that may provide philosophy with a false start; whether certain forms of wonder or surprise may not set philosophy up for a fall; and whether Schopenhauer's wonder – produced by assuming a vantage point that enables us "for a short time to marvel at the process of our own bodily action as miracle" (*WWR* II:248) – has not indeed already done so. For what we see as "miraculous," or "astonishing," or "sublime," as Wittgenstein would suggest in his later work, may itself need to be subjected to criticism or to therapy instead of being allowed to express its natural tendency and serve as the unquestioned stimulus of a train of philosophical questioning. To register this point, of course, is to raise a question as to whether the endings of philosophy ever do succeed in fully purging their beginnings. And this is a question with particular relevance for a philosophy that takes its task to be, not to perform sensational leaps of logic into the unknown – from familiar premises to obscurer conclusions – but rather to effect a leap from one modality of knowledge to another, and not to transcend its beginnings or wholly leap away from them, but rather to embrace them again in reflective form. With this in mind, it may not come as a great surprise to notice the otherwise singular fact that Schopenhauer's particular opening act has been far from purged by the time the curtain falls; it has merely been reappropriated. For when philosophy is done, among its chief conclusions is that our conduct *does* indeed "follow on presented motives with the constancy of a law of nature" – precisely like all other objects in the phenomenal realm in this regard. The act of sight with which philosophy opens – our will is an event – has been enshrined in the insight that consummates it.

Indeed, having made this observation, one will have little difficulty joining it to another no less seminal in reach, one that takes us back to Schopenhauer's own reflections on philosophy and its roots. For philosophy, Schopenhauer had written in his positioning essay "On Man's Need for Metaphysics" – seemingly echoing an established tradition of philosophical self-understanding – begins in wonder. Yet this, it is clear, is not the wonder of the child – the artless gaze turned outward, the face already quivering with readiness to convert the receptivity of an open mouth into a pleasured smile (a smile already present, it has been argued, in the word's root, given the links connecting the larger family that includes "miracle" and "admiration" to an Indo-European word for "smile").[37] This is a "wonder" – though let us now rather call it, more neutrally, an "astonishment" – that is already darkly brooding: for "it is the knowledge of death, and therewith the consideration of the suffering and misery of life, that give the strongest impulse to philosophical reflection and metaphysical explanations of the world"; "philosophical astonishment," thus, "is at bottom one that is dismayed and distressed" (*WWR* II:161, 171). In previous chapters, I argued that the unfolding of Schopenhauer's philosophy involves a particular kind of progression, one that we may recount as a shift in self-identification simultaneously presenting itself as a movement from one type of wonder to another. Yet if philosophy brings progression on one level, what should now be noticed is that the fundamental astonishment from which it begins is never fully purged or left behind. The act of sight that opens it – the world is a terrible place, full of suffering – survives to its end; it has not been explained away, but indeed only been etched more deeply into the phenomena by a philosophical insight that reveals it to constitute their essential character.

Schopenhauer's wonder is never dispelled. And it is precisely these unpurged philosophical beginnings, travelling from one end of philosophical inquiry to the other, that offer the strongest fuel to a suspicion or intuition that clings to it with equal tenacity, and that Simmel only recently voiced – an intuition that in these undigested presuppositions we have discovered a subterranean passageway that leads us, not to the thing-in-itself that lies beyond all phenomena, but to the inner heart of that particular phenomenon that is the individual philosopher turning the searchlight of his gaze inward. The gaze hits rock and it crumbles to the

---

[37] Lorraine Daston and Katharine Park, *Wonders and the Order of Nature, 1150–1750* (New York: Zone Books, 1998), 16.

other side; yet it is merely a new pass within the subterranean mine of his own soul. It is a danger that the turn inward, as suggested above in considering Schopenhauer's account of music, had clearly brooked – that such a turn would prove a deficient mode of transcendence, failing to lead beyond the merely personal to an insight vested with validity of a more universal kind.

Readers of Schopenhauer have thus kept rediscovering what Nietzsche would call "Schopenhauer as a human being," though there is a sense of shame to be overcome in order to articulate this discovery openly and lead philosophy back to its biographical roots. Back to Schopenhauer's relationship with his father: captious, never satisfied, inveterate in his dis-approval.[38] Back to his relationship with his mother: "He who has not received primary love, maternal love," writes Schopenhauer's biographer Rüdiger Safranski, "will very often lack love of what is primary, love of his own being alive," will lack "fundamental affirmation of life." Such a per-son is "inadequately born into his own body," "there remains a vulnerable aloofness and strangeness"; "the living element in himself" becomes "'the other', not his own."[39] Back to Schopenhauer's unlucky history of love: Schopenhauer (so again Safranski) had failed to experience a fulfilling relationship in which love and sexual desire might have been integrated and the character of sexual desire transformed, ceasing to be experienced as a brute need foreign to the self that places one in humiliating vulner-ability to the desired other.[40]

Such diagnoses are not without risk, and must be handled with cau-tion; one feels on slightly firmer ground with those reflections on Schopenhauer's character offered by Schopenhauer himself and by those on intimate terms with him. Schopenhauer is described and self-described as moody; anxious; depressive. Even during Schopenhauer's youth his mother decries his "scowling face," his "lamentations about the stupid world and human misery"; she speaks of "the melancholy brooding that you received as the inheritance from your father."[41] Schopenhauer echoes these very words in his private diary when he writes: "inherited from my father is the anxiety which I myself curse"; in conversation he confesses: "I was always very melancholy as a youth."[42] Even as a child, Schopenhauer

---

[38] See Cartwright, *Schopenhauer, passim.* Nietzsche's remark is from "Schopenhauer as educator," *Untimely Meditations*, 137.

[39] Safranski, *The Wild Years of Philosophy*, 16, 137–38. Compare Magee's balder remark: Schopenhauer's pessimistic views were "neurotic manifestations which had their roots in his relationship with his mother": *The Philosophy of Schopenhauer*, 13.

[40] Safranski, *The Wild Years of Philosophy*, 136.   [41] Cartwright, *Schopenhauer*, 108, 132.

[42] Schopenhauer, "Eis Eauton," *Manuscript Remains*, vol. IV, 506; Cartwright, *Schopenhauer*, 4.

dreads abandonment; as an adult, there are moments when he is seized by a nameless dread.[43]

To those interested in tracing Schopenhauer's philosophy back to its personal roots, his biographies offer sumptuous material, though to use it respectfully will demand reappropriating the notion of "sympathy" invoked at an earlier juncture of this chapter. To think oneself into Schopenhauer's philosophical standpoint will then involve an act of sympathy in the double sense earlier suggested: an act of feeling that is also an act of fellow-feeling.

Re-examining Schopenhauer's pessimism

On this sympathetic reading of philosophy-in-the-light-of-biography, the alienated regard that provides Schopenhauer's philosophy with its initial sight and final insight could find its interpretation. Yet something similar, as indicated in the terse biographical documentation above, could be said of that aspect of Schopenhauer's philosophy that has often presented itself to the world as its most gripping headline – namely, his pessimism. For both our present purposes and the purposes of the argument still to follow, it is important to pause to consider this headline with somewhat closer attention.

In referring to Schopenhauer's pessimism, what one often has in mind is a philosophical movement bearing a composite character, which one might propose to loosely dissolve into its constituents as follows. On the one hand, there is a characterisation we might call descriptive in kind: life is replete with suffering. On the other, there is a judgement openly evaluative in kind: non-existence – our own, the world's – is preferable to existence. And finally, there is a response that presents itself as the only appropriate reaction to this descriptive characterisation and evaluative judgement: the denial of the will to life.

Yet as readers of Schopenhauer's philosophy have sometimes remarked, an important distinction can be drawn within the first characterisation; and this is a distinction that raises a question about the exact nature of Schopenhauer's reason-giving and more specifically about the contribution of his metaphysical views to his pessimistic conclusions. For if life is full of suffering, this fact can be explained on two different levels, which carry different specifications of its modal force. On the one hand, there is the "deep" metaphysical explanation: the thing-in-itself – the inner nature

---

[43] Schopenhauer, "Eis Eauton," *Manuscript Remains*, vol. IV, 506–7.

of the world – is will; therefore we, as embodied manifestations of the will, are condemned to blindly strive and suffer without attaining satisfaction.[44] Yet this type of explanation seems to be complemented by another, one that presents itself rather closer to the "surface" and that indeed registers far less as explanation than as an observation of evident facts. These are facts we already partly brought into view in Chapter 1, when first considering Schopenhauer's philosophy in broad outlines. Aren't we always driven by desire – we asked – irresistibly driven forward by goals that are always immediately succeeded by new ones, moving ever forward in a never-ending Sisyphean march? Satisfaction always eludes us, and we continue to thirst on with insatiable desire and a bottomless sense of need. And in those rare moments when our desires are finally satisfied, boredom swiftly ensues to cause new suffering. Regimented more austerely, Schopenhauer's most decisive claims in this regard could be reformulated as follows: (a) happiness is negative: it consists in the satisfaction or relief of a previous desire, and is not a state that endures; (b) life oscillates between the suffering produced by unsatisfied desire, and the boredom produced by satisfied desire and the absence of new desire; (c) happiness always seems to exist only in the past and the future; as soon as a goal is attained, the happiness that had appeared within reach again recedes into the future.[45]

The two levels would seem to be related as a metaphysical reality to its expression: it is the deeper reality of the blindly striving will that expresses itself in the features captured by these propositions; the "surface" is grounded in the "deep." This is something that Schopenhauer signals

---

[44] This is the view taken by Copleston, who might have questioned my distinction between descriptive and evaluative levels given his view that Schopenhauer's theory of the will was not "purely descriptive, in the sense of being free from all judgements of value" (*Philosopher of Pessimism*, xi–xv). Copleston claimed that Schopenhauer's pessimism was "logically" based on his conception of the thing-in-itself as an irrational, blind impulse to existence: "if that metaphysic were actually true or if it were only held to be true, then from the logical standpoint, the one possible attitude towards life would be a pessimistic attitude" (*Philosopher of Pessimism*, 74–75). Magee criticises this type of position in *The Philosophy of Schopenhauer* (13–14) on the basis of the well-rehearsed view that descriptive facts do not entail value judgements – a criticism that leaves Copleston's specific position untouched given his denial that Schopenhauer's claims had been purely descriptive in nature. Janaway sides with Copleston in stressing the dependence of Schopenhauer's pessimism on his metaphysics: *Self and World in Schopenhauer's Philosophy*, 271–73; cf. Christopher Janaway, "Schopenhauer's pessimism," in Janaway, ed., *The Cambridge Companion to Schopenhauer*. Simmel's analysis goes in the same direction in *Schopenhauer and Nietzsche*, chs. 3 and 4, *passim*.

[45] My regimentation more or less follows the one offered by Young in *Willing and Unwilling*, 137–45. Young discusses a fourth "surface" claim that concerns the inevitable relations of hostility between human beings, in turn reflecting the pervasive presence of conflict within the natural world (Young earlier refers to this as "nature pessimism": the condition of nature is *bellum omnium contra omnes*, 74–76).

clearly in that concerted discussion of the *World as Will and Representation* in which he proposes to show that "all life is suffering" (*WWR* 1:310) and in which the "surface" features are one by one addressed. This discussion is signposted from the start as aiming to study human existence in order to "consider ... the inner and essential destiny of the will" within it (*WWR* 1:310). The import of this remark is brought out again crisply towards the end of his discussion of the surface features when Schopenhauer states:

> All that these remarks are intended to make clear, namely the impossibility of attaining lasting satisfaction and the negative nature of all happiness, finds its explanation in what is shown at the end of the second book, namely that the will, whose objectification is human life like every phenomenon, is a striving without aim or end. (*WWR* 1:321)[46]

Yet what is important to note is that, unlike the deeper metaphysical explanation, which will be unavailable to us pre-philosophically (on a reflective level at least) without accepting the truth of Schopenhauer's doctrine, the "surface" features are in the main ones that we can be expected to recognise prior to philosophical exposure – they are the ways in which the will expresses itself in our *experience*. Indeed, it is this phenomenological evidence, as already suggested in passing in Chapter 1, that could lend support to the metaphysical account and potentially lead us to acknowledge its truth. (The metaphysical account brings such phenomena into agreement, offering a coherent reading of the "ciphers" before us.) And it is this reference to our phenomenology that seems to offer a wedge that enables one to decouple the two levels to consider their reason-giving force in isolation, and most relevantly, to subject the reasons available prior to metaphysical commitment to closer critique. Focusing selectively on some of the above propositions as well as on Schopenhauer's phenomenology of suffering more broadly, I will here try to trace out what I take to constitute the most important stress fractures of Schopenhauer's account.

And perhaps no better starting point could be found than the Sisyphean notion of desire and its relentless march that Schopenhauer places at the heart of this account. To call it "Sisyphean" is to draw this march closer to the philosophical present and its specific tribulations, largely unfamiliar to a longer philosophical past despite its having provided the mythological means for designating them. Yet to accentuate these historical differences too sharply would be to ignore the ways in which this past would have found Schopenhauer's notion of infinite desire intimately, indeed

---

[46] The direction of the discussion is spelled out in fairly clear terms earlier in *WWR* 1:307–10.

dangerously, familiar. It was an understanding of desire that had haunted Epicurus, for example, when he had described human beings as living "in a state of painful stress and disturbance, buffeted as by a violent tempest," and had located the central cause of human misery in "the disturbance produced by the seemingly 'boundless' demands of desire" that allow us no rest.[47] It was a sense of the tempest within the human breast that had haunted Plato no less intensely before him: speaking of our desires in the *Gorgias*, he had used the telling metaphor of a "leaky jar" (493b) to convey the troubling insatiability that adhered to them. In the *Republic* he would refer to the "terrible, untamed, and lawless class of desires" (572b) that exists in every one of us, and that ceaselessly threatens to multiply into a "dense mass" of "countless unspeakable desires" and "countless needs" (573d–e). It was indeed against this disturbing vision of the darkness present in the soul that Plato's vision of the ideal society and of the highest form of life would unfold.[48]

Yet having noted this basic continuity of concern, it becomes possible for a discontinuity of a different type to be brought into relief. For in the ancient context, to observe that desire "goes off into infinity," in Epicurus' phrase – reaching out, as Martha Nussbaum reformulates, to a "'boundless' object that can yield no stable satisfaction" – was not to state a fact for its own sake. Registering the openness of desire was merely a prelude, or an adjunct, to engaging this characterisation in active terms; the statement of fact was closely connected to a normative ethical response. And this response, significantly, involved a concerted critique of desire that sought to order different types of desires in normative terms, distinguishing between good and bad, healthy and sick. Epicurus, thus, would proceed to divide desires into two classes, natural and empty, to suggest that the natural desires experienced by creatures uncorrupted by social influence do indeed have a limit and admit of satisfaction. It is only once perverted through socially acquired false beliefs that their boundaries become porous. And this was a diagnosis, of course, that held out the promise of a "therapy of desire," through a therapy of the beliefs that ground it.[49]

This normative stance found its immediate counterpart in Plato, whose distinction between necessary and unnecessary desires in the *Republic* (558d–559c) it directly brings to mind. Unlike Epicurus, Plato did not privilege the natural taken as a pre-social state (and in this, he would no

[47] Nussbaum, *The Therapy of Desire*, 104–5.
[48] The translation I draw on is Plato, *The Republic*, trans. T. Griffith, ed. G. R. F. Ferrari (Cambridge University Press, 2000).
[49] See the discussion in Nussbaum, *The Therapy of Desire*, ch. 4, esp. 111ff.

doubt have the sympathy of those unable to credit Epicurus' claim that "cravings for unlimited quantities of food and drink" are socially acquired, as through "the false belief that the stomach needs an unlimited amount to satisfy it").[50] Any therapy would have to be, not backward-looking rehabilitation, but forward-looking education. For the danger of desire does not come to us from without: it dwells within our very being. It dwells, indeed, in the body itself, and in the multiple appetites the body bursts with. It is in fact, not desire as such, but a more specific set of desires, namely those deriving from our physical nature, that Plato would link to the boundlessness that proves so deeply unnerving. "All of us, *insofar as we live an appetitive life*," Martha Nussbaum glosses the metaphor of the *Gorgias* cited just above, "are like vessels full of holes, vainly pouring into ourselves, again and again, a satisfaction that as promptly deserts us. Or, worse, we are like an especially loathsome sort of bird that excretes as rapidly as it eats, and is constantly doing both."[51] It is then to a different set of higher desires – to the *eros* that Plato, ascribing to the rational part of the soul its own desire and specific pleasure, makes a hallmark of the philosopher in the *Republic* and elsewhere – that such lower desires should yield and through which they should be transcended. For it is not, as Aristotle would suggest in his own terms in the *Nicomachean Ethics*, that pleasure should be rejected as such; the virtuous or contemplative activity that constitutes the good life is after all also attended by its proper pleasure. It is rather a matter of choosing the *right* kind of pleasure, and of "being right about what is *truly* pleasant" – not the pleasures of children or animals, but the pleasures of the wise man or *phronimos* who forms our ethical standard.[52]

With this perspective in place, certain of Schopenhauer's presuppositions now allow themselves to be dislodged from their background to become available to a more critical view. For in speaking of the infinite desire to which we are subject – "this body," writes Schopenhauer, "is nothing but the objectified will-to-live itself," and as the most perfect objectification of this will, man is "concrete willing and needing through and through; he is a concretion of a thousand wants and needs" (*WWR* 1:312) – it may now be noted, on the one hand, that Schopenhauer's attention is focused seemingly exclusively on a very particular class of desires, namely physical

desires deriving from our embodied state. Perhaps more important, however, is another observation concerning the nature of Schopenhauer's
focus; and this is that, in speaking of our desirous nature in descriptive
terms of this kind, Schopenhauer has adopted a spectatorial stance on the
phenomena that is significant for what it excludes. And what it notably
excludes, as suggested above, is a normative stance that many other philosophers would have argued should arrive as its sequel. But it is indeed
not merely as philosophers vested in a particular standpoint, but also as
laymen – and thus as subjects with whose phenomenological experience
Schopenhauer has declared a special concern – that we are entitled to
remark what Schopenhauer's spectatorial approach to desire leaves out of
view. For in bracketing the normative perspective, Schopenhauer seems
to overlook the fact that this is a perspective we ourselves often strive for,
and that our relationship to our own desires is pervaded by normative
terms. Some of our most important desires attach to objects or events,
not simply as means for satisfying desires experienced as brute itches or
throbs, but rather, as Jonathan Lear notes, under their aspect as "valuable,
beautiful, and good," as objects of a "yearning, longing, admiration" that
is tightly bound up with our limited condition.[53]

This point makes it easier to pick out more clearly another feature of
Schopenhauer's account that might otherwise escape attention, which
concerns the understanding of happiness that governs it. For the notion of
happiness at stake – the happiness whose possibility Schopenhauer denies,
and whose denial figures in his pessimistic conclusions – is in fact of a
very particular kind. Happiness has been collapsed into the satisfaction of
desire, a move plainly visible in Schopenhauer's remark that "the successive satisfaction of all our willing is what we think of through the concept
of happiness" (*WWR* II:634). And this is in turn linked with a construal of
happiness in predominantly experiential terms – as an *experience* of satisfaction that, Schopenhauer then goes on to claim, has only a lamentably
brief duration. What is deplored is that "all our *pleasures and enjoyments*
come to nought in our hands"; what is denied is that life is "here to be
thankfully *enjoyed*" and that man "exists in order to be *happy*" (*WWR*
II:574; emphasis added).

If this notion of happiness might fail to stand out for us, it is partly
because of its pervasive presence in our own ethical discourse, with its
Kantian and utilitarian foundations. Yet it contrasts strongly with the

[53] Jonathan Lear, *Radical Hope: Ethics in the Face of Cultural Devastation* (Cambridge, MA and
   London: Harvard University Press, 2006), 120.

notion of happiness at work in much of ancient philosophy where, as writers on ancient ethics have often stressed, the use of the term "happiness" to translate the term *eudaimonia* ("flourishing," "the good life") is misleading, to the extent that "happiness" is taken to designate a subjective or psychological state – a *feeling* of contentment, comfort, or pleasure. By contrast, John Ackrill suggests, in ancient ethics *eudaimonia* has a force like that of "the best possible life" – so that to deny, for example, that all human beings want *eudaimonia* would be as incoherent as denying that human beings seek to order their lives according to their conceptions about what are better and worse ways of doing so.[54] It is this non-experiential or non-subjective understanding of *eudaimonia* that makes it intelligible to consider, as Aristotle does, that our happiness – in this broader sense – can be affected by events after our death, as by fortunes or misfortunes that affect our descendants (*Nicomachean Ethics*, 1100a15–25).[55]

It is telling in this regard that precisely such a prejudicial understanding of *eudaimonia* appears to be expressed in Schopenhauer's remarks about ancient ethics throughout his work.[56] This understanding, as I have suggested, also ties in with Schopenhauer's emphasis on a diminished notion of desire and his neglect of the thicker evaluative descriptions that direct our desires. And one may then tie it to a further observation that concerns Schopenhauer's notion of pleasure, one that again throws out instructive bridges to more recent moral debates. For contemporary ethical theory, particularly of the utilitarian kind, has often come in for criticism over its proposal to deploy pleasure as a criterion for the evaluation of actions, relying on a notion of pleasure or utility that can be quantified prior to moral evaluation and that thereby allows us to compare the value of different actions through a comparison of their relative sums. Yet as writers on ancient ethics have pointed out, pleasure is not a notion that can be independently specified in value-free terms, let alone serve as a "single independently specifiable end." And this is because it is closely bound up with our evaluative conceptions. To the self-indulgent man, as Julia Annas notes,

---

[54] John L. Ackrill, "Aristotle on *eudaimonia*," in Rorty, ed., *Essays on Aristotle's Ethics*, esp. the remarks 23–24; cf. also the brief comment in Nussbaum, *Fragility of Goodness*, 6.

[55] Not all ancient philosophers, however, seem equally prepared to dismiss the relevance of experience in this manner, as indicated by Lucretius' well-known response to the fear of death, which rests on the premise that the value of an event depends on the possibility of a person's experiencing that event. See the discussion in Nussbaum, *The Therapy of Desire*, ch. 6, and also the collection of essays edited by John M. Fischer, *The Metaphysics of Death* (Stanford University Press, 1993), for some of the most interesting contemporary efforts to engage this type of question.

[56] See, e.g., *WWR* II:150–51; II:603; cf. Schopenhauer's definition of the term "eudemonology": "the art of getting through life as pleasantly and successfully as possible" (*PP* I:313).

it will be bodily pleasures that are enjoyable; to the temperate man, leading a life ordered by a different conception of the good, it will be restraint from bodily pleasures in which enjoyment is taken. It will then be misguided to seek to weigh the pleasures each of them experiences in order to raise a question about which of the two takes greater pleasure "from an objective point of view." For it is "one's conception of the good life which determines what counts for one as being pleasant"; thus "the good life and the truly pleasant life *must* be explained in terms of one another."[57]

It is just such a view of pleasure – as an independently specifiable and quantifiable notion – that can now be seen to be operating in Schopenhauer's thinking, and that indeed figures prominently in his pessimistic viewpoint, whose blanket constitutive statement that "*all* life is suffering" assumes a statistically more nuanced but also thereby more vulnerable inflection when transformed into a claim concerning the "*preponderating* magnitude of the evil and misery of existence" (*WWR* II:585). For if pleasure cannot be specified and quantitatively compared in value-free terms, then it becomes immediately questionable in what sense one is entitled to speak of "preponderance" in this connection. It becomes more questionable still whether we can respond to Schopenhauer's invitation to "let us for once calmly compare the sum of the pleasures which are in any way possible, and which a man can enjoy in his life, with the sum of the sufferings which are in any way possible, and can come to him in his life." And it becomes equally problematic to assent to his own conclusion: "I do not think it will be difficult to strike the balance" (*WWR* II:576). To then suggest, as Schopenhauer does in *Parerga and Paralipomena*, that in testing the truth of this claim we "compare the feelings of an animal that is devouring another with those of that other" (*PP* II:292) is to use a limited paradigm that – for all its devastating emotive appeal – is highly prejudicial even as it is highly diagnostic of Schopenhauer's intellectual bent, for it ignores precisely those ways in which the notions of pleasure and pain operate differently in the lives of human beings than they do in the lives of other animals.[58] To presume we may draw on a notion of shared

---

[57] Annas, "Aristotle on pleasure and goodness," 288, 289; cf. Alasdair MacIntyre's remarks in *After Virtue,* 3rd edn (London: Duckworth, 2007), 160–61.

[58] Schopenhauer certainly does draw some distinctions in this connection, stressing the important differences that result from the "addition of reflection," which brings a larger temporal horizon into view and quantitatively intensifies our susceptibility to happiness and suffering (see, e.g., *PP* II:293–97). Yet this distinction does not cut sufficiently deeply; and with the notable exception of our susceptibility to a source of suffering unshared by animals – namely, shame – Schopenhauer emphasises that this is an intensified set of sensations directed to "the same result," to "the same things which even the animal obtains, and indeed with incomparably less expenditure of emotion and distress" (*PP* II:295).

biological susceptibilities to support such a comparison would indeed be to buy into a myth of "man without culture" that is hard to sustain. For as Alasdair MacIntyre has remarked in a related context, our biological nature may constrain cultural possibility, yet "man who has nothing but a biological nature is a creature of whom we know nothing."[59]

But it is now crucial to note yet another feature of Schopenhauer's account the element just discussed is linked with, and to which it strongly points. For in the context of ancient philosophy, the recognition of the thick relations between pleasure and notions of the good was joined to an equally important reflection concerning the relationship between pleasure and activity. If it makes no sense to speak of pleasure *simpliciter*, this is because pleasures depend on conceptions of the good – conceptions expressed in different activities. Put more broadly, pleasures differ according to their respective activities.[60] Hailed by readers of Aristotle's ethics as one of his deepest insights, in his works this reflection was connected with a seminal emphasis on the importance of activity within the good life. For while it has often been debated how to reconcile two seemingly conflicting specifications of the good life that coexist in the *Nicomachean Ethics* – the ethical and the contemplative – more noteworthy is what unites these ideals rather than what divides them, and this is their shared character as modes of activity. As such, both evoke a definition of happiness that appears early in the work, as an "activity of soul in accordance with complete excellence" (1102a5–10), and as a sort of "living well and *doing* well" (1098b20–25).[61]

Significantly, one of the competing viewpoints Aristotle engages in this connection is the view that the good life might consist, not in activity – activity according to excellence – but rather in excellence taken as a state. This, as Martha Nussbaum remarks, is a position with great appeal for those wishing to secure the good against the instabilities of luck, given the vulnerability that the commitment to activity – in demanding an engagement of the world through a performance that can fail or succeed – would seem to carry. It is in this background, one organised by a concern with the role of luck in the good life, that one needs to read a remarkable passage in the *Eudemian Ethics* in which Aristotle raises the question of

---

[59] MacIntyre, *After Virtue*, 161.
[60] I am again drawing on Annas, "Aristotle on pleasure and goodness." This is not to say that all pleasure is internal to activity; see, e.g., MacIntyre's relevant remarks in *After Virtue*, 197–98, and 188ff. for the distinction between internal and external goods at stake in these remarks.
[61] I draw on the translation of the *Nicomachean Ethics* by Christopher Rowe, with introduction and commentary by Sarah Broadie (Oxford University Press, 2002).

suicide. "After talking about those who kill themselves because of some chance catastrophe," Nussbaum writes,

> Aristotle asks what *are*, after all, the things that make life worth the living. In general, he concludes, if you collect together all the things that a person does and suffers because of luck, rather than voluntarily, no combination of these, even prolonged to an infinite term, would suffice to make a person choose living rather than not living (1215b27–31). Life is made worth living for a human being only by voluntary action; and not simply the low-level voluntary action of a child (1215b22–24), but action shaped overall by adult excellence and its efforts.

Thus, to exclude the role of effort more broadly, and accomplished activity more narrowly, from our understanding of the good life is to impugn "a belief so deep and basic that we hold it to be a condition of our continued willingness to remain in existence."[62]

What the above now brings out is the fact that it is indeed the notion of activity, and the vital importance attaching to it, that seems to have been occluded in Schopenhauer's account. This occlusion comes as a natural adjunct of Schopenhauer's focus on happiness as a psychological state – as an experience of pleasure or enjoyment in relation to which human beings stand in a passive role. Yet I would suggest that this emphasis on passivity runs down the length of Schopenhauer's work as a far broader conceptual frieze. If we have just seen it expressed in Schopenhauer's specification of happiness, we had earlier seen it in his specification of unhappiness, defined by a particular view of the relationship of human subjects to their own desires. The will is a foreign presence irrupting from within to master us, an autocrat whose imperious decree our conscious mind can only meekly submit to.

It is an image of passivity that reappears in Schopenhauer's redemptive proposals – ascetic and aesthetic – for transcending the realm of suffering, including the experiential specification of happiness that governs it and that proves deeply disappointing. In articulating these redemptive solutions – solutions that, on Ackrill's more generous construal, we might agree to call Schopenhauer's considered view of *eudaimonia*[63] – Schopenhauer's dominant tendency is to accentuate our limited ability to voluntarily control them. We cannot achieve them through effort; they come to us as if from the outside. We saw this in connection with aesthetic experience in

---

[62] Nussbaum, *Fragility of Goodness*, 321.
[63] Schopenhauer himself, indeed, speaks of the denial of the will as the *summum bonum* and human *telos* at *WWR* I:362, though he signals this is merely "metaphorically and figuratively."

the first chapter, where we noted the prevailing (if ultimately modified) emphasis on the subject's passivity: the aesthetic object "snatches" us from ourselves (*WWR* I:197); the human eye awaits the object to carry out the "act of procreation" upon it (*PP* II:428). And whether it can do so or not further depends on the possession of an extraordinary disposition granted to few, reflecting an intellectual "aristocracy" established by nature (*WWR* II:146) and thus subject to its lottery. The aesthetic transformation of our regard, ultimately, "cannot rest with us" (*WWR* II:367).

Something similar holds for the metaphysical insight that leads to the denial of the will. For "all knowledge and insight as such," Schopenhauer asserts, "are independent of free choice"; and thus the denial of the will "is not to be forcibly arrived at by intention or design," but rather "comes suddenly, as if flying in from without" (*WWR* I:404). The domain of *eudaimonia*, such as it is, is utterly consumed in luck. And indeed this observation stands to be placed in an even sharper perspective. For the route to resignation that passes through knowledge, Schopenhauer notes, is anyway open to few; in practice, more frequently tread is the route that passes through suffering, when "fate and the course of things" confront us with relentless mortifications that lead us to see through the illusions of happiness, so that our will eventually turns away from the world (*WWR* II:638–39). Salvation is thus to be reached neither by knowledge nor by action, but rather by suffering. Standing some of the central traditions of philosophy on its head, it is in our very passivity that Schopenhauer locates our redemptive prospects. There is nothing you need to do; sit back and life will do it for you.

The emphasis on passivity in these "eudaimonic" proposals follows naturally, of course, from the problematisation of the will that gives them context, which problematises any appearance of voluntary control in their realisation. Yet Aristotle had already anticipated why, having placed an overwhelming emphasis on our passive capacity – and whether we are considering a state of virtue or a state of experience is immaterial to the point – we should not be surprised to find that "our continued willingness to remain in existence" has been placed in question. Writing in the *Nicomachean Ethics*, Aristotle had suggested that it counted against the understanding of happiness as a state of excellence that one could then be happy while asleep (1095b30–1096a1). Whether Schopenhauer had this remark in mind when he stated that "the happiest moment of the happy man is that of his falling asleep" (*WWR* II:578), the inversion could not be more telling for the displacement of activity from Schopenhauer's account.

Where it appears in Schopenhauer's discussion, in fact, activity registers, not as a component of happiness, but rather as a form of suffering. It reflects a striving that can be found everywhere in the natural world – in forces of nature, plants, and animals, no less than human beings. This restless striving is simply an expression of their nature as will, which "always strives, because striving is its sole nature, to which no attained goal can put an end" (*WWR* I:308). And in striving, we suffer:

> [A]ll striving springs from want or deficiency, from dissatisfaction with one's own state or condition, and is therefore suffering so long as it is not satisfied. No satisfaction, however, is lasting; on the contrary, it is always merely the starting-point of a fresh striving. We see striving everywhere impeded in many ways, everywhere struggling and fighting, and hence always as suffering. (*WWR* I:309)

Activity is the phenomenal condition through which our inner nature as will inexorably expresses itself in our lives, compelling us to move from goal to goal when all we thirst for is rest. "We resemble a man running down hill who would inevitably fall if he tried to stop, and who keeps on his legs only by continuing to run" – "pushed from behind" and "driven forward against [our] will," there is little chance of "that rest for which we are always longing" (*PP* II:284; *WWR* II:359–60). Activity is thus something to which we are condemned – a reality we must passively suffer. This characterisation of activity, importantly, brings out something that may already have been evident but can now be stated more plainly, namely that happiness always arrives as its aftermath. Schopenhauer's thinking appears to be organised throughout by a hypnotic disjunction between means and ends, between striving and attainment, desire and its satisfaction. Our striving is the suffering "before," and satisfaction the coveted "after," which becomes a "now" for only an infinitesimal moment before being extinguished.

Yet this binary division would seem to place itself at loggerheads once again with some of the most important phenomena. For certainly, we go to the gym to lose weight, we avoid the sun to preserve our skin, we take a side job to pay the bills, build up savings for old age. But is all of our activity of this order, directed to ends external to the activity? The means–end model describes many of our actions, but not all. It excludes, significantly, all of those activities that we do, not for their consequences, but for their own sake, whether it is learning the violin or learning to carve wood, spending time with our family or participating in a community project, going for cross-country walks or gardening, reading books or writing them. And these are activities in which the pleasure is located, not at the end of the activity, but within its very body. For a more complex model that would accommodate the different types of motivations expressed in our actions, in fact, Schopenhauer need have done little more than consider the threefold division Plato had proposed in the *Republic*, between activities one does for their own sake, activities one does for their sake *and* their consequences, and activities one does *solely* for their consequences (357b–d). In naming the first class of activities, Plato was exhibiting a concern that would typify many philosophers after him, and that may once again be situated against a preoccupation with the stability of the good, rendering activity self-sufficient by locating its ends within it. Aristotle would later elaborate on this notion of perfect activity further; and it is philosophical contemplation that would serve as its paradigm instance.[64]

But to remark the pleasure taken *in* activity and to bring the limitations of Schopenhauer's means–ends model into view, is simultaneously to bring into view the serious shortcomings attaching to his conception of the relationship between activity and suffering. For if we take pleasure in activity, activity and suffering cannot simply be identified. Indeed, Schopenhauer's unargued equation of the two, it may be objected, ignores not only our general pleasure in activity, but the heightened enjoyment we specifically take in *difficult* activity – activity that requires struggle of some kind to be accomplished, and paradigmatically activity involving a skill that must first be mastered. Whether we think of the silky violin note emerging out of a long history of dissonant scratches, the poetic word that triumphs in its struggle to capture its object, or the cross-country run in whose bounds strain and exhilaration stand combined, the resistance of one's material and the joy one experiences in mastering it are irrevocably intertwined. Far from being a form or cause of unhappiness, striving is integral to the joy one takes in acting. The pleasure we take in the difficult is one that ancient philosophers might have accounted for through the psychology of *thumos*, or the spirited part of the soul that takes pleasure in conquest and victory. It is not incidental that when Aquinas – drawing heavily on Aristotle in developing his ethical positions – analysed the passion of hope, he should have subsumed this within the irascible appetite. For hope addresses itself to a future good that is possible yet difficult to

---

[64] Schopenhauer's emphasis on the instrumental in fact appears to reflect another prejudicial understanding of the notion of *eudaimonia*. For Schopenhauer presumes that when identifying the good life with the life of virtue, ancient philosophers were arguing that virtue and happiness relate as means to end: that virtue *produces* happiness as its *experienced* result; see, e.g., the remarks in *WWR* II:150–51. This relation, as has been persuasively argued, should be understood not in instrumental but in constitutive terms: see, e.g., Ackrill, "Aristotle on *eudaimonia*."

attain, and *qua* difficult, it appeals to our desire to conquer it through struggle.[65] With his monocular focus on passive enjoyment and his construction of human motivation in terms of a predominant desire for rest, Schopenhauer seems to have thrown out this aspect of our psychology altogether, and with it the acknowledgement of the complex relations in which pleasure and pain are locked in activity.[66]

I have been suggesting that in cementing his pessimistic perspective, Schopenhauer disregards the pleasure attaching to activity, and more narrowly to difficult activity. It is interesting to note, however, that this insight finds direct expression elsewhere in his work. It is present, for example, in Schopenhauer's remark that "there is really no other pleasure than in the use and feeling of our own powers" (*WWR* I:305). Yet it stands out nowhere more starkly than in his late "Aphorisms on the Wisdom of Life," where Schopenhauer states:

> Activity to do something, if possible to make something, at any rate to learn something, is … absolutely essential to a man's happiness … Effort, trouble, and struggle with opposition are as necessary to man as grubbing in the ground is to a mole. The stagnation that results from being wholly contented with a lasting pleasure would be for him intolerable. The full pleasure of his existence is in overcoming obstacles … The struggle with them and the triumph make him happy. (*PP* I:438–39)

Here, struggle is recognised not as a mode of suffering or an impediment to happiness, but as a positive ingredient that happiness requires within its content.[67] And if this insight is here explicitly expressed, the same insight had been implicit in the heartland of Schopenhauer's aesthetics, the sublime – that aesthetic experience, tellingly, where the accent on active contribution was most strongly sounded, modifying the image of passivity elsewhere enforced – in which aesthetic pleasure was directly proportional to the resistance overcome. It is similarly a joy of this kind – one deriving from the "use and feeling of our own powers" of active understanding – that, as I have suggested, provides Schopenhauer's entire philosophy with its own affective backbone. Writing in *Beyond Good and Evil*, Nietzsche would later reject in disdain the ideal of a "happiness of rest, of

---

[65] See René A. Gauthier, *Magnanimité: l'idéal de la grandeur dans la philosophie païenne et dans la théologie chrétienne* (Paris: J. Vrin, 1951), 318ff.; and see also Chapter 6 below.

[66] Cf. Simmel's relevant remarks in *Schopenhauer and Nietzsche*, 55–56, contesting Schopenhauer's claim that all volition is painful.

[67] One might raise a question, however, as to whether Schopenhauer's endorsement of this view is aligned with the specific – "conditional" or "compromised" – perspective that governs this essay; for more on this perspective see the next chapter.

tranquillity, of satiety."[68] Yet Schopenhauer had already said it before him: what we desire is motion, not rest.

Such insights, however, do not appear to be integrated within the body of Schopenhauer's philosophy and the characterisation of human life that enters into his pessimistic viewpoint. As such, they are among several facets of his account that, as I have sought to show, open his pessimism to critique. Several of the above criticisms, of course, presuppose the licence to decouple the "surface" and "deep" levels of Schopenhauer's pessimism specified at the outset. Schopenhauer's concentration on the physical desires we share with other animals, for example, seems less surprising once Schopenhauer's metaphysics is brought back into view, with its programmatic abolition of the separators dividing human beings from the rest of nature, and its focus on the blind force at work in animate and inanimate beings alike. Similarly, if Schopenhauer ignores the higher pleasures that philosophers from Plato to Mill have counterposed to the lower pleasures of the body – and if, similarly, he never entertains the possibility that the second pole of suffering, boredom, could be addressed by cultivating such higher pleasures – this is surely intrinsically connected to the fact that, in the light of Schopenhauer's metaphysics, such pleasures can only appear as an anomaly and never as a generally accessible, actively pursuable ideal. It could be said that many of the philosophers who have prized these pleasures in the past have been haunted by the ghost of an intellectual elitism not unlike Schopenhauer's, and thus by similar questions concerning the accessibility of their ideals. Yet Schopenhauer's metaphysics seems designed to engrave this elitism rather more deeply into the fabric of reality – deeply enough, indeed, to cast a serious shadow over what was earlier referred to as Schopenhauer's "humanism" (Mann), and to make us question its force. Schopenhauer's inconsistent acknowledgement of the pleasure taken in activity may in fact be far from incidental in this connection. For it may ultimately reflect a more self-conscious distinction between types of enjoyment and their respective availability: a passive kind of pleasure typifying the happiness of the many, and an enjoyment characteristic of the highest aesthetic and philosophical activity generated through the exercise of mastery and reserved for the few.

To those unprepared to argue from Schopenhauer's metaphysical premises, however, the grounds of his pessimism would seem to be mined with philosophical difficulties, laying themselves open to question at every turn. It is thus equally questionable whether, offered as *reasons* for

---

[68] Nietzsche, *Beyond Good and Evil*, §200.

adopting Schopenhauer's pessimistic viewpoint in its composite character – life is full of suffering; non-existence is preferable to existence; denial of the will is the only appropriate response – these grounds would suffice to secure assent. And it is precisely the insufficiency of reasons, to recover our thread, that has set readers on the scent of causes – causes that bring biography into philosophy to locate the deeper sources of philosophical conclusions in the "temperament" or "specific being" through which such conclusions are filtered.

If, as suggested above, there can never be an "objective" way of measuring the sum total of pleasure in the world and comparing it against the sum total of pain, this betokens all the more strongly the subjective element at work when such a comparison is undertaken and settled by assigning particular weights to each side. It is a view that has often been echoed in the history of philosophical discussion. The nihilistic outlook, writes Donald Crosby in his *Specter of the Absurd*, "is not arrived at solely on the basis of intellectual arguments," but rather, or also, "from visceral and ill-defined intimations that are sometimes overpowering in their effects."[69] In Simmel's view, it was precisely the rational fracture points of a philosophical system that revealed its non-rational, expressive nature.[70] Nietzsche would put the point more strongly when asserting that such totalistic standpoints on life could *never* be appropriately assessed in the critical terms of a study of "reason-giving": "Judgements, value judgements concerning life, for or against, can in the last resort never be true: they possess value only as symptoms."[71]

How we respond to this way of reading a philosopher's intellectual vision – in expressive or "symptomatic" terms – will no doubt depend on the significance and reach of what we judge to be expressed within it. Simmel speaks of a "specific being" receiving philosophical expression, and he refers more narrowly to the "being of the philosopher himself" yet also more broadly "of the human type that lives within him." In talking about Schopenhauer the man earlier in this discussion – moody, anxious, prone to dread – the emphasis fell on the narrower way of reading his philosophy's expressive reach. Yet it has been a wider reading that has sometimes figured as the most interesting way of specifying it, and accounting for its significance.

[69] Donald A. Crosby, *The Specter of the Absurd: Sources and Criticisms of Modern Nihilism* (Albany, NY: State University of New York Press, 1988), 118.
[70] Simmel, *Schopenhauer and Nietzsche*, 58.
[71] Friedrich Nietzsche, *Twilight of the Idols*, trans. R. J. Hollingdale (London: Penguin Books, 2003), §2.

Nietzsche's own diagnostic reading of Schopenhauer's philosophy, which he came to see as a symptom of the *décadence* of the times, forms the topic of a longer discussion.[72] It is a more specific form of decadence or corrosion, by contrast, that has been picked up by an interpretation of Schopenhauer's philosophy assuming its sharpest form in Terry Eagleton's *Ideology of the Aesthetic*, which sets out to consider from an overtly ideological Marxist perspective the fascination with aesthetics in post-Enlightenment philosophy. In an intriguing and (for all its polemical tones) highly insightful essay, Eagleton invites us to read Schopenhauer's metaphysics in the light of the rise of capitalism and its intellectual fallout. Schopenhauer, he remarks, "is perhaps the first major modern thinker to place at the centre of his work the abstract category of *desire itself*, irrespective of this or that particular hankering." And it is, he argues, the new role that appetite has assumed in bourgeois society with the emergence of possessive individualism, in which desire has come to be enshrined as governing principle and dominant practice, that enables this dramatic shift, leading to "the construction of desire as a thing in itself."

Reified in this manner, desire is constituted as an event or force to which human beings themselves stand in subjection as mere "obedient bearers or underlings." It is this reification that allows desire as such to become the object of moral judgement for the first time. And it is in the same context that Eagleton places the character of endless striving that attaches to the will in Schopenhauer's philosophical understanding. This reflects "the perceived *infinity* of desire in a social order where the only end of accumulating is to accumulate afresh. In a traumatic collapse of teleology, desire comes to seem independent of any particular ends" and from this emerges the Schopenhauerian will, as "purposiveness without purpose."[73] Schopenhauer's will, on this reading, is thus nothing more

---

[72] For an excellent starting place, see the volume of essays edited by Janaway, *Willing and Nothingness*.

[73] Eagleton, *The Ideology of the Aesthetic*, 158–59. As David Cartwright notes (*Historical Dictionary of Schopenhauer's Philosophy* [Lanham, MD: Scarecrow Press, 2005], 89–90), there is a longer history of Marxist critiques of Schopenhauer against which Eagleton's reading may be situated. One of the best-known exemplars is Georg Lukács' *The Destruction of Reason*, trans. P. Palmer (London: Merlin Press, 1980), which sees in Schopenhauer a "bourgeois irrationalist" providing "an indirect apologetic of the capitalist social order" – notable about Schopenhauer's pessimism, for example, is the way it nullifies the value of action and history, and thus of political activity. Note also in this connection Michael A. Gillespie's account of Schopenhauer's philosophy (including its pessimistic elements) in ch. 6 of his *Nihilism before Nietzsche* (University of Chicago Press, 1995), in the context of a broader argument that nihilism originates in the idea of an omnipotent God in whom the will has primacy over reason, the modern notion of will thus representing a "secularization of the idea of divine omnipotence" (xxii).

than "the uncouth rapacity of the average bourgeois, elevated to cosmic status and transformed to the prime metaphysical mover of the universe," so that "the whole world [is] recast in the image of the market place."[74]

From Eagleton's perspective, indeed, the criticisms of Schopenhauer's pessimism outlined above could have been expanded to include another. For when Schopenhauer describes people as toiling and labouring without cease as a result of their inner nature, when he speaks of the "meaningless" and "insignificant" lives most people lead, one might retort that by reading these phenomena as an essential expression of timeless metaphysical facts he has evaded a recognition of their eminently contingent character. If people run about "like clockwork that is wound up and goes without knowing why ... to repeat once more its same old tune" (*WWR* I:321–22), if "nine-tenths of mankind live in constant conflict with want, always balancing themselves with difficulty and effort on the brink of destruction" (*WWR* II:584) – if, indeed, people labour in activities that they can desire only for their consequences, and not for any intrinsic pleasure or meaning they contain for them – this reflects particular social conditions that require reform, not further entrenchment through metaphysical reification.

Yet it is perhaps another expressive reading of Schopenhauer that for many others would carry a far deeper appeal, one that takes Schopenhauer's philosophy to express a predicament separate from, though not unconnected with, the one discussed by Eagleton, and indeed figuring among its broader repercussions – the displacement of the religious world-view that, with the collapse of social hierarchies and traditional values, heralded the arrival of the modern "secular age." Schopenhauer's biographers have often picked up on an experience of homelessness that figures as a leitmotif in both Schopenhauer's private life and his philosophical writings. And Safranski has not been alone in suggesting that we read this sense of homelessness as carrying a more than personal signification, pointing rather to a "metaphysical homelessness" connected to the "pain of secularisation."[75] Schopenhauer, Nietzsche had suggested before him, offers us a "horrified look into a de-deified world." This view has been echoed frequently since, as it was by Simmel, who took Schopenhauer's philosophy to reflect the larger cultural crisis – the profound crisis of meaning – provoked by the loosening hold of the Christian world-view. Schopenhauer's

---

[74] Eagleton, *The Ideology of the Aesthetic*, 160.
[75] Safranski, *The Wild Years of Philosophy*, 345; cf. Cartwright's opening remarks in *Schopenhauer*, 1.

philosophy, in this light, constitutes "the absolute philosophical expression for this inner condition of modern man."[76]

Discussing Schopenhauer's "cosmic" viewpoint or view *sub specie aeternitatis* earlier, I characterised it as one proposing to survey the world from a magisterial perspective seemingly located somewhere outside it – a quality aptly captured by Thomas Nagel's idiom: a "view from nowhere." Having then connected this viewpoint to the sublime, I suggested we read it in its character as a conquest or overcoming. Yet it may now be asked whether this same viewpoint could not also be read differently, retelling it to recount its character as one, not of victory, but defeat. For with the above in mind, one might wonder whether this non-locative location – this Archimedean "outside" typifying an extremity of detachment – may not reflect, not a sublime act of voluntary self-extraction from the ordinary world, but rather a forcible expulsion produced through the collapse of the evaluative structures that had formerly kept one's feet lodged on firm ground. To wonder this is to wonder whether the conquest of the eye may not in this case rest on a defeat of the heart; and it is similarly to wonder whether, in the Archimedean standpoint offering a vertiginous image of the boundless world, the vertigo has not been expelled to the content of its vision, but continues to internally define it.

"Awakened to life out of the night of unconsciousness," Schopenhauer had written with brutal dreaminess in one of the focal passages carrying the viewpoint *sub specie aeternitatis*, "the will finds itself as an individual in an endless and boundless world," and then "hurries back to the old unconsciousness." Yet till then "its desires are unlimited, its claims inexhaustible, and every satisfied desire gives birth to a new one. No possible satisfaction in the world could suffice to still its craving, set a final goal to its demands, and fill the bottomless pit of its heart" (*WWR* II:573). This image of infinite desire, I earlier suggested, refers us to the tenets of Schopenhauer's metaphysics, which it simply recapitulates. Yet should one put metaphysics to the side and listen to the words in their most immediate meaning, one could be forgiven for hearing in them a poignant statement, not of the tyrannical desires of the flesh, but of the deeper needs of the spirit – of a desire for meaning that surpasses anything that the world

[76] Friedrich Nietzsche, *The Gay Science*, trans. J. Nauckhoff and A. del Caro (Cambridge University Press, 2001), §357; Simmel, *Schopenhauer and Nietzsche*, 5, and see generally ch. 1 and the translators' introduction. Cf. Max Horkheimer's description of Schopenhauer as the philosopher of abandonment, who by exposing this abandonment gives us "the motive for solidarity shared by men and all beings": "Schopenhauer today," in Fox, ed., *Schopenhauer: His Philosophical Achievement*, 32.

has to offer, not in quantity and in serial succession, but in quality and kind. Our bottomless "craving" might be stilled by an understanding of our good and of the *telos* to which our striving is ordered that would make striving less frantic, and life worth living. Yet that possibility is no longer "in the world"; and so our only place is now outside it.[77]

I have been suggesting that there are broader and narrower ways of fleshing out the view that Schopenhauer's philosophy can be approached in expressive terms. Most broadly, Schopenhauer's philosophy can be taken to express a larger predicament which continues to define our own present, and in which many of us may recognise the image of our philosophical and spiritual struggles. It is a way of situating Schopenhauer, to be sure, that offers us crucial resources for appreciating the significance of his intellectual vision. Yet to return to the theme that has given this discussion its backbone, there is now a question to be raised as to how such an expressive understanding can enter fruitfully into our philosophical engagement of his work, and relate to the notions of excellence that govern it.

Simmel, on his part, seemed to indicate that the expressive understanding of philosophy offers a way of constituting our notions of philosophical excellence anew, contributing its own unique standards and peculiar notion of truth. This would still be a truth of adequation or correspondence, but an adequation not between the statements of philosophy and the world, but the statements of philosophy and the being of their author. It is doubtful that Schopenhauer himself would have taken the same view. Given the aspiration to objectivity that dominates his epistemic ideal, the reduction of his philosophical insights to the subjectivity of their individual author could only have been experienced as a defeat. Many modern philosophers would share the unwillingness to accept a reconstitution of philosophical excellence in expressivist terms, to the extent that this entails abdicating the notion of reason-giving and nullifying the importance of argument within philosophical practice.

Now to trace a philosophy to its personal or biographical roots, as Copleston has suggested, need not entail that we abandon the effort to rationally examine its content.[78] Yet as David Cooper recently remarked

---

[77] Note in this context Schopenhauer's remark in *On the Will in Nature* (4–5) that the "steady growth of unbelief" forms one of the chief reasons why progress in philosophy is needed; it is thus against the backdrop of a newly secularised world that Schopenhauer self-consciously places his own philosophy.

[78] Copleston likewise linked Schopenhauer's pessimism to his character, yet did not take this to constitute an exhaustive explanation, or to fully determine the way one engages his philosophy; see his preface to the second edition of *Philosopher of Pessimism* (cf. 74).

in a context not unrelated to this one, it is questionable whether, if a certain philosophical debate is sustained by roots deeper and more affective in kind – if the confrontation that masks itself as argument at bottom constitutes "a confrontation between *visions* or *moods*" – argument could serve at all as a means to dispel it, and whether it might not be fruitless (as fruitless as most forms of evasion) to attempt to resolve it through such means.[79] In our case, what should be added or rehearsed is that the expressive reading of Schopenhauer's work came in the background of registering Schopenhauer's self-conscious demotion of argument as a philosophical excellence, as also in the background of recording the vulnerabilities of Schopenhauer's arguments, which often embarrass the effort to engage them through a notion of philosophical excellence that assigns to argument the highest virtue. The investigation of the expressive character of Schopenhauer's philosophy was indeed closely conjoined to a perception of the limitations of its rational character.

Why read Schopenhauer? I asked at the opening of this chapter. Over the course of the above discussion, this question has often shifted its inflection from a "why" to a "how." Yet we are back where we started, at the foot of a mountain we had been considering whether to climb. It will be the task of the next chapter to articulate a different response, and way forward.

---

[79] Cooper, *The Measure of Things*, 14.

CHAPTER 5

From aesthetics to ethics

Engaging Schopenhauer ethically: a leap?

I suggested in the last chapter that efforts to approach Schopenhauer by engaging the argumentative or reason-giving component of his philosophy were liable to collide with its limitations – both those Schopenhauer himself self-consciously espoused and those which he did not, and which he would have counted as a philosophical defeat. Yet the question cannot then be avoided: if not argument, what instead?

To this question, we have already seen several alternative ways of responding. For those not specifically concerned with the stakes of contemporary relevance, the less disputatious approach to past philosophers that Rorty refers to as "historical reconstruction" naturally remains open. For those who choose, on the other hand, to engage philosophy in expressive terms – whether as the expression of an individual or a type, of socio-economic realities or a spiritual condition – philosophy can be read as Nietzsche proposed: as a documentation of symptoms, and potentially a means to self-knowledge, whose uses will be as various as the uses to which self-knowledge is generally put. And as Nietzsche's medical metaphor suggests, this kind of self-knowledge cannot be expected to be inert, for diagnosis often serves as the prelude for therapeutic intervention. By the same token, sympathetic understanding of the other and the self-in-the-other may need to be balanced with more ruthless forms of confrontation.

This is not a reading whose ingredients I will be wholly leaving behind, and in my own approach, both the concern with self-knowledge and its therapeutic undertones will re-emerge as important themes. If Arthur Danto is right in suggesting that philosophy constitutes a mode of self-knowledge, and one inherently transformative in kind, this should not come as a surprise.[1] Yet my proposal will be that it is those limitations

---

[1] For Danto's remarks, see Chapter 3.

of reason that Schopenhauer himself would have counted, not as a defeat, but as an achievement – and similarly, the self-knowledge implicit in this achievement – that need to be made central to the way we approach his philosophy and appraise the relevance and power of its vision. And doing so, as I will be suggesting, must involve a similar effort to bring sympathy and critical confrontation into equilibrium.

And it is in fact the notion of "vision" just invoked – along with the notion of "achievement" attending it – that here affords us the best point of entry, or indeed re-entry. For in deliberately demoting the role of argument in philosophy, we will recall that what Schopenhauer had set in its place was a task described as one of articulation, or the rational articulation of feeling. There were different ways of giving content to this broad notion, but the reading developed in Chapters 2 and 3 had centred on one important way of specifying it. Schopenhauer's philosophical standpoint, I argued there, needs to be understood as fundamentally aesthetic in character. Philosophy takes its point of departure from an aesthetic mode of vision that it then seeks to express in philosophical form. And it is the aesthetics of the sublime that offers the best resources for appreciating the more specific character of this standpoint, including its character as a conquest, or an achievement. It is in this context that one should locate the viewpoint *sub specie aeternitatis* whose physiognomy expresses itself sometimes more weakly and sometimes more strongly in Schopenhauer's writings, and more strongly in some parts of his work than in others – more strongly in his discussion of aesthetics in book 3 than in the first two books and even more strongly in his discussion of ethics in book 4, and more markedly in the second volume of the *World as Will and Representation* than in the first – yet which is tied programmatically to Schopenhauer's conception of the holistic perspective of philosophy and its demand for a distant viewpoint and an ascent.[2]

Yet if this was a proposal for reading Schopenhauer's standpoint, it could now be questioned how exactly it stands to be related to the issues

---

[2] See Hübscher, *The Philosophy of Schopenhauer in its Intellectual Context*, ch. 7, for a general discussion of Schopenhauer's style, and see especially the remarks on the difference between the two volumes on 229. It is in the second volume, Hübscher notes, that Schopenhauer's style fully comes to fruition and, using a wide range of stylistic devices, gains "its unsurpassed precision, music and power of imagery." The tendency to single out book 4 for special treatment is exemplified early on by the editor of Kant's work, Karl Rosenkranz, who described it as a "lofty, moving poem, created with a grandiose mysticism" (344). Nietzsche likewise singled this book out for mention, speaking of its "power to uplift" and draw one into "the mood ... that seizes us on hearing noble music" (quoted in Janaway, "Schopenhauer as Nietzsche's educator," 17). Schopenhauer himself exhibited a similar attitude, as suggested by the remark cited by Cartwright: "in the fourth book there are a few sections that could be regarded as inspired by the *Holy Ghost*" (*Schopenhauer*, 541).

raised in the last chapter. On the one hand, this proposal might be heard as offering an answer of some kind to the question "how" thematised there. "How read Schopenhauer's philosophy?" – "Read it in aesthetic terms." Yet this answer could only satisfy for a moment before leading to deeper perplexities. For what might it mean, after all, to read a philosophy "aesthetically"? To respond to it, perhaps, in the way one might to a pretty picture or a poem – allowing ourselves to be carried away by a kind of feeling described earlier as a "thrill" or "intoxication"? And is a poetic "as if" and temporary suspension of disbelief the way one would envisage its basis?

It will now be recalled, in fact, that the philosophical readings surveyed in the last chapter had not wholly left the aesthetic qualities of Schopenhauer's philosophy out of view. These qualities, however, appeared precisely where the rational force of Schopenhauer's philosophy reached its sheer drop, and as a fall-back option for floating over the abyss, if not safely then at least enjoyably. Copleston, for example, had begun by refusing to "treat metaphysical systems simply as though they were analogous to pictures or poems or symphonies." Yet having examined Schopenhauer's claims and found them lacking, he had couched the remaining alternative precisely in such terms, suggesting Schopenhauer's philosophy might "be profitably viewed as an aesthetic whole, a work of the creative imagination."[3] Similarly, Magee had asserted that there is "much to admire in the sweeping grandeur of the argument as a whole," even as the whole underwent seemingly fundamental criticisms. In taking this stance, Magee and Copleston were exhibiting a motif that had emerged early on in the reception of Schopenhauer's philosophy, which involved drawing a distinction between the form of his work and its content, and rejecting the content while acclaiming the form.[4] This, of course, was a distinction that surgically disconnected its claims of beauty from its claims to truth. Writing about Schopenhauer, Thomas Mann had suggested that these kinds of claims were intimately linked: "The pleasure we take in a metaphysical system," in an "intellectual organisation of the world into a closely reasoned, complete and balanced structure of thought, is always of a pre-eminently aesthetic kind ... Truth and beauty must always be referred the one to the

[3] Compare Nietzsche's already-cited remark concerning Schopenhauer's reliance on "poetic intuition" ("On Schopenhauer," 260); for Nietzsche too, the poetic was the fall-back approach to Schopenhauer's metaphysics after its logical proofs had been shown to fail.
[4] See Cartwright, *Schopenhauer*, 392, in connection with the review by Jean Paul; and 526, in connection with the British reviewer John Oxenford, who played a catalytic role in Schopenhauer's rise to prominence.

other."[5] Yet the necessity conveyed by this "must" is one that other readers of Schopenhauer have placed in question, in a way that may remind us of Danto's pragmatic observation that, for philosophical texts, "their status as literature" forms "a consolation prize for failing to be true."[6]

On the reading of Schopenhauer's standpoint I proposed, of course, these two kinds of claims were not decoupled but rather preserved in close connection. Indeed, as I pointed out in Chapter 3 when first presenting the viewpoint *sub specie aeternitatis*, this viewpoint in certain respects simply compounded and re-expressed through visionary means the core elements of Schopenhauer's metaphysics expounded in the larger body of his philosophy in more discursive form. In doing so, it reflected what Schopenhauer had elsewhere explicitly told us: aesthetic experience and metaphysical insight are closely interlocked. The affective undertone of Schopenhauer's philosophy, correspondingly, was not *mere* feeling or thrill – a thrill blind to reason – but feeling informed by substantive philosophical beliefs. Yet in tying Schopenhauer's aesthetic standpoint to the doctrinal content of his philosophy, this reading would also seem to tie its fortunes umbilically to the latter's vulnerabilities. The idea of engaging Schopenhauer aesthetically would thus seem to confront us with an unenviable choice of interpretations: either we understand the aesthetic appeal of Schopenhauer's philosophy in terms that decouple it from its claim to truth – thereby expelling his philosophy from the "properly philosophical" universe – or we insist on maintaining its aesthetic character in close connection to its doctrinal content and thereby saddle ourselves with all the difficulties that attach to the latter.

My argument will be that the choice just stated represents a false dilemma; and my own task will be to articulate a different way of understanding how this aspect of Schopenhauer's standpoint – an aspect that philosophers focusing on Schopenhauer's arguments and the doctrinal content of his philosophy tend to obscure – allows itself to be engaged. Engaging it, I hope to show, need not entail a capitulation to mere form or mere feeling, or an abdication of the enterprise of critique; yet that involves recognising that there is a way of critiquing Schopenhauer's philosophy that does not solely address itself to its doctrinal content. Taking the first step in that direction, however, involves a move that to some may appear as a leap – a leap past "pretty pictures" and merely poetic "as ifs" to see the aesthetic act in its ethical character.

---

[5] Mann, "Schopenhauer," 372.   [6] Danto, "Philosophy and/as/of literature," 66.

Just why this should register as a leap is a point that the early Nietzsche is helpful in getting us to appreciate, even as he reveals that his own discovery of Schopenhauer emerged through a leap already ethical in texture. It was a texture evident in the very title of his essay "Schopenhauer as Educator," written in 1874 – a couple of years before he formally broke with Schopenhauer – in which Nietzsche looked back at that event of cataclysmic importance in his philosophical life that was his discovery of Schopenhauer. For it was precisely an "educator," Nietzsche explains, that he had been on the look-out to find, searching desperately for a "true philosopher" to function "as an educator who could raise me above my insufficiencies in so far as these originated in the age and teach me again to be *simple* and *honest* in thought and life."[7] To seek an educator was to seek a philosopher who could serve as an "example," in a way that involved disregarding the distinction between philosophy and biography, between a philosopher's works and his person. For "this example must be supplied by [a philosopher's] outward life and not merely in his books" (*UM* 136–37). And Schopenhauer's life delivered testimony to his freedom and independence; his solitude; his passion. It is accordingly "Schopenhauer as a human being" (*UM* 137) that we meet in Nietzsche's remarks concerning his "calm, good-natured discourse," his "rough and somewhat bear-like soul," his honesty, cheerfulness, and steadfastness (*UM* 134–36).

Yet to dissolve the distinction between life and works was not to abolish the importance of the latter. And as Nietzsche's next remarks suggest, it is precisely against the vision expressed in his works that the philosopher's own qualities stand to be appraised. For if Schopenhauer the human being commands our admiration with his passion and calm, his honesty and steadfastness, it is relative to the terrible philosophical vision that he holds before himself: "*The Schopenhauerean man voluntarily takes upon himself the suffering involved in being truthful*" (*UM* 152). It is in confronting the terrible truth that Schopenhauer-the-man exhibits his character. The undertones of the sublime present in this understanding of Schopenhauer may already be palpable. They become more palpable elsewhere, when Nietzsche offers his acclaim to Schopenhauer's ascent "to the heights of tragic contemplation, to the nocturnal sky and its stars extended endlessly above us," where he "set up before him a picture of life as a whole" (*UM* 141).

---

[7] Nietzsche, "Schopenhauer as educator," *Untimely Meditations*, 133; hereafter cited as *UM* in the main text.

What is crucial in this connection is that these undertones emerge only to have a problematisation of the ethical as their immediate effect. For how, Nietzsche asks, is it possible to derive "a new circle of duties" through the vision Schopenhauer makes available to us – is it clear "how one can proceed towards so extravagant a goal through a practical activity"? Put differently: does Schopenhauer's vision have the resources to generate a renewed praxis? Or again: can Schopenhauer *educate*? I quote the most relevant passage in full.

> One might otherwise think it nothing but an intoxicating vision granted us only for moments at a time, and then leaving us … prey to an even deeper dissatisfaction. And so we have seriously to ask the definite question: is it possible to bring that incredibly lofty goal so close to us that it educates us while it draws us aloft? – that Goethe's mighty words may not be fulfilled in us: "Man is born to a limited situation … but as soon as he oversteps his limits he knows neither what he wants nor what he ought to do, and it is all one whether he is distracted by the multiplicity of the things he encounters or whether his head is turned by their loftiness and dignity. It is always a misfortune when he is induced to strive after something which he cannot proceed towards through self-initiated and regulated activity" … [The Schopenhauerean man's] dignity and loftiness can only turn our heads and thereby exclude us from any participation in the world of action; coherent duties, the even flow of life are gone. One man perhaps at last accustoms himself to living discontentedly according to two different rules of conduct, that is to say in conflict with himself. (*UM* 156)

The ascent to the intoxicating vision of Schopenhauer's philosophy, this sumptuous passage suggests – the ascent to that sublime vantage point *sub specie aeternitatis* from which the whole of life presents itself to view – becomes a problem when it comes to the question of redescent. It is a problem that Thomas Nagel, writing in a related context, formulated in similar terms when commenting on the dangers of cultivating a standpoint of detachment in the ethical domain. "The pursuit of objectivity with respect to value," he remarks in *The View from Nowhere*,

> runs the risk of leaving value behind altogether. We may reach a standpoint so removed from the perspective of human life that all we can do is to observe: nothing seems to have value of the kind it appears to have from inside, and all we see is human desires, human striving – human *valuing*, as an activity or condition … The problem is to know where and how to stop … a detached view of our own existence, once achieved, is not easily made part of the standpoint from which life is lived.[8]

⁸ Thomas Nagel, *The View from Nowhere* (Oxford University Press, 1986), 209.

Having withdrawn to a distant viewpoint, where all we can see is not this action or the other but "the whirl and tumult of life," where all we can hear is not particular things said but a "continual humming" that is "like the roaring of the sea" (*WWR* II:381–82), re-entering this diffuse roar by raising our voice, to say one thing as against another, has become problematic. Given the detachment constitutive of the sublime vantage point of philosophy, the ethical can only appear as a leap: having mastered being by an act of such magisterial seeing, it is unclear how a return to being could be achieved.

Yet this last formulation now allows us to bring into view a separate difficulty attaching to Nietzsche's approach – one that problematises the project of looking towards Schopenhauer's philosophy with an ethical concern at a rather more fundamental level. For if Schopenhauer had assumed this kind of magisterial position in the realm of seeing, this was linked with the fact that his "exit to objectivity" was a one-way ticket that made no provisions for a return. The vision of philosophy did not lead to praxis; at best, it led to the dissolution of praxis – or to a praxis directed entirely to self-abolition. Equally important is a second point, which addresses itself to the notion of "leading" just employed. For central to Schopenhauer's understanding was an emphatic disavowal of the possibility that philosophical insight could seek to educate action and affect the way we lead our lives. The task of philosophy, Schopenhauer would write opening his discussion of ethics in the *World as Will and Representation*, is "to inquire, not to prescribe"; "to become practical, to guide conduct, to transform character, are old claims which with mature insight it ought finally to abandon" (I:271).

This stance was rooted, on the one hand, in a familiar anxiety about prejudicing the contemplative stance through a practical concern with its effects. Yet its roots ran deeper, striking into an understanding of human action that briefly came into view earlier and may now be fully spelled out. For in so far as individual human beings dwell in the phenomenal domain, their actions and individual acts of will are subject to the causal necessitation that governs all phenomena. Taking over a notion introduced by Kant, Schopenhauer would assert that every individual has an "intelligible character" that represents the law of his willing. Readers of Hume would find much to recognise in the resulting picture of human motivation. For the ends one wills and strives for can never be changed, being determined by one's intelligible character; it is only the particular form these ends assume or the means one uses to achieve them that may change as one's beliefs about the world are revised. Motives can never change "the will itself"; all that the outside influence of motives can do is to "bring it about that the will pursues the goal to which it aspires once for all in accordance with its inner nature, by quite a different path, and even in an entirely different object, from what it did previously" (*WWR* I:294). As Schopenhauer would put it in his main ethical work, *On the Basis of Morality*, "everyone will be powerfully stirred by *those* motives to which he is predominantly susceptible, just as one body reacts only to acids and another only to alkalies"; a change in the basic orientation of one's nature is "more impossible than changing lead into gold."⁹ This view was linked with a broader understanding of the relationship of the mind and the will, and the subordinate role of the former, that we have already seen. With this background, the possibility that reflection in general and philosophical reflection in particular could enter fruitfully into the way we lead our lives would seem to be foreclosed in advance.

Now on the one hand, it is clear that the adoption of a deterministic view need not spell the end of ethical endeavour. For as Schopenhauer himself remarks, it does not entail that we must simply "submit to the inevitable" and abandon our efforts to resist inclinations or improve our character; all effects must after all happen through their proper causes (*WWR* I:301–2). Ethics does not stop; and thus even ethical prescription – *pace* Schopenhauer's disavowal – might have its place taken as a "proper cause." Equally importantly, commentators have argued that the denial of the transformative power of philosophy is one that Schopenhauer cannot consistently maintain.¹⁰ Schopenhauer, indeed, appears to exhibit a certain vacillation regarding the power of philosophical reflection to affect our emotional and practical lives. It was certainly a presumption of immense power that was implicit in what David Cartwright describes as Schopenhauer's "messianic sense of his philosophical mission" and his understanding of its "philanthropic" nature, in providing comfort for mankind.¹¹ Schopenhauer's proposal for resolving our fear of death, as we saw this earlier, seemed to reflect a similar presumption. "A philosophical knowledge of the nature of the world," Schopenhauer states in this context, could "overcome the terrors of death according as reflection had

---

⁹ Arthur Schopenhauer, *On the Basis of Morality*, trans. E. F. J. Payne (Indianapolis and Cambridge: Hackett Publishing, 1995), 193.

¹⁰ Young makes such a suggestion regarding the *morally* transformative effect of metaphysical knowledge, arguing that Schopenhauer himself "denies the possibility of separating a person's moral will from their metaphysical knowledge" (*Willing and Unwilling*, 105). Cf. *WWR* II:600: "to be just, noble, and benevolent is nothing but to translate my metaphysics into action."

¹¹ Cartwright, *Schopenhauer*, 504, 528. Compare the remarks in Schopenhauer, "Eis Eauton," *Manuscript Remains*, vol. IV, 484.

power over direct feeling in the given individual," so that, "armed with the knowledge we confer on him, he would look with indifference at death hastening towards him" (*WWR* I:283). Excessive passions, he remarks more generally elsewhere, are based on "an error and delusion," and thus "could be avoided by insight" (*WWR* I:317–18).

Yet such remarks are sprinkled in a setting dominated by far more sceptical notes as to whether reflection *can* indeed have power over feeling: for "a powerful control of the faculty of reason over directly felt suffering is seldom or never found in fact" (*WWR* I:315).[12] And whatever the countervailing winds, it is ultimately the disavowal of prescription, coupled with an embrace of resignation as the un-praxis-like praxis and way-of-unliving that philosophy *should* lead to if it *could*, that define the texture of Schopenhauer's philosophy. Nietzsche's proposal to attune himself to Schopenhauer's ethical address cannot but strike us thus as a remarkable one. And it is considerations such as these that have prompted commentators to suggest that "when Nietzsche first sees Schopenhauer offering a 'philosophy to live by', he fails to understand clearly that Schopenhauer did not present a 'philosophy to affirm life by'."[13] For certainly, one may recognise in Nietzsche's positive reading of the educational significance of Schopenhauer's vision – its return to being, to "regulated activity" and the "even flow of life" – many elements present in Schopenhauer's scheme. In a reading that unfolds at two levels, individual and communal, Nietzsche suggests that for the individual, this vision of the whole can serve as a map that he may use to orient himself and "learn from it the meaning of [his] own life," allowing him to "gain insight into his own want and misery, into his own limitedness, so as then to learn the nature of his antidotes and consolations: namely, sacrifice of the ego, submission to the noblest ends, above all those of justice and compassion" (*UM* 141–42). On the communal level, this vision can form the basis for the constitution of a community that will justify the blind suffering of nature by promoting the

---

12 Cf. the remarks at *WWR* II:498–99 apropos the fear of death.
13 David Cartwright, "Nietzsche's use and abuse of Schopenhauer's moral philosophy for life," in Janaway, ed., *Willing and Nothingness*, 131. Given the difficulty of ascribing to Nietzsche such a profound oversight, this inevitably raises larger questions concerning the depth of Nietzsche's adherence to Schopenhauer's philosophy prior to his formal break with it. Janaway quotes a letter dated 1876, written at the time of Nietzsche's formal break, in which he states, "when I was writing on Schopenhauer, I already noticed I had left behind everything concerning dogma; for me what mattered was the *human being*" ("Schopenhauer as Nietzsche's educator," 13). Referring to the 1868 notes entitled "On Schopenhauer," Janaway suggests that given the numerous problems Nietzsche found in Schopenhauer's metaphysics, it is hard to believe he was ever a serious adherent of it (18–19). The distinction between Schopenhauer's person and Schopenhauer's philosophical system seems to have been made from early on.

existence of extraordinary human beings who wrest themselves from their uncomprehending suffering and the unreflective pursuit of goals deriving from their animal nature to reflect on life as a whole. It is the creation of this extraordinary class of reflective individuals – the philosophers, the artists, and the saints, to whom we ourselves may aspire to belong whether "in our present or in some future incarnation" (*UM* 161) – that gives the ideal for which we may henceforth strive. If we recognise several of these constituents, however, we will also recognise that an intention to return to being – let alone one that could be framed in normative ethical terms – had not defined the context in which they had found their original deployment.

Yet if Schopenhauer's philosophical vision was not intended to enter fruitfully into the way we lead our lives – if Israel Knox was thus right in suggesting that Schopenhauer "*could* have been among the greatest and most beneficent philosophers" had he not failed to formulate a normative ethics[14] – then it may come as a surprising discovery to find that Nietzsche has cut a far from lonely figure in looking to Schopenhauer for ethical guidance, and in deeming himself to have found it. For he has been joined by a larger group of readers who at different times have acclaimed the life-changing effects of Schopenhauer's philosophy. In his intellectual biography of Schopenhauer, Arthur Hübscher already provides some interesting evidence in this regard. Describing the impact of Schopenhauer's philosophy on his first acolytes, he calls attention to the fact that its dominant effect was not withdrawal, but engagement – a more forceful re-engagement of life on new terms.

> Schopenhauer's first disciples are neither escapists, hermits nor any other sort of pessimists inept at the business of life … Following Schopenhauer's direction, they march along their lives' paths undaunted and self-assured. They view their troubles, their sufferings not as a unique misfortune, and gain from it not only catharsis and consolation, but a "genuine elixir of life," a stimulus to selfless deeds and to a courageous mastering of their life's mission. In contact with Schopenhauer and his work, the gentlest and most susceptible of these early followers, Adam von Doss, gains strength and zest for life. He says that henceforth he moves forward, "not despondently and unwilling, but proudly and joyfully."[15]

The focus here is on the *de facto* effect of Schopenhauer's philosophy. Yet Hübscher puts the point more strongly when he turns to speak of an

---

[14] Israel Knox, *The Aesthetic Theories of Kant, Hegel, and Schopenhauer* (London: Thames and Hudson, 1958), 164; emphasis added.

[15] Hübscher, *The Philosophy of Schopenhauer in its Intellectual Context*, 265.

intended effect – the aim of Schopenhauer's philosophy being "to have a direct effect on our life," so that it "is meant to be, just as the great thinkers of antiquity wanted it, a signpost to the formation and mastery of life."[16]

Hübscher's emphasis on intended effects, and his elliptic gesture to the philosophers of antiquity, have in turn been developed more programmatically and all the more strikingly by several recent writers who have proposed to find in Schopenhauer a philosopher, no less, "of the art of living." Schopenhauer's name thus makes an appearance next to those of Kierkegaard, Pascal, Emerson, and Thoreau in Alexander Nehamas' *Art of Living*, where Nehamas enumerates some of the torch-bearers of a conception of philosophy with deep roots in the ancient world – as a practice and way of life, rather than a theoretical discourse or set of abstract teachings.[17] It is in the same context that Joshua Dienstag has more recently offered to place Schopenhauer's philosophy in his book-length study of pessimism. Dienstag's objective in this work is to argue for a restored interest in a broad range of thinkers united by their pessimistic outlook. Schopenhauer inhabits this list along with Rousseau and Leopardi, Freud and Camus, Cioran and Unamuno, Nietzsche and Cervantes. One of the greatest impediments to a more widespread interest in these thinkers, in Dienstag's view, is an enduring perception concerning the negativity or sterility of their outlook: whatever its other merits, their pessimism comes with no constructive or positive message. Thus, "they interest us; but, it is believed, they cannot possibly orient us."[18] In staking a claim for the ability of these pessimist writers to orient us, notably, Dienstag aligns them with pre-modern philosophers like the Stoics and Epicureans, for whom philosophy represented not a body of teachings, but an art for negotiating our lived responses.

This understanding of philosophy provides the horizon within which Dienstag similarly offers to engage Schopenhauer's work. "Like Stoicism," he writes, "his is a philosophy of the self, a guide to practical existence on Earth, not a set of moral duties." The view of Schopenhauer expressed

---

[16] Hübscher re-expresses this resoundingly: "It is possible to live with his philosophy, and it is possible to die with it" (*ibid.*, 425–26). I cannot discuss Hübscher's understanding of this point in detail, but his remarks on 330–32, in combination with his discussion of Schopenhauer's relevance in ch. 12, provide helpful orientation; the main question to be raised in connection with Hübscher's view would concern its character as appropriation as against interpretation.

[17] Alexander Nehamas, *The Art of Living* (Berkeley and Los Angeles: University of California Press, 1998), 4; his own focus in the book is on Montaigne, Nietzsche, and Foucault. Nehamas' construal of Schopenhauer as a philosopher of living seems clearly indebted to Nietzsche's reading.

[18] Dienstag, *Pessimism*, 3.

here is echoed in several other locations, as in Dienstag's characterisation of the "life that Schopenhauer envisages" as "one of constant efforts
at self-fortification through efforts at self-denial," or his remarks about
Schopenhauer's "inherent modesty of purpose in [his] attempts to aid
human beings." It finds direct expression again in Dienstag's account of
the resignation that Schopenhauer proposes as constituting, "not an emotion or even a stance of passivity, but instead an art of living or technique
of the self that prescribes a set of activities for human beings to pursue."[19]

The above discussion will already have tuned us into the awkwardness
these statements carry, inviting us to place a question mark over talk of
Schopenhauer's "purpose" and a double question mark over talk of his proposal as a positive "life" or "way of living." These difficulties cast a cloud
over Dienstag's interpretation; but it is now instructive to consider why
this may have occurred. One reason is immediately clear, and it relates to
a decision concerning which aspect of the reason-giving associated with
Schopenhauer's pessimism to prioritise. For as pointed out in the last
chapter, there are two distinct ways in which the force of this reason-giving
could be approached, one grounded in Schopenhauer's metaphysics of the
will (the "deep" account) and another ("surface" account) that moves at a
level largely phenomenally available to us. Dienstag focuses on one specific "surface" feature, namely the problematic relationship of happiness
to time, in line with his identification of the preoccupation with tempor-
ality as one of the unifying typological features of modern pessimism.[20]
Crucially, this involves a decision to dismiss the metaphysical aspects of
Schopenhauer's view of time, including its basis in Kant's transcendental
idealism, as part of a philosophical fashion – a historically contingent "passion for metaphysical finality that gripped nineteenth-century Continental
thinking" – which leaves the truer foundations of Schopenhauer's pessimism untouched. Since, in our own times, "it is probably Schopenhauer's
metaphysics that strikes us as the least plausible element of his overall
philosophy," this allows us to appreciate "the strength and significance of
pessimism" in a way that does not take it to "stand or fall along with the
credibility of Schopenhauer's account of will and phenomena."[21]

Next to this self-conscious decision, however – a decision, significantly,
to eclectically engage certain parts of Schopenhauer's philosophy while sift-
ing out others – there is an additional ground, one perhaps less wittingly

[19] *Ibid.*, III, 107, 116; and see generally ch. 3.
[20] See *ibid.*, 19–36, for an initial overview of these features.   [21] *Ibid.*, 97–98.

leaned upon, which concerns the particular work of Schopenhauer's that Dienstag draws on heavily for his interpretation. This work is the "Aphorisms on the Wisdom of Life" (*Aphorismen zur Lebensweisheit*), which appears in Schopenhauer's late *Parerga and Paralipomena*. Yet it is now important to note the specific position that this treatise occupied in Schopenhauer's life and works. For it was one of the ironies of Schopenhauer's intellectual history that the long-awaited moment of fame that had eluded his major works for years finally came to Schopenhauer with the publication of the two-volume *Parerga and Paralipomena*, with this particular treatise as a lodestone of special attraction in the new surge of response. If there was irony in this event, that was because the wave of renown should have reached the feet of the fame-starved exponent of an unworldly and unliveable pessimism through a work that proposed to offer a "philosophy for the world," to show people how life might, after all, allow itself to be lived.

Abandoning the standpoint of his true metaphysics – "the higher metaphysical ethical standpoint to which my real philosophy leads," from whose objective viewpoint the worth of living was denied – in this work Schopenhauer staked out an approach that "remains at the ordinary empirical standpoint and firmly maintains the error thereof." And within this conditioned standpoint, Schopenhauer proposed to consider how life might be most "pleasantly and successfully" led (*PP* 1:313). Schopenhauer called it a "compromise"; Rüdiger Safranski describes it as a hypothetical, almost poetical, yet ultimately deeply practical "as if." *Supposing* that life were worth living, what would be the best way to live it? This work – which as Safranski notes quickly became the bible of the educated bourgeoisie –

> set aside the metaphysical scandal. It reduced the esoteric No to life to a muted exoteric Yes: if we cannot avoid participating, then let us at least do so with all necessary scepticism, with resistance to disappointment; let us at least keep our stakes in the game low and give as little credit as possible … Schopenhauer encourages an attitude of the "as if." Today we might say: "You don't stand a chance, but take it anyway."[22]

It is this work that in great part seems responsible for Dienstag's construal of Schopenhauer's ethical viewpoint, where it appears to be taken as a seamless continuation of the philosophy expressed in the *World as Will*

---

[22] Safranski, *The Wild Years of Philosophy*, 335. Cf. Hübscher's remarks on this work in *The Philosophy of Schopenhauer in its Intellectual Context*, 222–26.

and Representation.[23] What must be conceded, however, is something that makes this unwitting presumption of continuity a little less surprising and easier to sympathise with. For certainly, there are numerous features of the "Aphorisms" that serve to distance it from the "higher" perspective of Schopenhauer's true philosophy. The morality we find here, for one, is a far cry from the morality of love and compassion that Schopenhauer had made central to his "true" account, describing it (without prescribing it) as the corollary of grasping that the difference between self and other is merely a phenomenal illusion. In the "Aphorisms," as Safranski notes, "all his advice presupposes society as a network of latent hostility, of reciprocal ill will."[24] This much is clear: the reader of the "Aphorisms" is not expected to have seen through the veil of individuality. Similarly, the brooding seer of book 4 of the *World as Will and Representation* who had seen galaxies and stars collapse into " – nothing" now instead counsels us – courage: our motto should be "Do not give way to the evil, but face it more boldly" (*PP* 1:475). The view *sub specie aeternitatis* itself only figures in the treatise once, and there in the sedate significance of the (rational) capacity to see "particular things as manifestations of universal law," that is, to grasp generality (*PP* 1:478).

And yet these discontinuities coexist with certain important continuities. For if the "Aphorisms" openly departs from the *World as Will and Representation* in adopting a normative accent, in the body of Schopenhauer's normative proposals we may recognise a set of reflections that had already been present in his main work, framed as metaphysical claims and voiced in a descriptive cadence, and that now reappear in prescriptive tones and with a corresponding shift away from metaphysical necessity to a contingent factuality more amenable to control. "Those who by aspiring and hoping live only in the future and always look ahead and impatiently anticipate the things to come – things that are first to bring them true happiness," Schopenhauer trenchantly comments, are "comparable to those donkeys in Italy whose pace is quickened by their having a stick with a truss of hay fastened to their heads ... They defraud themselves of their whole existence" (*PP* 1:414). In the *World as Will and Representation*, the perpetual straining for the future had registered as a universal human feature that reflects our deeper nature. In holding it up to criticism, Schopenhauer implicitly brackets the relevance of this deeper

---

[23] Note Dienstag's important reference to this work at the start of his discussion in *Pessimism*, 107.
[24] Safranski, *The Wild Years of Philosophy*, 337.

ground, as he does again explicitly in the open prescription that "we should never forget that the present alone is real and certain," and "should always consider it worthy of a cheerful reception" (*PP* I:414–15).

In a text heartily peppered with prescriptive "should"s, we watch as the formidable metaphysical Will is domesticated into something that may be managed pragmatically using the principle "the less the will is excited, the less we suffer" (*PP* I:417), and the *velle non discitur* ("willing cannot be taught") is superseded by the counsel that "we should set limits to our wishes, curb our desires, and subdue our anger" (*PP* I:438). The ephemerality of human life is not now the object of a saturnine vision on cosmic scale, but registers sedately in the admonition: "We should constantly bear in mind the effect of time and the transient nature of things" (*PP* I:470). The insight that all phenomena are causally necessitated takes its place as a therapeutic reflection that will "better enable us to bear with composure the misfortunes that befall us" (*PP* I:473). Yet what is important to notice in these serial subversions is the familiar set of reflections at work within them, only now shorn of their metaphysical depth, and combined with an overt confidence – implicit in the normative stance – in the power of reason to affect the way we lead our lives, by submitting them to critical examination. Philosophy, in this process, has taken on a very traditional task: to offer relief from suffering and a therapy of the passions by educating the faulty judgements that ground them. The Schopenhauer of the *World as Will and Representation* did not believe in a "therapy of desire"; the Schopenhauer of the "Aphorisms" does.

This is the background, I would suggest, in which we may locate the seeds of Dienstag's positive reading of Schopenhauer, and potentially the reading of several others for whom this late work has served as the main portal to Schopenhauer's philosophy. And granted that this positive reading may not be grounded in a fully judicious interpretative grasp, it is high time to ask why an interpretative grasp should after all be our principal concern. Writing in a related context, Nietzsche would remark: "The philosopher believes that the value of his philosophy lies in the whole, in the building: posterity discovers it in the bricks with which he built and which are then often used again for better building: in the fact, that is to say, that the building can be destroyed and *nonetheless* possess value as material."[25] The significance of this point for our context will be clear. For to the extent that we approach philosophers with a concern for their relevance – for the ways in which their work can service our philosophical or more narrowly

---

[25] Friedrich Nietzsche, *Human, All Too Human*, trans. R. J. Hollingdale (Cambridge University Press, 1996), II/I §201.

ethical needs – there is after all nothing to prevent us from approaching the total edifice in an eclectic manner. We are under no obligation to imprison ourselves within Schopenhauer's terms or his "intentions" – whether his determinism or his negative ideal of resignation, whether his denial of the power of reflection or his deeper metaphysical explanations – and we may simply isolate those of its "bricks" that seem to us to have enduring value as material. In this spirit, we might isolate the local edifice that is the "Aphorisms," and appropriate it as a source of normative ethical guidance that speaks to our needs. The result, as Dienstag suggests in his discussion, would be an ethical framework with distinct affinities to Stoicism.

My argument will be that this proposal does not bear good fruit. But a closer consideration of the reasons for its unfruitfulness can offer us the very resources we need for an alternative way of making the leap to the ethical that we have been seeking. And here, no better foothold can be found than the notion of Schopenhauer's Stoic sympathies or affinities just invoked. The discussion of Schopenhauer's pessimism in the last chapter provided an earlier opportunity to comment on some of the continuities linking Schopenhauer's concerns with those at work in ancient philosophy. These are continuities that, given Schopenhauer's profound admiration for Plato and his wide-ranging familiarity with ancient philosophy, should not seem all that surprising. In the last chapter, my focus had been on a perception of the dangerous infinity of desire that many ancient philosophers would also have recognised as their own, even as this experience of recognition turned out to belie important contrasts. Yet in this context, the continuity that should engage us is a broader one, relating to a preoccupation about the stability of the good that already stepped briefly into view in the last chapter, and to which the Stoics would offer a particularly dramatic resolution.

It is a preoccupation with the vulnerability of the good life to luck that, as Martha Nussbaum has documented it, was negotiated in the context of both philosophy and literature, receiving some of its most poignant expressions in the works of the Greek tragedians. It would form a standing motif in the work of Plato, who would be animated throughout by a profound concern to secure the best human life against different sources of vulnerability.[26] And it would then find an important place in Aristotle's ethics, which would strive for a middle ground by acknowledging the

---

[26] Nussbaum groups these sources under three main headings: the threat posed to the good life by the instability of external goods; the threat posed by the potential conflict between different goods and different components of the good life; and the internal threat posed by the passions and bodily desires. My above remarks are made primarily with the first category in mind. See Nussbaum, *Fragility of Goodness*, ch. 1, for this grouping.

dependence of the good life on factors beyond human control – recognising the importance of external goods such as health, wealth, beauty, or honour – while seeking to delimit this dependence and to specify the good life in ways that would invest it with greater stability. The life of virtue, taken as an exercise of stable dispositions, and the life of contemplation, taken as an activity directed to pre-eminently stable objects and perfect at any given moment – both centrepieces of Aristotle's ethical account – can be seen as proposals oriented precisely by this deeper demand to secure the good against easy subversion.

For "how," as Cicero would characteristically ask, "can the man who is without assurance be happy? ... No one can be happy except when good is secure and certain and lasting." Cicero would not be alone among ancient philosophers in qualifying security as "that object of supreme desire and aspiration."[27] Yet Cicero's continuation would be diagnostic concerning the position that Stoic philosophers in particular – whose views would often find themselves re-expressed in Cicero's works – would adopt on this debate. For how, he would go on, can one "hold his head erect, in disdain of all the vicissitudes of man's lot, in the spirit we wish the wise man to show, unless he shall think that for him all things depend upon himself?" Marking a sharp distinction between inner and outer – between the moral and intellectual life involving an exercise of reason fully in our control, and the outer domain of fate that lies outside our power to control – the Stoics would stake their claim for the invulnerability of the good by identifying happiness exclusively with virtue and thus with the goods of the soul, sweeping all values conclusively into the safety of the inner "citadel" where none the vicissitudes of fate could reach them. All that truly matters depends upon oneself alone.

It is a yearning for invulnerability that we will not be meeting in this argument for the last time. Yet what is now important is that it is this same yearning and its corresponding ideal whose reflection we may recognise in the pages of Schopenhauer's "Aphorisms," receiving pervasive expression within it and indeed providing it with one of its defining motifs. It is no accident that it should appear at its very curtain-raising moment, where Schopenhauer approvingly cites the Epicurean philosopher Metrodorus' formulation: "The cause of happiness that lies within us is greater than the cause that comes from things" (*PP* I:315). It makes several other appearances throughout the work. "What a man is and has in himself,"

27 Cicero, *Tusculan Disputations*, trans. J. E. King (London: W. Heinemann; New York: G. P. Putnam's Sons, 1927), 5.40–42.

we hear, "is the sole immediate factor in his happiness" (*PP* 1:323). And again, expressing a familiar scepticism about the external domain that is governed by fortune, in the significant context of glossing a remark by Aristotle that foregrounds the notion of self-sufficiency: "all the external sources of happiness and pleasure are by their nature exceedingly uncertain, precarious, fleeting, and subject to chance" (*PP* 1:333). A powerful attachment to the ideal of self-sufficiency breathes through these pages: the true sources of happiness lie within oneself. And if Schopenhauer does not avail himself of the granite image of a citadel to re-express that vision of inner entrenchment, the one he uses is no less evocative in its contrasts. In a world where fate is so cruel, he writes, "the man who has much within himself is like a bright, warm, cheerful room at Christmas amid the snow and ice of a December night" (*PP* 1:333).[28]

Even if one had not been prepared to discover the Stoic sympathies of Schopenhauer's ethical approach, it would have been hard to miss them. It is not long, however, before this response of recognition cedes its ground to a new surprise; for on closer inspection, the apparent continuities turn out to conceal rather starker divergences. For on the one hand, the Stoic-sounding maxims dispersed through Schopenhauer's discussion seem to dovetail naturally with his central claim that, within the threefold division of goods he outlines – "what a man is," "what a man has" (his property and possessions), and "what a man represents" (his honour, rank, and reputation) – our true happiness is vested in the first. Yet that is before we attend rather more closely to the way Schopenhauer specifies this category. This category refers us to "personality in the widest sense," and thus, Schopenhauer clarifies, it includes "health, strength, beauty, temperament, moral character, intelligence and its cultivation" (*PP* 1:315). To readers of Stoic ethics, it will be instantly evident that our seemingly Stoic maxim has been filled in a highly unconventional manner, one that notably cuts across the inner–outer divide as the Stoics had framed it. The remarkable juxtaposition of moral character to health and beauty speaks for itself. On the Stoic understanding, these two would have stood on opposite sides of the divide. Our moral character is within our control; health and beauty certainly aren't.

Yet this allows us to place our finger more precisely on the point where the deeper difference lies. For if Schopenhauer's way of stocking the

---

[28] Schopenhauer's deep sympathies with this ideal are attested equally eloquently in the private compilation of maxims appended to "Eis Eauton," *Manuscript Remains*, vol. IV (517–20), which among quotations from several ancient writers includes one by Cicero that re-expresses the essential Stoic stance.

category of "what a man is" does not follow the seams between inner and outer as the Stoics had drawn them, this reflects the fact that the distinction between what we can and cannot control – which these seams had tracked – does not hold the same relevance for him; indeed, it seems to hold little relevance altogether. That fact is already indicated with unmistakable clarity when Schopenhauer, having outlined the category "what a man is," goes on to state: "the differences under [this] heading are those established by nature herself between one man and another" (*PP* 1:315). The most important factor in human happiness, Schopenhauer remarks elsewhere, is one's individuality; yet that is fully determined. Thus "the measure of [one's] possible happiness is determined beforehand by his individuality" (*PP* 1:317). No more astounding inversion of the Stoic perspective could in fact be found than the one carried by a remark that appears in the same vicinity: "The objective half of the present reality is in the hands of fate and is accordingly changeable; we ourselves are the subjective half that is ... essentially unchangeable." Our happiness lies "inside" us; yet this "inside" does not define the domain of our control, but is precisely what is least within it. The inner has been consumed by necessity; or by what, considered from another standpoint, we might also call "luck."

This, of course, would seem unsurprising from the perspective of the *World as Will and Representation*, where moral character and intellectual abilities were said to be wholly determined, and the blessed were those whom nature included in its order of intellectual aristocracy; and it is this understanding, thus, that the discussion in the "Aphorisms" directly resumes. Yet this was an understanding intimately linked with the non-normative perspective of Schopenhauer's major work. Appearing in this context, it might make us wonder whether sufficient space has been opened in which ethics can be done, and whether this ethics of the "as if" amounts to more than a self-congratulating description of the blessed, which those excluded can only respond to by slinking away in despair to "the snow and ice of their December night." The good, Aristotle had written in the *Nicomachean Ethics*, must be "doable or capable of being acquired by a human being" (1096b30–35); yet more than that, the good life must be "something available to many; for it will be possible for it to belong, through some kind of learning or practice, to anyone not handicapped in relation to excellence" (1099b15–20). Schopenhauer does not share Aristotle's constraints on the notion of happiness and his notion of reasonable handicap; nor the ethical space they carve open.

And indeed just how slender that space is can be fully appreciated once we recall that the external domain (the "objective half" of the world) is in reality, in Schopenhauer's view, no less subject to causal determination than its subjective correlate. If external goods such as wealth or honour have an advantage over those belonging to the "subjective" class, Schopenhauer suggests elsewhere, this is in the sense that "everyone has before him at least the possibility of coming into possession of them, whereas the subjective is certainly not given into our power" (*PP* 1:319–20). Yet this comparison, of course, is fully compatible with the recognition – too obvious to gainsay, and forming the root of the ancient preoccupation with the vulnerability of the good – that these goods, in another sense, are certainly *not* within our firm control. And this recognition is one that Schopenhauer himself openly expresses in many other locations: "all the external sources of happiness and pleasure are by their nature exceedingly uncertain," we have already heard; "fate is cruel" (*PP* 1:333).

The choice we are thus presented with seems to be one between different ways of *not* being in control. There is certainly more that could be said about Schopenhauer's discussion – with its slippery notions of "fortune" and "fate," "luck" and "necessity" – in this connection and more specifically about the precise space, slender yet existent, that it opens up for ethics to be done.[29] Yet overall, it seems to me that, if we were looking to Schopenhauer for an ethics that "speaks to our needs," it could be questioned to what degree it truly addresses us. For my purposes, however, it is a second and rather different level of responding to Schopenhauer's ethical stance that holds greater relevance. It is a response that directs itself to a part of Schopenhauer's treatise – the chapter "Counsels and Maxims" that follows his discussion of the tripartite scheme mentioned above – in which a normative tone *does* in fact appear to be more forcefully struck, and Schopenhauer turns to offer a series of prescriptive recommendations addressed, it would seem, to an audience that includes us. This was the particular context in which many of the positive recommendations we saw above made their appearance: "we should never forget that the present alone is real and certain"; we should "set limits to our wishes, curb our desires, and subdue our anger"; "we should constantly bear in mind the effect of time and the transient nature of things."

---

[29] The most important space – beyond the one deriving from our limited ability to control external goods – would seem to concern our limited ability to realise our character fully, exploiting its potential and developing the tendencies that best cohere with it; see the brief remarks in *PP* 1:320. This seems to correspond to what Schopenhauer refers to as our "acquired character" in his main work; see *WWR* 1:303–7.

Yet it is to a more specific aspect of Schopenhauer's normative address in this context that I would now like to invite us to attend. It is an aspect that can be located within the same horizon that was limned above in broad strokes – a horizon defined by a keen awareness of human vulnerability faced with the world, and the fragility of human happiness within this world. And what I would like to consider is the particular character that takes shape within it, and that Schopenhauer proposes to us as a response to it. It is a response, this much is clear, that immediately registers in its character as a withdrawal; a contraction; a self-limitation. We should "set limits to our wishes, curb our desires," we heard (*PP* I:438). We should "reduce to very moderate proportions our claims to pleasures, possessions, rank, honour" (*PP* I:408); we should guard against "making many demands" (*PP* I:411). Our desires – unbounded, we may recall, in metaphysical reality – should contract. This contraction of our demands on the world, Schopenhauer's remarks make equally clear, is one fundamentally grounded in a project of self-defence. If we withdraw our claims, it is to inoculate ourselves against the harsh rejection of our claims that is always in preparation. It is because the "striving and struggling" for pleasures, possessions, and so on, "entail great misfortunes" (*PP* I:408); because a happiness founded on many demands "is very easily overthrown, since it offers many more opportunities for accidents" (*PP* I:411). Fate – in its now familiar aspect as the uncontrollable world lying outside us – always lies truculently in wait. "The whole of life is a struggle, every step is contested" (*PP* I:475). Wayfarer, beware.

It is this spirit of wariness, and its concomitant representation of a world ready to frustrate our hopes from every side, that permeates Schopenhauer's "Aphorisms" and lends it its ethical pitch; and in doing so, of course, it naturally proclaims the affinities between this treatise and the pessimistic perspective of Schopenhauer's main work. The first virtue in a world understood in such terms will be distrust. "Demosthenes is right," notes Schopenhauer in his private diary *Eis Eauton*, "when he says that ramparts and walls are a good bulwark, but that the best is *apistia* (distrust)." And again: "It's safer trusting fear than faith."[30] Stamping the normative ethics of the "Aphorisms" with its character is indeed an emphatic embrace of the virtues of suspicion and distrust. Have no trust in the world; no trust in people; in what you hope for; in the present. Prepare for the worst; arm yourself; do not let yourself be deceived. We

---

[30] Schopenhauer, "Eis Eauton," *Manuscript Remains*, vol. IV, 492, 495.

need a "temper of iron, armour against fate, and weapons against man-kind" (*PP* I:475) to get around safely in a world such as this one.

And if suspicion is the primary virtue, it is prudence that undoubt-edly constitutes its indispensable adjunct. Certainly, moderate your claims to minimise your capacity to be touched by misfortunes; yet do not just stand still – do your best to avoid such adversities. And prudence requires cunning, industry, and concerted machinations: "we should not be afraid to spend time, trouble, and money, to put up with formalities and incon-venience ... in order to shut the door on the possibility of misfortune" (*PP* I:472). In the dirty warfare between fate and ourselves, we need to stalk fate as slyly as it stalks us. "We should practise caution," Schopenhauer writes, "by forestalling or averting misfortunes, whether they come from people or things, and should become so refined in this that, like a clever fox, we neatly slip out of the way of every misfortune, great or small" (*PP* I:473).

It is a deep and familiar concern with vulnerability, I have been suggest-ing – a concern that thematises the relationship between human beings and the world, between their aspirations and the world's readiness to meet them – that underlies Schopenhauer's ethical proposal; and his proposal then arrives as a response to it. Yet if this concern is familiar to us, it will be possible to raise a question about the capacity of Schopenhauer's response to satisfy us. And this, indeed, will be to raise a positive eth-ical question concerning the character that has just been placed before us. He is suspicious; he is distrustful; a "wily fox" that slips under fences, through traps, out of barnyards; a prudent housekeeper who keeps his books in order.[31] He is preoccupied with self-protection, with self-defence; he nurses his wounds and anxiously guards against incurring new ones. He desires nothing positive – he does not dare; his only desire is to pre-serve himself from harm.

The character just held up before us as an ethical ideal, I would sug-gest, does not, or should not, satisfy us. Preoccupied with the self, inward-looking, lacking the courage of desire, aspiring to nothing but a safe escape – it is an image I doubt many of us would like to recognise, let alone aspire to, as our own. The "we" that I have been drawing upon in my discussion might here begin to visibly shake. For what is at issue

---

[31] I have in mind Schopenhauer's practical recommendation elsewhere in the "Aphorisms" that one "be careful to preserve what has been earned and inherited" (*PP* I:350); Schopenhauer seems to suppress a blush in making this statement – hardly surprising given its oddly prosaic character.

is clearly a substantive ethical criticism that cannot be offered without equally substantive defence. It will be the task of the discussion that follows to articulate this defence. And for this purpose, I would like to suggest that it is precisely to Schopenhauer's philosophical standpoint as I earlier sought to characterise it – to that standpoint located specifically within the aesthetics of the sublime – that we need to turn back, in order to place it in its larger, and then its ethical, context.

The cosmic viewpoint in context: flights of the soul in ancient philosophy

It was a standpoint, I suggested in Chapter 3, accomplished through an exercise of philosophical imagination that placed before one a spectacle of the infinite world – a spectacle of "countless luminous spheres" spinning in infinite space, of innumerable beings "restlessly and rapidly arising and passing away in beginningless and endless time" (*WWR* II:3) and projected as a "vanishing quantity" in the "endless and boundless world" (*WWR* I:311; II:573), which simultaneously foregrounded the flight of time and the infinite flight of desire. In summoning the infinitely vast to view, this was an act of vision whose nerves stretched out to connect it with the aesthetics of the sublime. And it was, I argued, the notion of conquest or overcoming which figured centrally in the sublime that likewise reproduced itself within this standpoint, placing us beyond the reach of suffering through the very act of representing it.

Yet if this magisterial act of summoning and summation threw out living nerves to Schopenhauer's own aesthetics, what must now be observed is another set of nerves stretching out from this visionary act – and thus equally from the heartland of Schopenhauer's aesthetics – to connect it to a location outside his philosophy, and to a rather different episode in the philosophical past. For if the philosopher was here seen to be in flight, his soul soaring aloft to behold grand totalities, this was not for the first time in his history. It was a flight, after all, to which the philosopher had already been launched long before that by Plato. The philosopher's body, Socrates had said in the *Theaetetus* in a set of well-known (though not always well-received) lines, might dwell in a fixed place; yet his soul,

> considering all these things petty and of no account, disdains them and is borne in all directions, as Pindar says, "both below the earth," and measuring the surface of the earth, and "above the sky," studying the stars, and

investigating the universal nature of every thing that is, each in its entirety, never lowering itself to anything close at hand. (173e–174a)[32]

The notion of flight would re-emerge as a topos in other parts of Plato's writings, as in the myth recounted in the third speech of the *Phaedrus*, which would describe the flight that all souls had performed prior to their earthly existence, travelling to the edge of the cosmos to attain a vision of the truest reality – a vision only fully accessible to the gods. This is the vision – gained when the soul "journeyed with God and, lifting its vision above the things which we now say exist, rose up into real being" – that philosophers would later strive to recollect, in doing so regaining the "wings" by which this cosmic ascent had formerly been accomplished and "standing above human concerns" to draw closer to divinity (249c–d).[33] While not a flight into the heavens, it was likewise a vivid notion of journeying ascent that had formed a climactic moment in the allegory of the cave in the *Republic*, when the prisoners broke free to climb out to the open air and behold the sun – the Form of the Good – in all its brilliance. And if these forms of flight or ascent might seem to unfold in the realm of mere literary figure and myth, it was a far less mythical image of the soul's wondering and wandering – and a far more telling specification of its contemplative reach – that was offered elsewhere in the *Republic*, where the philosopher's soul was qualified as one equipped to "spend all its time reaching out for the wholeness and totality of things – divine and human," contemplating "the whole of time and the whole of reality" (486a).

It is a form of philosophical relocation, as the work of Andrea Nightingale suggests, that we would do well to anchor more broadly in the ancient ideal of philosophical contemplation and its development. For ancient philosophers seeking to articulate the notion of contemplation or *theoria*, she has argued, modelled it on a pre-existing notion of *theoria* in which the relocation at stake carried rather more concrete connotations. In its traditional meaning, it indicated a "journey or pilgrimage abroad for the purpose of witnessing certain events and spectacles," paradigmatically, oracles and religious festivals, from which one returned to one's community to deliver a first-hand report of what one had witnessed.[34] Like

---

[32] I draw on the translation of Harold N. Fowler in Plato, *Theaetetus, Sophist* (London: Heinemann, 1921).

[33] The first translation is Fowler's, in Plato, *Euthyphro, Apology, Crito, Phaedo, Phaedrus* (Cambridge, MA and London: Harvard University Press, 1914); the second adopts Christoph Jedan's rendition of *eksistamenos tōn anthrōpinōn spoudasmatōn*, in his *Stoic Virtues: Chrysippus and the Religious Character of Stoic Ethics* (London and New York: Continuum, 2009), 110.

[34] Nightingale, *Spectacles of Truth*, 3.

the traditional *theoros*, the philosopher undertook a journey marked by a threefold progression: an outward travel, an experience of sacred sights abroad, and a repatriation. The philosopher's journey, however, was not physical but metaphysical, and indeed involved an activity of reason that left the senses behind. And it was a journey away, not from this or that social community, but from the human community as such, to travel to the realm of the divine.

Equally crucial for our context, as with the traditional traveller, the philosopher's experience was one that could be narrated in terms of a progressive shift of vision, and an attendant shift in self-understanding. Stepping away from one's native community, one stepped back to find that detachment and contact with the radically other had estranged the familiar and made one regard it with new eyes. And in doing so, it had alienated one from the location one had hitherto experienced as one's home. One returned, in Nightingale's phrase, "as a different man" and now "a stranger to his own kind," one who would henceforth "dwell in a world where he is never fully at home."[35] Yet in the case of philosophical *theoria*, this was a loss of community and spoliation of identity that was directly conjoined to the discovery of a truer one. For in leaving the human realm behind to travel out to the divine, one was re-establishing contact with a divine element that was already within one, and in which one's truer identity resided. The journey outward was thus also a journey inward, and upward within the soul, transcending the body to reason and one's "egoistic, passionate individuality" to the higher aspect of one's being "open to universality and objectivity, and participating in universal nature or thought," in the words of Pierre Hadot.[36]

As this defining moment of self-transcendence suggests, the transformation of vision produced through this journey was one that carried a fundamentally ethical dimension, calculated to leave one's evaluative standards transformed. It may be unclear in the context of the *Republic*, as Nightingale remarks (echoing a not unfamiliar observation), "how metaphysical contemplation generates a moral theory with a specific content."[37] Yet having ascended out of the cave to behold the Forms, and "having seen the truth of what is beautiful and just and good" (520c), it is evident that one redescends with a sharper understanding of these evaluative truths

---

[35] *Ibid.*, 107 and 97.
[36] Pierre Hadot, *Philosophy as a Way of Life: Spiritual Exercises from Socrates to Foucault*, trans. M. Chase (Malden, MA: Blackwell Publishing, 1995), 103; cf. 242.
[37] Nightingale, *Spectacles of Truth*, 128; an emphasis on the ethically and epistemically transformative effects of the journey of philosophical *theoria* is indeed central to Nightingale's account.

than the one available to those who have spent their lives underground enthralled by a play of shadows. Hence, indeed, the imperative that those successfully redescending should then be appointed to rule. It is a revision of evaluative standards whose sweeping reach is indicated strongly elsewhere in the *Republic* in the continuation of a remark already partially seen above. "Do you think," Socrates asks, "that the mind which ... can contemplate the whole of time and the whole of reality, is likely to regard human life as of any great importance?" (486a). For the life to be henceforth led was not human, but divine, embodying an ideal of godlikeness that would be among Plato's many bequests to later philosophy.[38]

It is the above emphasis on the "flight of the soul" as a notable topos in Plato's works, and a related understanding of the transformative effects and objectives of philosophy more broadly, that has in turn framed Pierre Hadot's important discussion of this philosophical topos and its later development. Hadot has come to be known to us as one of the most vocal exponents of a view of philosophy that dominated the ancient context, even as it has been eclipsed in our own outlook, according to which philosophy constitutes, not an enterprise devoted to the production of abstract theoretical truths, but a deeply practical project to transform our way of life. Taking its point of departure from an awareness of human suffering, and having connected this to the problematic play of the passions, philosophy seeks to offer a "therapy" that will rectify the latter. The medical undertones of this aim – adeptly studied by Martha Nussbaum in her *Therapy of Desire* – achieve paradigmatic expression in Cicero's statement that philosophy "is a physician of souls, takes away the load of empty troubles, sets us free from desires and banishes fears."[39]

The change of vision and way of being that philosophy proposes in pursuit of this aim is indeed so far-reaching that, as Hadot suggests, here we should speak, not of an "ethical" or "intellectual," but rather of a *spiritual* transformation.[40] Central to Hadot's account of the philosophical practices of the Platonists, Stoics, and Epicureans, accordingly, has been a notion of "spiritual exercises" that all ancient schools had in common even as they might vary in form. These exercises included the memorisation of

---

[38] For more on this, see as a starting point Julia Annas, *Platonic Ethics, Old and New* (Ithaca, NY: Cornell University Press, 1999), ch. 3; and David Sedley, "The ideal of godlikeness," in G. Fine, ed., *Plato 2: Ethics, Politics, Religion, and the Soul* (Oxford University Press, 1999).

[39] Cicero, *Tusculan Disputations*, 2.11.

[40] See Hadot's discussion of the term in *Philosophy as a Way of Life*, 127, and *La philosophie comme manière de vivre: entretiens avec Jeannie Carlier et Arnold I. Davidson* (Paris: Albin Michel, 2001), 150–52.

maxims and the meditation on aphorisms encapsulating school dogmas, the anticipatory reflection on possible evils (*praemeditatio malorum*), the cultivation of heightened modes of attention, or even the interpretation of dreams. It is precisely in this context that Hadot situates the spiritual exercise that concerns us most directly. For to see things correctly, in the view of these ancient philosophers – to place things in their true perspective – it is necessary to raise oneself above them, to consider them from higher ground. Regimenting the notion of flight already weaving itself through the works of Plato, all schools would make central to their philosophical practice a spiritual exercise that would allow them to be programmatically transported to that higher ground. Hadot calls it a "cosmic flight" or "view from above," or again a "practical physics."[41]

If we were looking for illustrations of this type of practice, there are few works that could afford richer evidence than Marcus Aurelius' *Meditations*. It is an admonition to relocate ourselves to high ground that addresses us clearly, for example, in the following remark:

> Watch and see the courses of the stars as if you ran with them, and continually dwell in mind upon the changes of the elements into one another; for these imaginations wash away the foulness of life on the ground. Moreover, when discoursing about mankind, look upon earthly things below as if from some place above them. (7.47–48)[42]

Yet the attainment of a mere position "above earthly things" may indeed represent the task in far too modest terms. To see things aright a more dramatic ascent, and more extensive journey, may be required – a sweeping journey through the regions of the universe as a whole, traversing the expanse, not only of space, but endless time:

> You have the power to strip off many superfluities which trouble you and are wholly in your own judgement; and you will make a large room at once for yourself by embracing in your thought the whole Universe, grasping ever-continuing Time and pondering the rapid change in the parts of each object, how brief the interval from birth to dissolution, and the time before birth a yawning gulf even as the period after dissolution equally boundless. (9.32)

---

[41] Much of Hadot's discussion of this can be found in chs. 6, 9, and 10 of *Philosophy as a Way of Life*. See also Engberg-Pedersen's helpful account of the view from above in his "Marcus Aurelius on emotions"; and for another discussion of the cosmic vantage point and its function in Stoicism, also John Sellars, "The point of view of the cosmos: Deleuze, Romanticism, Stoicism," *Pli*, 8 (1999).

[42] All translations are taken from Marcus Aurelius, *The Meditations of the Emperor Marcus Antoninus*, vol. I, trans. A. S. L. Farquharson (Oxford: Clarendon Press, 1944).

We find comparable invitations in Seneca: "Place before your mind's eye the vast spread of time's abyss and embrace the universe; and then compare what we call human life with infinity."[43]

Elsewhere, this moment of cosmic aviation confronts us, not in the content of protreptic invitations to undertake it, but as the subject of descriptive statements that remark its performance in matter-of-fact terms. "The rational soul," states Marcus in the *Meditations*,

> goes over the Whole of the Universe and the surrounding void and surveys its shape, reaches out into the boundless extent of time, embraces and ponders the periodic rebirth of the Whole and understands that those who come after us will behold nothing new nor did those who came before us behold anything greater. (2.1)

The vision beheld, accordingly, stands before us as a matter of fact, as a spectacle readily present to the gaze:

> Asia and Europe are corners in the Universe; every sea, a drop in the Universe; Mount Athos, a clod of earth in the Universe; every instant of time, a pin-prick of eternity. All things are petty, easily changed, vanishing away. (6.36)

The same descriptive cadence is present in Seneca's words when he writes: "As the mind wanders among the very stars it delights in laughing at the mosaic floors of the rich and at the whole earth with all its gold."[44] Yet the protreptic elements that elsewhere frame such images allow us to hear this kind of cadence more judiciously, signalling clearly that this viewpoint requires active effort to be attained, and betraying the character of the cosmic viewpoint as an achievement. And it is through an exercise of the imagination, Hadot suggests more specifically, that this viewpoint stands to be achieved.[45]

In the context of Stoic philosophy, the view from above effects a transition whose significance can be appreciated in light of the Stoic understanding of the passions, taken as judgements of value that indicate our attachment to things that are not dependent on our control. The aim of philosophy is to liberate us from these attachments and direct us towards the pursuit of what does lie within our control, namely virtuous action that conforms to reason. Displacing us from our ordinary viewpoint, the view from above relocates us to the perspective of the entire cosmos that

---

[43] Hadot, *Philosophy as a Way of Life*, 182.   [44] Sellars, "The point of view of the cosmos," 20.
[45] Hadot, *Philosophy as a Way of Life*, 184; cf. 242.

is animated by reason, allowing us to reappraise our attachments from the broader perspective of reason or universal nature. In doing so, it places us in contact with the higher aspect of our own being – the divine element of reason that we share with the cosmos as well as with all other human beings, and in which our passionate individual subjectivity is overcome.

It is an experience of overcoming, or transcendence – an experience of transgressing natural limitations that nevertheless reveals our truer nature and our consanguinity to the gods – that finds itself reflected in expressions of this viewpoint as a recurrent motif. "How closely in accord with nature it is," Seneca writes in one of his *Epistles*, "to let one's mind reach out into the boundless universe! The human soul is a great and noble thing; it permits of *no limits except those which can be shared even by the gods.*"[46] Epicurus, writes Lucretius in his *De rerum natura*, "desired passionately to burst through the narrow confines of the gates of nature ... he advanced far beyond the blazing walls of the universe and traversed the immense whole with his mind and soul, whence, a conqueror, he brought back to us the account of what can arise and what cannot ... *he makes us, with his victory, equal to the heavens.*"[47] The philosophical *theoros* is here seen undertaking his characteristic journey out to the cosmos and returning with his report of the sacred sights encountered. Yet what is important in this connection is that if this act of contemplation comes as a victory or conquest, this is because it involves an identification with the divine in which the lower aspect of one's being stands transcended.

Many of the points discussed above are brought together in a particularly potent unity in a rich passage of Cicero's *Tusculan Disputations*, which it will be helpful to consider briefly. Giving context to Cicero's remarks is a thesis that had defined the Stoic viewpoint and Cicero here takes upon himself to defend: virtue is sufficient for happiness. What follows is a portrait of the wise man engaged in the philosophical life and the philosophical curriculum in all its plenitude that is calculated to arouse the conviction that happiness – here, indeed, an *experiential* happiness

---

[46] Seneca, *Ad Lucilium epistulae morales*, vol. III, trans. Richard M. Gummere (London: Heinemann; New York: G. P. Putnam's Sons, 1925), 181 (epistle 102); emphasis added.

[47] I draw on Nussbaum's limpid translation of this passage in *The Therapy of Desire*, 215; emphasis added. Nussbaum argues, however, that the longing for the transcendence of natural boundaries and the attainment of a godlike condition expressed in this passage conflicts with the Epicurean emphasis on the importance of attuning ourselves to nature and striving to live within its limits. Note that Nussbaum similarly stresses the evaluative effects of this vision of the whole: this "grasp of the whole takes the knower ... beyond the mortal condition, into the value system, therefore the security, of the god"; it "teaches her to see and care in such a way that she really is no longer bounded" (216–17).

realised as a strongly felt sense of joy – attends his every step. The philosophical curriculum, notably, includes the study of physics, ethics, and logic, which had typified the Stoic way of determining its content. And it is indeed first as a theoretical contemplator of nature – considering nature with what today we might call a scientific form of interest – that the wise man first takes the stage. The wise man looks out to the universe with all the excitement of a scientist eager to understand its workings:

> With what joy … must then the soul of the wise man be thrilled when in such company [the study of physics, ethics, and logic] he spends his life and passes his nights in their study! When for instance he discovers the movements and revolutions of the whole heaven and sees the countless stars fixed in the sky in unison with the movement of the vault itself as they keep their appointed place, seven others preserving their several courses … no wonder the spectacle of all this stimulated those men of old and encouraged them to further search. Hence sprang the investigation into the beginnings and as it were the seeds from which all things got their origin, propagation and growth, to find out what was the beginning of each kind … what life is, what death, and what the change and transmutation from one thing into another, what the origin of the earth.

This passage will remind us of the opening of Aristotle's *Metaphysics*: men look out to the world, and the phenomena of nature provoke them to wonder. They ask "why?" questions and seek to grasp their causes, replacing ignorance with understanding, and wonder with self-evidence. Yet it is a different kind of contemplation, and different kind of wonder, that appears in the very next moment.[48] And it is a transition, significantly, that registers as a sudden turn that may now strike as evocatively, provocatively familiar: a turn away from the spectacle of the cosmos, to the soul that contemplates it. "To the soul occupied night and day in these meditations," Cicero continues,

> there comes the knowledge enjoined by the god at Delphi, that the mind should know its own self and feel its union with the divine mind, the source of the fulness of joy unquenchable. For meditation upon the power and nature of the gods of itself kindles the desire of attaining an immortality that resembles theirs, nor does the soul think that it is limited to this

---

[48] My discussion here is not meant to take sides on the complex debate concerning the relationship between the different parts of the Stoic curriculum – particularly physics and ethics – and the nature of Stoic motivation for the study of the natural world, by implying that this study is exclusively ordered to ethical objectives. See Brad Inwood, "Why physics?" in R. Salles, ed., *God and Cosmos in Stoicism* (Oxford University Press, 2009), for a strong argument against this narrow view that affirms the intrinsic value of such study, emphasising the way it unites us with our true (divine) nature.

short span of life … As the wise man gazes upon this spectacle and looks
upward or rather looks round upon all the parts and regions of the universe, with what calmness of soul he turns again to reflect upon human
affairs and what used to be nearer to him! Hence comes his knowledge of
virtue; the kinds and species of the virtues break into blossom, discovery is
made of what nature regards as the end in what is good and the last extremity in what is evil, the object of our duties and the rule for the conduct of
life that must be chosen.[49]

The turn outward – reaching out to discover the universe – has here become
a turn inward; and it has done so bringing a momentous self-discovery in
its train. One's true nature – eloquently expressed in the ability to make
the cosmic spectacle an object of understanding – is unlimited; it is divine.
The subject has recognised his nature as identical to the nature expressed
in the cosmos. In this process, we may notice that the heavens have transformed themselves from an object of scientific explanation to the object
of a different kind of contemplation that we might be tempted to describe
as aesthetic in texture: one's eyes are now roving over the universe in a
way seemingly unarrested by particular phenomena and unchecked by the
desire to explain them.

And this change in the character of one's gaze, we may also note, has
been accompanied by a dramatic shift in one's own location. The cosmos as a scientific spectacle was one from which one seemed to stand
divided, still rooted to the ground as one stared upward to the "countless stars fixed in the sky." Yet now one is no longer looking *upward* but
around (one "rather looks round upon all the parts and regions of the universe"): and this means one has soared upward to the heavens to assume
one's place within them, merging with the object one formerly surveyed
from afar. This dramatic turn – from outward to inward, from upward
to around (and then downward to one's former position) – engenders a
similarly radical change in one's evaluative mode of seeing. What used
to be near is now far; the ordinary world has been re-evaluated, and the
true ethical standards and the nature of virtue have come into view. The
ascent to the cosmos – one marking an ascent to the higher function of

---

[49] Cicero, *Tusculan Disputations*, 5.68–72; I have adopted a couple of Christoph Jedan's minor modifications of this passage. See his illuminating discussion of this passage and its context in *Stoic
Virtues*, ch. 10, to be read with ch. 9. Jedan argues that the assumption of the divine perspective – which he takes Cicero to be expressing here – plays a central role in the acquisition of Stoic
virtue, and he suggests that this change of perspective needs to be read in strongly religious terms,
as one that "would have stood closer to a religious experience than to doctrinal theological teaching" (108), more a form of conversion and a ritual of mystical initiation than a conviction obtained
through systematic argument.

one's being – has come with a sharp revelation of one's highest aim and *telos*: to become who one is; to imitate God and realise one's own divinity. Self-knowledge has brought aspiration. And what is crucial is that this unfolding self-discovery has simultaneously arrived as a discovery of the true meaning of one's ardour and thrilling joy.[50]

It is a type of joy that many of Cicero's fellow philosophers would have recognised in the moment of the mind's stretching forth to the world, to range freely over it and return – a "conqueror," Lucretius had said – with new understanding. It was this joy that Lucretius had named in a famous passage of his *De rerum natura*, when discussing the power of philosophy – embodied in Epicurus' piercing philosophical insight – to reveal the nature of things. "The terrors of the mind are dispelled, the walls of the world dispart"; the gods themselves become visible in their majesty, and the calm realms in which they reside ("buffeted by no wind, sprinkled by no storm cloud's shower") come into view. "At this experience, at this realization that by your power nature has been so completely exposed and unveiled on every side, I am thrilled by a kind of divine ecstasy and quaking awe [*divina voluptas ... atque horror*]" (III:14–30).[51] The power manifested by Epicurus is a power of the human mind to unveil the truth that strikes the human mind itself with a thrill at its own capacities and boundless freedom. It is the thrill of a self-discovery: for these powers reveal to us who we are.

We are far from the wonder that opens Aristotle's *Metaphysics*. But it will be evident that we have been drawing nearer to a more familiar topography for some time. For if Lucretius' awe does not remind us of Aristotle's wonder, it will remind us of a kind of wonder that we had earlier considered closely when bringing the character of Schopenhauer's philosophical standpoint into view. In confronting Cicero's remarks in particular, it will be hard to avoid the uncanny sense of a sudden *anagnorisis*: for the composite philosophical happening that Cicero depicts would seem to form nothing less than a mirror image of the structure of that happening

---

[50] Compare a related moment in the *Phaedrus*, discussed by Nightingale, in which the philosopher's awe upon encountering the Forms – distant, awesome, divine – leads the philosopher to recognise his kinship with them, discovering the self in the other and the familiar in the foreign – a self-discovery that prevents him from being "debased or annihilated by his encounter with divine reality" (*Spectacles of Truth*, 261). It is this joyful celebration of human dignity and power that would seem to be missing from what is perhaps the best-known rehearsal of the cosmic standpoint in later literature, namely Pascal's comparison of the two infinities in his *Pensées*, which terminates not in exaltation but mortification, and in an emphasis on the limits of human reason and the discontinuity between the human and the divine. But that is the topic of a longer story.

[51] I draw on the translation by Martin Ferguson Smith: Lucretius, *On the Nature of Things* (Indianapolis: Hackett Publishing, 2001).

Schopenhauer had described as the aesthetic sublime. The turn outward to the cosmos; the turn inward; the self-discovery; the exultation. And it is indeed the philosophical enactment of the sublime that here finds itself more narrowly resumed, for what strikes the mind with awe is its own capacity to make the world an object of understanding, and conquer it through this same act.

In this parallel structure, the family resemblance stands loudly proclaimed; yet there had been numerous physiognomic features that had already provided rich evidence of the underlying kinship in the foregoing discussion. It will take little, thus, to recognise in Schopenhauer's governing philosophical ideal as characterised earlier the echoes of an ideal with deep roots in the ancient discourse. We may think of the privilege attaching to the notions of rising and ascent (the soul "lifted its vision," we heard in the *Phaedrus*, it "rose up into real being," "standing above human concerns" in a way it later sought to recapture, thereby regaining its "wings"). We may think of the aspiration to a cosmic vantage point in which one "speeds through the infinite vastnesses of the universe" (Hadot's phrase), and of the use of the imagination in doing so;[52] of the perception of the finitude of human existence linked with this, and the transformation of ordinary perception in the shift from a subjective to an objective viewpoint. We may think of the self-transcendence at stake in this shift of viewpoint, which raises us from our passionate, egoistic subjectivity to the higher aspect of our being that represents our true nature. We may think, finally, of the exulting tone that forms the subtext of such endeavours.

In picking up on these connecting ligaments, it is not my intention to enter into a more complex debate concerning the place of Schopenhauer in the history of the ancient contemplative ideals and their later vicissitudes. It has become a topos in our understanding that these ideals were eroded at a critical moment of our philosophical history, as the convictions that had underpinned them gave way. The notion of "mind as mirror" and of human beings relating to reality as spectators – spectators who "could and should acquire insight into the order of reality as God has disposed it" – was to cede its ground, on one dominant telling of this story, to the notion of human beings relating to reality as agents who actively shape their world.[53] One feels that in this history, Schopenhauer could not but occupy a maverick position. For having shed the belief in a world

---

[52] This is not, of course, to identify the notions of imagination at stake.
[53] The remark is from Edward Craig, *The Mind of God and the Works of Man* (1987), quoted in Cooper, *The Measure of Things*, 23.

governed by reason and constituting the expression of a rational order – an order created by God according to divine Ideas – Schopenhauer's attachment to a spectatorial ideal of objective contemplation resting on the faith that our minds (even if by way of exception) can succeed in mirroring the true order of reality may strike us as a remarkable one, and as a throwback to an earlier era. This ambiguous position would seem to reflect the unusual amalgam of influences at work in Schopenhauer's philosophy, in its effort to syncretise the insights of Kant with those of Plato. Yet it is in fact Plato's influence – as Nietzsche would point out indefatigably in sharp polemical tones – that would register more strongly in the notion of contemplation figuring as Schopenhauer's pre-eminent ideal. The gods may have passed out of the world; yet when Schopenhauer nevertheless describes the person endowed with great intellectual powers as living the life of the gods – his ability to take the "liveliest interest on the path of mere *knowledge* … places him, so to speak, in the atmosphere where the gods live easily and serenely" (*PP* I:337–38) – he succumbs to an impulse that is immensely revealing about his relationship to the ancient ideal.

I have been emphasising the physiognomic continuities between Schopenhauer's philosophical understanding and one widely attested in ancient philosophy. Yet it will be a concern rather with the discontinuities that will provide the next stage of my argument with its impetus. My focus in the following will fall on a very specific discontinuity – a discontinuity that, having placed Schopenhauer's philosophical standpoint in its larger context, can be brought into view by simply adding to this context a further layer of characterisation. And with this characterisation, we finally make the leap to the ethical to which this discussion has been looking ahead for some time.

Greatness of soul: a standpoint and its ethical character

To pick out this additional layer, all we need to do indeed is to return to some of the statements already heard above to put our ears against them with more judicious attention. "Tell me rather how closely in accord with nature it is," we heard Seneca state, "to let one's mind reach out into the boundless universe! The human soul is a great and noble thing." And we may now recall that it was a statement posing as the precise inverse of this one, yet also as its most natural complement, that we had heard Socrates make when qualifying the nature of the philosopher in the *Republic*. "Do you think," he had asked, "that the mind which is not afraid of great things, and can contemplate the whole of time and the whole of reality, is likely to regard human life as of any great importance?" (486a). These words would be echoed elsewhere in the same work when discussing the need for responding to misfortune with composure: for "nothing in human affairs is worth taking that seriously" (604b–c). Earlier I suggested that the assumption of the "cosmic" standpoint, in its manifold expressions within ancient philosophy, marked the occurrence of important shifts of evaluative vision. Here, the central shift is laid bare before our eyes in a very simple anatomy: it consists in a displacement of grandeur. It is not human life as we know it that is "great"; what is great is the human soul as it can reach out to the boundless world.

Yet we will only be able to hear these statements in their fullest ethical accents once we allow ourselves to place Plato's remarks next to the ones Aristotle would later make that would directly resume them. For the declaration that "nothing is worth taking seriously" would appear in the *Nicomachean Ethics* almost verbatim; and it would do so at that specific juncture of the *Ethics* when, having completed his discussion of several virtues, Aristotle would turn to consider that particular virtue that we have sometimes translated as "magnanimity," "high-mindedness," or "pride," but that we translate best as "greatness of soul" or *megalopsychia*. "The great-souled man," Aristotle would state there, is "not given to admiration" – or: "wonder" – "since nothing is great to him" (1125a1–5).[54]

The ideal of greatness of soul has sometimes seemed hard to unify; and to many, its disunity has served as an eloquent testimony to its composite origins, to a set of moral ideals in the process of seismic change, and to a culture still struggling to effect the transition from the warrior to the citizen of the *polis*, from the Homeric hero to the philosopher, from Achilles to Socrates. Aristotle's discussion of the great-souled man in the *Nicomachean Ethics* has often been read as a bid to articulate a unified account of this virtue in the background of such tensions, one that would reconcile the meaning carried by this virtue in its Achillean embodiment – an intolerance of insults, and a claim of honour to be defended to the death – and the meaning it carried in its Socratic form – a supreme indifference to fortune, honour included.[55] Within these extremes, Aristotle

---

[54] Here I follow the translation of this statement by Robert C. Bartlett and Susan D. Collins: Aristotle, *Nicomachean Ethics* (University of Chicago Press, 2011).

[55] A key passage of the *Posterior Analytics* (97b15–25), outlining two seemingly conflicting conceptions of greatness of soul – embodied respectively by Achilles, Ajax and Alcibiades, and Socrates and Lysander – has often been taken to set the context for Aristotle's systematic discussion of the virtue in the *NE* and the problem to which it seeks to respond. See briefly Roger Crisp, "Aristotle on greatness of soul," in R. Kraut, ed., *The Blackwell Guide to Aristotle's "Nicomachean Ethics"* (Oxford: Blackwell, 2006), 169, and Michael Pakaluk, "The meaning of Aristotelian magnanimity,"

would seek to carve out his characteristic *via media*: between demanding and renouncing; between claiming too much and claiming too little; between the different kinds of things to which one's claims should be properly directed. Accepting the Achillean privileging of honour above all external goods, Aristotle would reject the violence of Achilles' attachment; accepting the Socratic under-privileging of external goods, he would refuse to go all the way to indifference.[56] For while one should be neither overjoyed by good fortune nor over-pained by bad, external goods are not immaterial to the good life and have the power to affect it.

It will already be clear from the last formulation that greatness of soul was a virtue that stood at the heart of a debate that has already come into view, concerning the stability of the human good or the role of luck in the good life. This is the context in which we may understand R. A. Gauthier's comment, in his book-length study of this virtue, that Aristotle's account of greatness of soul sought to address "the problem which is the crucial problem of Greek ethics in its entirety: that of the relationship between human beings and the world."[57] In Aristotle's account, this relationship would be thematised most directly through the notion of honour, identified as the highest external good, but shadowing it would be a broader concern with the individual's relationship to the goods of fortune.

If we were looking for a conceptual handle that would allow us to approach this virtue insightfully, in fact, it is the basic notion of a "relationship" that might best serve in this role. For this virtue would seem to present itself fundamentally as a composite structure of relationships, or correspondences. Greatness of soul, Aristotle writes, "seems to belong to the sort of person that thinks himself, and is, worthy of great things" (1123b1–5); and since "worth is stated in terms of external goods," and since honour "is in fact the greatest of external goods" (1123b15–25), it is honour that greatness of soul is most concerned with. There is thus a twofold correspondence at stake in this virtue: between one's judgement of one's worth and the facts of one's worth; between the facts about one's worth and the facts in the external world that respond to it. What one is; what one thinks; what the world offers. One's worth, in turn, is more specifically to be understood in *ethical* terms; for it is to the extent that one realises the virtues or excellences that one is worthy of such great things.

Oxford Studies in Ancient Philosophy, 26 (2004), 169–70; and see more substantially, Neil Cooper, "Aristotle's crowning virtue," *Apeiron*, 22 (1989), and Gauthier, *Magnanimité*, part 1, ch. 1 and *passim*.
[56] I draw heavily here on Cooper's formulation in "Aristotle's crowning virtue," 195.
[57] Gauthier, *Magnanimité*, 303.

Hence the fact that greatness of soul is described as a kind of "adornment" or "crown" of the virtues (1124a1–5).

It is an account that has been said to conflict with the terms of Aristotle's own general understanding of the virtues; that has been said to be in tension with Aristotle's annunciation elsewhere of friendship, and not honour, as the highest good. It has been similarly debated whether Aristotle is here reporting *endoxa* or endorsing them; whether greatness of soul can be coherently reckoned as a virtue in itself, as against a "meta-virtue," or merely a matter of form or "grand style." Beyond these internal questions and criticisms, it has been decried by many as a morally problematic ideal. There will be something more to say about the latter type of criticism in the next chapter. Yet it will be relevant for the purposes of our immediate argument to consider a point that has often surfaced in this crossfire.

The great-souled man as drawn up by Aristotle has struck many as smug, self-satisfied, arrogant – his pleasure the pleasure of self-contemplation in the worst possible sense.[58] He knows what he is ethically worth; and firmly established in this sense of self-worth, he claims his dues of honour accordingly from his fellow human beings, over whom he seems to tower in a spirit of self-sufficiency and superiority. There may be nothing generally objectionable, as David Horner notes, about being aware of the condition of one's character. The problem with the great-souled man, however, has to do with the fact that "he (albeit accurately) recognizes his own condition to be *great*"; and that this occurs in the absence of "sufficient balancing factors of moderating humility and positive concern for others."[59] For our immediate context, Horner's point may be reformulated more relevantly as follows: the problem with the great-souled man is that his character appears as a finished possession, a settled fact – a fixed term that it now only remains for the world to move towards and adequately respond to. The ethically right way of relating to one's character, by contrast, can never be in terms of a descriptive judgement that represents it as a fixed fact; it can only be as an object of aspiration.

In thematising the notion of aspiration, this criticism touches on questions of fundamental importance for interpreting Aristotle's account – above all, questions concerning the exact balance in which it proposes to place demand and renunciation, or again the inner and the outer

---

[58] See Harry V. Jaffa, *Thomism and Aristotelianism: A Study of the Commentary by Thomas Aquinas on the Nicomachean Ethics* (University of Chicago Press, 1952), 137, 140, for the remarks that inspire this statement.

[59] David Horner, "What it takes to be great: Aristotle and Aquinas on magnanimity," *Faith and Philosophy*, 15 (1998), 427.

(virtue as against its reward) as objects of interest and objects of one's claims. For on the one hand, as the reading outlined above suggested, part of Aristotle's aim was to balance Socratic indifference to external goods by a greater emphasis on their importance, and the importance of honour in particular – it is great honour, as already noted, that specifically interests the great-souled man as the prize he deserves for his virtue. Yet in seeking to maintain these sides in balance, it nevertheless seems to be contempt that often emerges in his discussion as the stronger pitch. Towards honour, and similarly (and *a fortiori*) towards lesser external goods such as power or wealth, the great-souled man will be "moderately disposed" and "moderately pleased" – "neither over-pleased" at good fortune, nor "over-distressed" at bad (1124a5–20), registering neither difference too strongly. In a word (we might reasonably restate): indifferent. Accordingly, it is a movement *away* from the world rather than a movement *towards* it that seems to define the great-souled man's relationship to his surroundings. It is not incidental that the portrait of the great-souled man has often struck readers as uncannily empty of activity: the great-souled man stands aloof among those he considers his inferiors; he does not walk – he *stands still*.[60] He is a finished product; he does not aspire. To him, "nothing is great."

Yet this picture of contraction cannot wholly satisfy us. It cannot be overlooked, for example, that in the *Rhetoric*, greatness of soul is linked with emulation (whose Greek term, *zēlos*, gives us our modern "zeal"), taken by Aristotle as the very opposite of contempt, and defined as a "kind of distress at the apparent presence among others like him by nature of things honored and possible for a person to acquire" (2.11.1) which the emulator lacks and thus strives to acquire.[61] Here, greatness of soul is associated with a strong element of demand and entitlement that moves decidedly towards the world, not away from it. Aristotle's remarks on emulation appear to focus principally on external goods and the striving movement to obtain them.[62] Yet it is the notion of virtue standing at

---

[60] As W. F. R. Hardie notes – framing a criticism echoed by other readers – the character of the *megalopsychos* is drawn up as a collection of overwhelmingly "negative, and sometimes unattractive, attributes": "he does *not* seek danger, has *few* needs, is *rarely* moved to action, is *not* given to praise or admiration or the pursuit of grudges, *eschews* gossip or personal talk." See his discussion in "'Magnanimity' in Aristotle's *Ethics*," *Phronesis*, 23 (1978), 66.

[61] I draw on the translation by George A. Kennedy: Aristotle, *On Rhetoric: A Theory of Civic Discourse* (Oxford University Press, 2007).

[62] Not exclusively, however; note for example the remark at 2.11.4, which explicitly refers to the virtues as objects of emulation. The inner and the outer, inner worth (virtue) and its reward (honour), are locked in exquisitely close relations.

the heart of Aristotle's account of *megalopsychia*, and indeed underlying the claim to external goods, that would seem to build the notion of a "movement toward" even more integrally into his account.

For the contempt at stake in the great-souled man's orientation, Michael Pakaluk has recently argued, is the contempt that consists in the "power of dismissing goods as of no worth" in comparison with virtue. Virtue, however, involves action; it involves movement towards what is considered fine; it involves aspiration. The central attitude of the great-souled man, accordingly, should be understood as an "attitude of idealistic moral aspiration" – an attitude constituted not by possession, but by striving. For virtuous activity, as Aristotle himself suggests in the *Ethics*, "is not something that we can hold on to as 'a kind of possession.'" The aspiration tied to greatness of soul, as Pakaluk puts it, is to "do something truly great with one's life."[63] It is not irrelevant in this connection that greatness of soul should make an appearance in Aristotle's discussion of the different characters of the young and the old in the *Rhetoric* (2.12–13), where it is incorporated in the description of the character of the young. For the attitude of the young is defined precisely by a powerful and confident movement towards the world, and an idealistic aspiration towards the fine. If the great-souled man "thinks nothing is great," thus, this can apply only to the external domain (and even there, with due measure), not to the domain of virtue. If *he* is great, it is because he thinks that *something else* is.

The difficulties one encounters in seeking to capture the precise balance between movement towards and movement away – between indifferent withdrawal and zealous approach, between the value of the outer and the inner – in Aristotle's account, it could be said, reflect Aristotle's programmatic concern to preserve such fragile and fruitful tensions within his ethics. For to strike the right balance in one's response (to be "neither over-pleased" at good fortune, nor "over-distressed" at bad) will be as difficult as striking the mean that typifies virtue. Similarly, if we take this virtue to be addressing "the problem of the relationship between human beings and the world" more broadly, the willingness to tolerate the absence of exact definitions and clear-cut boundaries may be seen as a stand against other attempts to solve this problem that proceed by drawing a sharp boundary around the self and locating value exclusively in the inner as against the outer domain.[64]

---

[63] Pakaluk, "The meaning of Aristotelian magnanimity," 244–46.

[64] Not everyone would thus agree with Pakaluk if his understanding of Aristotelian greatness of soul in terms of a "capacity to dismiss competing [i.e. external] goods as of *no* account" ("The meaning

It was this sharper segregation that typified the Socratic approach, and the approach that, as Martha Nussbaum has shown, finds wide expression in much (if not all) of Plato's work.[65] Socratic greatness of soul, as Pakaluk again suggests, can be understood in more unambiguous terms as a capacity to hold goods of the body in contempt in favour of goods of the soul. It can be described as "an exaltation of the soul over the body, which consists in a readiness to reject anything whatsoever that is incompatible with the indications of what is *kalon*." Greatness of soul is thus "a virtue that expresses, not simply by acknowledging but also by actually displaying, the power of the soul over the body."[66] It is a sharp boundary of this kind, as mentioned earlier in this chapter, that similarly typified the Stoic solution to the broader problem that greatness of soul can be seen as addressing. To the extent, indeed, that greatness of soul designates an ability to disdain external goods – vulnerable to the vicissitudes of luck – for the goods of the soul – residing within the fortified area of one's control – it is the virtue that would serve to epitomise the entire Stoic ethical ideal, not one virtue among many, but the central virtue in the philosophical life.[67]

With this crisper boundary in place, the composite "movement away" and "movement toward" at issue stands out in correspondingly sharper terms. It is an act, clearly, that is still defined by what it leaves behind and what it reaches for, rejecting apparent or lesser goods – typically goods of the body – for the higher goods of the soul. A galvanising "movement toward" thus remains at its heart. Yet the movement away now stands out more sharply as an act of transcendence, one whose performance brings a starker exercise of power into play. Pakaluk, accentuating this display of power just above, spoke of a moment of "exaltation"; Gauthier in his own discussion would employ headier language to speak of "domination." For contempt, his remarks suggest, is a form of domination. In disdaining the power of external goods, the sage disdains the world, and in disdaining it, he dominates it – overcomes it.[68] And having drawn closer to these notions, it may now be easier to finally perform the leap that allows us to join the different stages of our discussion more firmly together, to suggest

---

of Aristotelian magnanimity," 245; emphasis added) was taken to translate directly into the view that external goods are of *no* account for the good life.

[65] See the discussion in *Fragility of Goodness*.

[66] Michael Pakaluk, "Socratic magnanimity in the *Phaedo*," *Ancient Philosophy*, 24 (2004), 116.

[67] As Gauthier points out, however, it shared this privilege with the virtues of perseverance and courage, which were invested in Stoic ethics with a broad signification that gave them a similarly central role in the moral life. See *Magnanimité*, part 1, ch. 4, esp. 144ff., for discussion.

[68] *Ibid.*, 40 (cf. 127, 303).

that it was precisely the virtue of greatness of soul that was at stake – in sometimes more and sometimes less pronounced ways – in the philosophical vantage point described earlier.

Now on the one hand, it has been a matter of some debate how Aristotle's account of greatness of soul in particular stands to be related to the other ideals receiving expression in the larger body of his work. This includes the ideal of friendship, but it also includes, more significantly, the ideal of theoretical excellence developed in later books of the *Nicomachean Ethics*. In the *Ethics*, the relationship between greatness of soul and the activity of philosophical contemplation remains overall obscure, and this virtue seems to be most visibly linked to the narrower class of excellences or "goods of the soul" that belong to the practical, and not the theoretical sphere.[69] If this conclusion has been debated, however, that reflects the stronger connection into which other ancient philosophers have drawn greatness of soul with theoretical excellence and contemplative activity.

It is a connection, as more than one writer has suggested, deeply stamped in Plato's understanding. And indeed this connection – couched, this time, in the vocabulary of *megaloprepeia* ("magnificence") rather than *megalopsychia* – is nowhere more plainly evident than in the passage of the *Republic* already referred to several times above. "Do you think that the mind which is not afraid of great things" – or in a more evocative translation: "a mind habituated to thoughts of grandeur" – "and can contemplate the whole of time and the whole of reality, is likely to regard human life as of any great importance?" (486a). Hence Gauthier's claim: for Plato, magnificence represents the philosophical virtue *par excellence*, and its exercise is identical with contemplative activity – though this is indeed an activity not "merely" theoretical in kind but deeply suffused with evaluative significance, as it is deeply suffused with aspiration and desire. The reality to which the philosopher directs himself is not an object of inert knowledge but of erotic love (485b).[70] Yet what needs to be marked in this context is the particular specification of contemplative activity that is present in this passage. For that, as suggested earlier, is a specification that expresses a more widely instanced understanding of the philosophical standpoint

---

[69] Gauthier has been one of the strongest exponents of the view that the great-souled man in the *Nicomachean Ethics* is to be identified with the philosopher (*Magnanimité*, part 1, ch. 3), yet his view remains eccentric. See Hardie, "'Magnanimity' in Aristotle's *Ethics*," 67–69, for a succinct criticism of Gauthier; and Jaffa, *Thomism and Aristotelianism*, ch. 6, for a statement of the alternative view.

[70] See Gauthier's discussion of Platonic greatness of soul in *Magnanimité*, part 1, ch. 2. Hadot makes the same link between greatness of soul and the philosophical attainment of cosmic/universal vision; see e.g. *Philosophy as a Way of Life*, 97, 242.

in terms of ascent, cosmic journeying, and command of the universal whole. The remarks from Seneca's *Epistles* that opened this section, tying the nobility (or "grandeur") of the human mind to its capacity to reach through the boundless universe, provide another ready testimony to the same underlying link connecting the contemplative standpoint thus specified to the character trait of *megalopsychia*.

Taken as an ascent, and a magisterial ascent that brings the totality of being and the infinite cosmos into view, the act of contemplation thus expresses a capacity to transcend the lower for the higher – the physical for the metaphysical, the subjective for the objective, the body for the soul – that we can now recognise as an instance of the kind of transcendence at stake in the virtue of *megalopsychia*. What this means is that the conquest performed by the mind is a conquest that constitutes an expression of character; it is a conquest that realises a possibility fundamentally ethical in kind. And having brought this ligament into view, it is important to bring out another, which the tell-tale vocabulary of "conquest" and "domination" above has already flagged.

For this, as we may recall, was a vocabulary we had called on heavily to describe the experience of the sublime as Schopenhauer – no less than Kant – had articulated it, and to characterise the dialectic of powerlessness and power, vulnerability and mastery, that formed its heart. In articulating his view of the sublime, Schopenhauer, like many of those beginning to think more rigorously about the sublime before him, had drawn on the ancient treatise on rhetoric by (pseudo-)Longinus, *On the Sublime*. And this is a treatise, as any reading immediately reveals, that is suffused with the philosophical ideal of grandeur spelled out in the ethic of *megalopsychia*. Longinus would ground himself directly in this ideal when making the capacity for grand thoughts one of the most important sources of the sublime style.[71] Sublimity, Longinus would declare in a key remark, "is the echo of a noble mind" (*hypsos megalophrosynēs apēchēma*) – or in another

---

[71] Longinus, "On Sublimity," 467 (8.1). D. A. Russell suggests that the philosophical background of Longinus' treatise is "predominantly Stoic" ("Greek criticism of the Empire," in G. A. Kennedy, ed., *The Cambridge History of Literary Criticism*, vol. 1, *Classical Criticism* [Cambridge University Press, 1989], 307). For a stronger characterisation of this philosophical background, see Alain Michel, "Rhétorique et poétique: la théorie du sublime de Platon aux modernes," *Revue des Études Latines*, 54 (1976); and see 288ff. for some relevant remarks concerning the differential emphasis on the movement *towards* versus *away*, or withdrawal versus positive aspiration, in different forms of the ancient sublime. See also the suggestive discussion in Charles Segal, "Writer as hero: the heroic ethos in Longinus, *On the Sublime*," in J. Servais, T. Hackens, and B. Servais-Soyez, eds., *Stemmata: mélanges de philologie, d'histoire et d'archéologie grecques offerts à Jules Labarbe* (Liège and Louvain-la-Neuve: L'Antiquité Classique, 1987).

translation: "an image reflected from the inward greatness of the soul."[72]
The vision of humanity that inspires writers of the sublime style, he would
later state, is an understanding of human possibility and the human vocation in which our aspiration to surpass ourselves – the "irresistible desire
for anything which is great and, in relation to ourselves, supernatural" –
plays a central role. And so, crucially, does the capacity of the mind to surpass or transcend, which Longinus describes in terms that will now seem
intimately familiar: "The universe therefore is not wide enough for the
range of human speculation [*theoria*] and intellect. Our thoughts often
travel beyond the boundaries of our surroundings." Or in a more telling
translation: human thought "passes the bounds of the material world and
launches forth at pleasure into endless space."[73]

The connection between the sublime and the ancient ethical ideal of
greatness of soul, indeed, had been strongly preserved in Kant's account of
the sublime in his *Critique of the Power of Judgment*, where the experience
had been analysed precisely in terms of a discovery – prompted by, and
succeeding, an initial terror before spectacles of nature's might or magnitude – of the human capacity to disdain nature for something greater
belonging to the moral domain. Nature is judged sublime, Kant had written, in so far as it calls forth "our power (which is not part of nature) to
regard those things about which we are concerned (goods, health and life)
as trivial, and hence to regard its power ... as not the sort of dominion
over ourselves and our authority to which we would have to bow if it
came down to our highest principles."[74] In this disdain of the physical for
the metaphysical, of the lower goods for the higher, and our lower identity
as natural beings for our higher identity as rational beings with a moral
vocation – and in the sense of human sublimity that forms its concomitant – many ancient philosophers would have been justified in recognising an echo of their ideal of grandeur.

Yet it is finally time to turn back to our trajectory to consider where the
forgoing discussion has brought us. I began by arguing that the standpoint
sub specie aeternitatis expressing itself in Schopenhauer's work – intimately
linked with Schopenhauer's understanding of the aesthetic sublime – is
connected by significant bonds of kinship to a philosophical ideal widely
attested in ancient philosophy. This ideal, I then argued, in turn stands to
be connected with the ethical ideal of greatness of soul, whose influence

---

[72] Longinus, "On Sublimity," 468 (9.2); the second rendition is William Smith's (1740).
[73] Longinus, "On Sublimity," 494 (35.2–3); the second translation of the latter remark is again
Smith's.
[74] Kant, *Critique of the Power of Judgment*, §28, 145.

is indeed manifest in the work that provides the later aesthetics of the sublime with its most immediate pedigree. The conquest performed by the mind, as I suggested above, realises an ethical possibility; it forms an expression of character. Yet it is important now to pause to spell out more fully the implications of this last point.

For to declare that an action admits of ethical qualification is at the most elementary level to signal the fact that failure of some kind is possible with respect to it. To describe this conquest as an ethical possibility is thus to recognise the possibility that failure might occur. What kind of failure might that be? Here, I think that we may allow ourselves to draw some distinctions. For the acts of magisterial detachment, free accelerations through the universe, and exulting ascents above the earthly that ancient philosophers, and Schopenhauer in their footsteps, would describe and prescribe can be taken to constitute merely a heightened instance and particularly festive celebration of a more basic human capacity for detachment available to all: an ability to step back from what is initially given that comes in infinitely varied and finer degrees, yet whose basic form is simply the act of representing, or remarking (an act of remarking that, after Wittgenstein, one feels compelled to locate in language and as a linguistic event). This basic act of transcendence – the act of picking out what is given which Sartre might have described as "nihilating" it, tracing out a boundary of non-being around it, to see its being in the light of its possible non-being – would seem to constitute a possibility distinctively human, even if in its finer forms it might require a process of cultivation or education to be realised. The practice of cosmic voyaging and ascent described above – developed and propagated within philosophical tradition, and employed programmatically as a space for reflecting on human nature and the values that should govern human life – evidently belongs to the latter kind.

With this in mind, I would then argue that it is not the intellectual act of transcendence itself, isolated in this manner, that might fail to be performed; or if it did, its failure would not constitute a failure specifically ethical in kind. The specifically ethical possibility of failure can be picked out by saying that this act of transcendence might be performed in better or worse ways; that there might be better or worse ways of relating to the space that is open to us as a distinctively human possibility, and in particular to the standpoint of magisterial detachment open to us as a more developed human possibility. Characterising Aristotle's ethical method, Martha Nussbaum has outlined a two-step approach in which we first "isolate a sphere of human experience that figures in more or less any human life, and in which more or less any human being will have to make *some* choices rather than others, and act in *some* way rather than some other," and then go on to ask: "What is it to choose and respond well within that sphere? What is it, on the other hand, to choose defectively?"[75] I am suggesting that we count the ability to assume a vantage point of heightened detachment on human life as isolating such a sphere, in relation to which different choices and different ways of responding are possible. And I would suggest that talk of "better" or "worse" ways of responding can be understood – as Nussbaum, following Aristotle, similarly understands it – in terms of their expressing better or worse kinds of character. As the ancient discussions already signal, to recognise the mind's conquest as an expression of character is to recognise the possibility that this character may fail to be achieved.

Aristotle himself had detailed carefully, in the *Nicomachean Ethics*, the different ways in which greatness of soul could fail to be achieved. One may fail to be great-souled through conceit or presumption – through thinking one is worth more than one is. One may fail to be great-souled through smallness of soul (*mikropsychia*) – through thinking one is worth less than one is (1123b5–15). Yet in turning back to consider Schopenhauer, it is Aristotle's discussion of the contrasting character of the young and the old in the *Rhetoric* (2.12–13) that can provide us with the most concrete and potent grip. Our focus here should fall on a core theme of this discussion that revolves around a by now familiar contrast between movement away and movement toward, between withdrawal and zealous approach. The young, Aristotle writes,

> are not cynical but guileless, because of not yet having seen much wickedness. And [they are] trusting, because of not yet having been much deceived. And [they are] filled with hopes; for like those drinking wine, the young are heated by their nature, and at the same time [they are filled with hopes] because of not yet having experienced much failure … And they are easily deceived for the reason given; for they easily hope for the best … And they are great-souled;[76] for they have not yet been worn down by life but are inexperienced with constraints, and to think oneself worthy of great things i[s] greatness of soul and this is characteristic of a person of good hopes. And they choose to do fine things rather than things advantageous [to themselves].

---

[75] Martha Nussbaum, "Non-relative virtues: an Aristotelian approach," *Midwest Studies in Philosophy*, 13 (1988), 35.
[76] I substitute "great-souled" for Kennedy's "magnanimous" here.

Yearning for the fine and attached to honour; driven by aspiration; bright-eyed with trust and hope – impulsive, desirous to a flaw, powerfully outward-moving. The character of the old stands in sharp contrast:

> [T]hey are cynical; for a cynical disposition supposes everything is for the worse. Further, they are suspicious because of their distrust [*apistia*] and distrustful because of experience. And for these reasons they neither love nor hate strongly ... And they are small-minded because of having been worn down by life; for they desire nothing great or unusual but things necessary for life ... And they are cowardly and fearful ahead of time about everything; for their disposition is the opposite of the young ... And they are more fond of themselves than is right; for this is also a form of small-mindedness. And they live for what is advantageous [to themselves] (not for what is fine).[77]

In a state of recoil and suspicion, on their defence against strong attachments, hoping warily only for what they can gain through prudent calculation – the contrast could not be sharper.

These, of course, are extremes; and as Aristotle's continuation suggests, the fully good character is in fact exhibited by those in the prime of life who combine what is best of both ages and thereby strike the mean. Yet with this stark contrast in view, we can now return to the normative standpoint of Schopenhauer's "Aphorisms" we outlined earlier to consider it with keener eyes. We should "set limits to our wishes, curb our desires," we had heard, "reduce to very moderate proportions our claims to pleasures, possessions, rank, honour," guard against "making many demands." Our desires should contract. One will not, Schopenhauer states elsewhere, "ardently aspire to anything in the world, nor will he complain very much if he fails in any undertaking"; instead, he will be imbued with the spirit of Plato's words in the *Republic* (604c): "nothing in human affairs is worth

---

[77] See also Nussbaum, *Fragility of Goodness*, 337–39, for an illuminating discussion of this passage to which I am indebted for my appreciation of its significance, and whose thematisation of trust and hope as attitudes carrying positive ethical value provided me with one of the starting points of my own argument. To understand these attitudes in such positive terms need not involve misconstruing Aristotle's project in the *Rhetoric*, whose objective in this context is indeed not to articulate an ethical ideal but to offer potential orators material for achieving their persuasive aims – and for this kind of objective, the accuracy of character attributions taken as descriptive facts would suffice. Thus it would be a mistake to assume that Aristotle attributes to the young the virtues of courage and greatness of soul in their proper sense and his own voice (see Gauthier's discussion of this passage in *Magnanimité*, 30–35, for a clarification of this point; and Terence H. Irwin, "Ethics in the *Rhetoric* and in the *Ethics*," in A. O. Rorty, ed., *Essays on Aristotle's "Rhetoric"* [Berkeley and Los Angeles: University of California Press, 1996], for larger discussion). Even if the young are not exhibiting the full virtues, however, what is relevant is that the attitudes of hope, trust, and confidence are marked out as an ethically significant field, and as the field in which the modification of these attitudes that represents true virtue can be sought.

taking that seriously" (*PP* I:409). One will embrace the twin virtues of prudence and distrust (*apistia*), preferring to fear than to have faith. One will not trust in the world or in people; one will throw out hope to arm oneself against disillusionment. One will forestall misfortunes through cunning machinations that allow one to "slip out of the way of every misfortune, great or small," "like a clever fox." Self-defensive, preoccupied with the self, inward-looking, lacking positive aspirations beyond the negative aim of minimising harm – this is the character that Schopenhauer has commended to us.

It is now possible to say: what Schopenhauer has placed before us is the character of an old man – broken by experience, eyes empty of hope, withdrawn; small-souled. This is the character he has invited us to cultivate as the proper response to the picture of the world that emerges after the work of philosophy has been done. I mentioned earlier that the "Aphorisms" sought to prescind from the higher perspective of philosophy to consider how, "supposing" that life might be liveable, it might in fact be most happily lived. The character portrait proposed in the "Aphorisms" may thus seem to arrive as an "after" to this philosophy that is nevertheless not a logical consequent – and Schopenhauer, after all, had more generally disclaimed normatively consequential ways of relating philosophy to anything we go on to do after its consummation. At most, it is a *non sequitur* contrived to occupy our time in the aftermath of the millennium since the apocalypse has not occurred.

Yet on the one hand, it should be recalled that the picture of the world against which this character recommendation has been articulated – and from which it derives its relevance – is in fact substantially continuous with the perspective of that higher philosophy, whose pessimistic vision it re-expresses even while leaving its metaphysical underpinnings out of view. But there is certainly a stronger way of pressing the point, one that indeed entails drawing these underpinnings firmly back into the centre of our view. I suggested earlier that Schopenhauer's normative proposal arrives as a recommendation of withdrawal, contraction, self-limitation. Yet it is hardly incidental to note the peculiarly *quantitative* dimension on which Schopenhauer places his accent in stating this proposal. We should "limit" our claims, "reduce" our claims to "very moderate proportions," not make "many demands." It is not, it may be noticed, a question of drawing distinctions between *kinds* of desires, and encouraging us to cultivate certain kinds instead of others. It is rather a question of decreasing them *all*.

It might be tempting to read this omission to dwell on normative criteria for ordering desires as yet another token of the limited normative character of the "Aphorisms" – perhaps reflecting Schopenhauer's deeper conviction that the *qualitatively* higher goods are accessible only to those born under a happier star, and no amount of normative commendation can make them available to us if our nature is not already suitably disposed. Yet to read Schopenhauer's omission in this manner might be to miss a more significant way of explaining it, one that once again serves to place the Schopenhauer of the "Aphorisms" in far more seamless continuity with the Schopenhauer of the *World as Will and Representation*. The Schopenhauer of the "Aphorisms" says: "all desires should be decreased"; the Schopenhauer of the *World as Will and Representation* would have said: "all desires should be uprooted." Putting this basic difference aside, however, we may now recall that it was a very similar omission that had been caught in our headlights in the last chapter when examining Schopenhauer's pessimism and attending to the phenomenological description of the human condition that Schopenhauer had made central to his pessimistic conclusions in the *World as Will and Representation*. It was a condition shaped by the operation of a boundless desire: riven by infinite desire, we suffer. Yet to simply register infinite desire among the "facts" of the human condition, I had suggested – to remark it descriptively, like some non-human spectator, as a fact or given – was to overlook the ethical space that this remarking potentially opened up. For it could be argued that this is a fact to be treated after it has been observed; and it was just such a vigorous normative stance that had typified the way ancient philosophers had engaged this feature of the human condition.[78]

This was my proposal; yet in hindsight, it may seem as if there was one all-too-obvious response with which it could have been met – though indeed a response that would have involved abandoning the project of decoupling Schopenhauer's pessimism from its metaphysical foundations. For in Schopenhauer's philosophical vision, it could be said, there simply *were* no resources that would allow such a normative stance to be taken and such distinctions to be meaningfully made. In ancient ethics, such distinctions had been articulated against a set of thick conceptions of the good life and a thick understanding of the human *telos*. It has become a commonplace that these conceptions historically suffered

---

[78] Schopenhauer in fact refers briefly to Epicurus' distinction between different types of desire in *PP* 1:346; yet his engagement with this standpoint remains all too brief.

a holistic collapse that rendered them inaccessible to our present culture. This was a collapse, as Alasdair MacIntyre has suggested in *After Virtue*, in which philosophical and social developments were closely intertwined, one tightly connected with the broader social transformations that led to the breakdown of traditional social hierarchies and religious forms of belonging, and therewith the collapse of evaluative structures and their supportive context. Schopenhauer's philosophy, as mentioned in the last chapter, has indeed been situated by several of its most insightful readers against the horizon of these very changes. With its defining representation of a will that lashes forth blindly – movement without finality, purposiveness without purpose – Schopenhauer's vision can be taken as an eloquent expression of this sense of evaluative collapse. By the same token, it is not difficult to see why this vision of the world should lack the resources for articulating a normative standpoint that would enable us to draw meaningful distinctions between desires and to order different kinds of goods. All there is, is human willing. There is nothing outside it to which it is worth directing it. There is no *telos*. There are no criteria. There is no "outside." Or again, in a different sense: all there is, is now "outside."

It is precisely in these terms, and with this stark sense of an "outside," that I suggested at the end of the last chapter that Schopenhauer's philosophical standpoint *sub specie aeternitatis* might alternatively allow itself to be read. Its sublime cosmic viewpoint – its supremely detached "view from nowhere" – might be read not as a victory but a defeat, being an Archimedean "outside" to which we have been expelled through the dissolution of the evaluative structures that formerly retained our feet on solid ground. The intervening discussion has suggested that this was an "outside" that had been occupied before, and in doing so has offered a more positive way of characterising Schopenhauer's profound attachment to this location "outside" – taking it as an "outside" of the mind, and thus an "inside" on the ancient division – by connecting it to an aspiration to transcendence with a far longer lineage, and powerfully expressed in the ideal of *megalopsychia*, particularly in its Stoic form. Yet having remarked Schopenhauer's participation in this philosophical tradition, it becomes possible to attend all the more acutely to the significant ways in which he departs from it.

For certainly, like the ancient philosophers, Schopenhauer embraces the "outside" as a location in which suffering can be overcome by seeing, in which the passions can be mastered, in which the world can be seen in its true and objective significance and the subjective perspective of the individual can be transcended. Like the ancient philosophers, and to the extent that he understands this changed perspective in terms of a shift from the lower to the higher function of one's being in which one's truer identity lies – in Schopenhauer's terms, one's identity as the subject of knowing, which is the correlate of the aesthetic Ideas – Schopenhauer understands the occupation of this vantage point as a transformative one.[79] Yet notice, for one, the singular thinness of this new identity. One rises to identify oneself with – what? One's status as a conscious being; as a being capable of representing; of philosophically representing; of stepping back from the world, master of being by envisaging its non-being. (Schopenhauer, we may note, has dismissed Kant's more positive moral specification of this identity as so much sanctimonious humbug). We stand "higher," certainly; yet the ground is brittle, and the air almost too thin to breathe.

The ancient spectator journeying out to the cosmos, by contrast, had breathed the air of the gods. His gaze had travelled out to the heavens and returned with awed wonder to recognise the piece of heaven scintillating within him. The outward gaze had turned inward laced with new self-understanding. And this was no inert or sterile self-understanding; it was a self-knowledge that generated positive aspiration, and yielded new structures of value with which to re-engage life. One stepped away to step back; one ascended to again descend – though one would henceforth live one's life under the glow of that ascent. It was not the movement of ascent – the movement away, of withdrawal – in which greatness of soul was achieved. Greatness of soul was only fully achieved in the redescent, taken in the broader sense of an engagement, a positive aspiration, a movement powerfully towards the world (though to new aspects of the world), an expansion. The realisation that "nothing is great" among the things we formerly took seriously – whose Platonic formulation Schopenhauer had approvingly yet perhaps not so appropriately mouthed in the "Aphorisms" – only received completion in the discovery of what now *is*. Longinus had said it: nature brought man "into the universe as into a great festival, to be *both* a spectator *and* an enthusiastic contestant in its competitions." The grand human vocation betrayed in the human passion for greatness was expressed in participation after being expressed in contemplation from afar.[80]

---

[79] And thus, to resume a question raised earlier in this chapter concerning Schopenhauer's jaundiced view of the power of reflection to affect our practical and emotional lives ("a powerful control of the faculty of reason over directly felt suffering is seldom or never found in fact," *WWR* I:315): the power of philosophical reflection can indeed be more openly acknowledged once we understand it as an exercise, not of the faculty of reason, but of the more transformative mode of cognition that constitutes the aesthetic.

[80] Longinus, "On Sublimity," 494 (35.2); emphasis added.

Schopenhauer's sublime fails to complete this movement – it does not redescend. The philosophical subject remains a spectator, never leaping down to the ring to become an active contestant. The identity to which this sublime vantage point connects us, correlatively, appears to be sterile, incapable of generating positive aspiration. It is this lack of aspiration, it may now be stated more clearly, that we find reflected in the character commended in the "Aphorisms" – preoccupied with self-defence, nursing old wounds and guarding against new ones, desiring nothing positive beyond escape from harm. The negative character of this ideal is far from incidental; it expresses the fundamental sense of metaphysical destitution that the "Aphorisms" had proposed to leave outside the gates. Yet with the foregoing discussion behind us, this lack of aspiration can be characterised in more substantive, and more thickly ethical, terms. We may call it a failure in *megalopsychia*.

To characterise Schopenhauer's philosophical act in these terms is to bring ethics into epistemology in a way that we can be certain Schopenhauer would have vigorously opposed, contaminating with practical qualifications a domain that he believed ought to remain wholly inaccessible to them. Here, we may simply have to beg to differ. For acts of mind often *do* express character; acts of mind can be and often *are* criticised in ethical terms, and more narrowly in terms that address the ethical character exhibited in their performance. As Linda Zagzebski points out in this context, we do not criticise beliefs solely by evaluating them through the kind of criterion with which philosophers have often been rather too narrowly preoccupied – namely, whether these beliefs themselves are adequately or inadequately justified. Our criticism often turns to the person himself and the qualities he has exhibited in forming or endorsing such beliefs. We call a person "short-sighted" or "obstinate," "vacuous" or "shallow," "dull" or "obtuse," "narrow-minded" or "careless," "intellectually cowardly" or "rash," "imperceptive," "prejudiced," or "rigid." And this kind of criticism, of course, is "much closer to *moral* criticism" than commonly supposed.[81] Intellectual acts and decisions in general provide an important arena for the expression of character. A similar premise, as I have suggested, was implicit in the ancient understanding of the particular act of mind at stake, which carried a qualification of character that located it in a fundamentally ethical field. And to accept this, of course, is to acknowledge that the same type of act could be undertaken from a different location within that field; that there might be other ways of

---

[81] Linda T. Zagzebski, *Virtues of the Mind* (Cambridge University Press, 1996), 5.

handling or responding to the same broad intellectual possibility, expressing a different kind of character.

In this case, however, it is not the interpretative problem of
Schopenhauer's anticipated dissent to the above proposal – a proposal to
read the ethical in the intellectual, and the ethics in the aesthetics – that
may seem to carry the greatest urgency. Even if we accept that there is a
space for the ethical appraisal of intellectual standpoints in general, what
might be questioned is the availability of a different ethical choice with
respect to this one. For if the character of Schopenhauer's standpoint is
given in a distrust and suspicion typical of old age, old age – it may now
be said – is always arrived at, never chosen. And if we propose to criticise
this character using the ethical terms of ancient philosophy, the question
to raise is whether these terms are any longer ones that belong to *us*. This
is not, or not only, a question about the actual absence of "greatness of
soul" from our current ethical vocabulary, provoking a linguistic discomfort betrayed in my occasional escape into the Greek transcription. Or if
this condition of linguistic desuetude is relevant, it is in so far as it points
to something deeper. For if we recognise our own image in Schopenhauer's
vertiginous Archimedean "outside," if his *specific* appropriation of the
ancient standpoint is an expression of a *specifically* modern predicament
that is still our own – in which the gaze journeys outward to a cosmos
empty of its gods and inward to a correspondingly empty citadel – it may
well be wondered how the failure to aspire, indeed to aspire *greatly* and to
"great things," could possibly come up for critique. *Megalopsychia* might
have been possible to a youthful philosophical past in which the gaze
turned to the heavens above and to the breast within and returned with
richer trophies; but that past is no longer our present.

It will be the task of the next chapter to sketch out, within its own limits, the beginnings of a response to this question, which will come both
as a development of the critique of Schopenhauer's standpoint already
broached, and a more positive statement of an alternative that finally
places this critique more clearly in the horizon of an appropriation.

CHAPTER 6

An ethics of redescent?

Regaining the open sea: certainty, vulnerability, humility

I suggested in the last chapter that the character Schopenhauer commended to us in response to his pessimistic vision – a character that we may connect to the broader nature of his philosophical standpoint – was one that Aristotle had already given us the resources for describing revealingly, if somewhat rhetorically, as the character of an old man. Yet it is important to recall the exact words Aristotle had used in doing so. The old, he had said, had been "worn down by life," and thus were small-souled, desiring "nothing great or unusual but things necessary for life." Or as Nussbaum has more suggestively translated these same words: they have been "humbled by life" and thus "desire nothing great or excellent, but only what is commensurate with life."[1]

If the thematisation of greatness and smallness of soul had not already made it plain, these words make it plainer. What this reference to the attritional effects of life makes clear is that, at stake in the different responses of the young and the old to the possibilities the world offers, is a deeper drama that centres on a concern with esteem and self-esteem, and is driven forward by reactions of pride and humiliation. The key contrast that forms the axis of this passage in the *Rhetoric* – between trust and distrust, hope and disillusionment – can indeed be seen as an expression of this underlying drama. It is precisely within the ethical field defined by this concern and its peculiar dialectic of pride and humiliation – and more particularly, within this field taken as a location for the manifestation of qualities of character – that I would propose that Schopenhauer's philosophical standpoint best stands to be critically engaged; and in being critically engaged, constructively appropriated.

---

[1] Nussbaum, *Fragility of Goodness*, 338.

It may not have struck Schopenhauer as wholly surprising to find that a heightened attention to esteem and self-esteem, and indeed to the ethics of esteem taken as a concern with character, should turn up as a prominent headline in approaching his philosophy. For on the one hand, and most broadly, a concern with character formed a central feature of Schopenhauer's own ethical approach, and indeed his caustic critique of Kant's ethics of duty has been heard as prefiguring Elizabeth Anscombe's later critique of modern moral philosophy (1958), which would mark the beginning of a renascence for the ethics of virtue and a restoration of philosophical interest in character.[2] Yet joined to this broader affinity is another – one narrower and indeed less theoretical kind, relating to that visceral struggle that provided Schopenhauer's own biography with its most poignant motif. For it was a dialectic of honour and shame, of esteem and its denial, that would define the way Schopenhauer the philosopher would experience the encounter between his philosophy and the world. This was a world that would absorb the event of his philosophical publications with the most deafening silence, leaving Schopenhauer's ears burning for decades for the sound of applause, and gradually leading him to retreat to a bitter Olympian seclusion from which he would henceforth release his thunderbolts implacably against his philosophical contemporaries, having constructed his self-understanding as an extraordinary voice of truth ahead of its time. (Whoever wishes to achieve something great must "direct his gaze to posterity," and meanwhile endure the present with all the loneliness of "an inhabitant of the desert."[3]) It is indeed through this poignant drama of a recognition yearned for and refused that the reader often makes contact with Schopenhauer the human being in his works, tasting his struggles but also his character in Schopenhauer's haughty and acerbic vituperations against Hegel and his like, and reacting with a mixture of embarrassment and compassion at his pompous cries of "I am read and will be read" and "the public has discovered me" when the waters of fame finally began to lap at his feet late in life.[4]

Yet if it is a drama of esteem that lends to Schopenhauer's biography its most emotive theme – causing Schopenhauer-the-individual to irrupt within Schopenhauer-the-philosophical-mirror-of-the-world with a biographical intensity that makes this mirror crack – even more relevant in this context is the way in which that drama appears enacted in the content

[2] See G. E. M. Anscombe, "Modern moral philosophy," *Philosophy*, 33 (1958), and Schopenhauer's discussion in "Criticism of the Basis Given to Ethics by Kant," in *On the Basis of Morality*.
[3] Respectively *PP* II:77 and "Eis Eauton," *Manuscript Remains*, vol. IV, 497.
[4] Schopenhauer, *On the Will in Nature*, 5, 6.

of his philosophy itself. For it is indeed a similar dialectic of honour and dishonour, or pride and humiliation, as I argued earlier, and an intense concern with the humbling experience of human vulnerability – faced, not this time with the social world, but with the world as such – that provides Schopenhauer's philosophy with its most important affective structure. Philosophy takes its beginning from a keen perception of the vulnerability of human beings in the world. And it is a vulnerability that is deeply etched into our being, for it comes to us through the body, which enmeshes us in the world and places us in a passive relation to it. We do not fly over the world like a "winged cherub"; on account of the body we are rather "rooted in that world" (*WWR* I:99). Through the body, desire pounds us; suffering eats away at the body and bores into our defences. Tied to the body, we watch helplessly as the birds of prey begin to circle: the prospect of great suffering, the prospect of death.

It is this sense of vulnerability and the craving for a condition that would transcend it – and in doing so place us in an active relationship to our suffering – to which philosophy seeks to respond; and it responds to it by what I earlier qualified as a double act of representation whose joint effect is to catapult us to a location beyond its reach. "The world is my representation" as the truth of transcendental idealism: the world that formerly terrified us is revealed to be nothing but an epiphenomenon of our (biological) nature; it is not we who depend on the world, but the world that depends on us. "The world is my representation" as a philosophical truth: I have fathomed the world through understanding. This act of cognition then finds its complement in an act of judgement in which the world thus understood is summoned to be judged and categorically rejected. Both acts of representation, I suggested earlier, perform an inversion that it is precisely the notions of pride and humiliation that allow us to characterise most perceptively, marking the transcendence of humiliation in pride, of vulnerability in mastery, and suffering by seeing. I am not in the world; I stand outside it – untouched by its action. In locating this composite philosophical happening in the structure of the sublime, this was the dialectic that bared itself more fully to view.

Yet in doing so, it can now be said, it simultaneously offered us the best handle for approaching this philosophical happening in more critical terms – terms that, bracketing the force of its reason-giving and its rational character, address themselves to these episodes of contracting and rebounding pride in their character as ethical events. This would not be the first time that the proposal to call up an ethical standpoint on intellectual decisions had been put forward, as already noted at the end of the last chapter. Nor would it be the first time this standpoint had been called up on philosophical decisions in particular. It is in fact precisely in connection with one of the central philosophical decisions at stake in Schopenhauer's own work – his transcendental idealism, corresponding to the first act of representation outlined above – that this proposal has been articulated most methodically in recent times.

For there are certain debates, as David Cooper has argued, in which it is doubtful whether the competing positions can be represented as a "straightforward confrontation between philosophical arguments," and in which these positions instead appear to be grounded in more "vital" affective or spiritual concerns; and it is by reference to such concerns that debates of this kind demand to be critiqued and more fruitfully resolved.[5] The debate concerning the relationship of the world to the structures of our thought or language – "Is there a way the world anyway is, irrespective of how we take it to be? Is an articulable world anything but the 'product' or 'construct' of human thought and attitude?" – belongs to this category, given the intensity with which the notion of human dignity is thematised within it. And indeed, as Cooper documents in staking out his proposal to engage this vital notion more programmatically, both sides of the debate have frequently exchanged charges bearing a pronounced ethical character, accusing each other of carrying the "dignity" of humanity to the lengths of arrogance and hubris. The charge of hubris has thus often haunted what Cooper calls the "humanist" decision to read the world in its dependence on human structures of thought or language, and it has attached with particular tenacity to several post-Kantian idealists who have accentuated the godlike nature of the human activity of constructing the world in tones of often ill-concealed exuberance. Fichte would speak of the "full feeling ... of absolute self-sufficiency" that "enables him to 'look down with ... disrespect' on the 'spiritual servitude' of the 'dogmatist' who still requires the crutch of a world separate from that activity." Friedrich Schiller would refer to the "God-like" character of humanity in a similar connection. Later down this ramifying line of philosophical descent, William James would acclaim our "divinely creative functions."[6]

Though the use of religious expressions to convey it might be absent, it is a similar sense of mastery and its accompanying euphoria, I suggested in Chapter 3, that is instinct in Schopenhauer's deployment of the first act of representation, which humbles the world by revealing it in its

---

[5] Cooper, *The Measure of Things*, 14; and see the introductory remarks in ch. 1.
[6] *Ibid.*, 156; and see generally the discussion on 153–60.

dependence on us. Yet it seems to me that it is in the second, composite
act of philosophical representation and judgement that this sense of mastery emerges more potently in ways that allow us to engage it in stronger
ethical terms. For it is here that Schopenhauer's philosophical position
stands out more sharply as one assumed against different possibilities, and
as a decision – to stand outside and exchange the deep enmeshment of
vulnerability for a wholesale withdrawal – that might have been differently taken. The modal horizon of this "might have" needs to be carefully
handled. Yet surely the most obvious way of giving it content is by once
again reviving the concern with rational justification raised in Chapter
4, where it was suggested that this magisterial stance outside – taken as a
representation of the world that is consummated in the judgement that it
ought not to be, and in the claim that the denial of the will to life is the
only appropriate response to it – cannot be given a fully satisfying rational
warrant. The decision to stand outside does not "follow" from the facts.
In establishing the "facts," indeed, the dice have already been loaded. The
cracks in the mirror of rational warrant had there pointed us on to the agi-
tations of Schopenhauer's own character behind it; as also to the tremors
of a predicament that might be more widely shared.

Putting the latter type of tremor aside for the moment, it is to the
former that the present context invites us to return – yet not, this time,
to Schopenhauer's pessimism as an expression of moodiness, anxiety, or
saturnine gloom, but as the expression of a different and rather more
philosophically relevant aspect of Schopenhauer's intellectual character. And to bring this into view, all we need to do is revisit with slightly
closer attention those particular seams in the "facts" that we had earlier
marked in distinguishing between the "surface" and the "deep" accounts
of Schopenhauer's pessimism. For certainly, as suggested in Chapter 4,
Schopenhauer's pessimism may seem to lack warrant if we confine ourselves to the surface level of the phenomena. Matters change, however,
if we confer our assent to Schopenhauer's metaphysical account – that
account which, having turned inward to self-experience and then outward
again to the external world, had raised a flag of philosophical victory and
declared the Kantian thing-in-itself conquered and revealed: it is will. If
philosophy ended up at a magisterial standpoint outside the world, it was
this *terra firma* – no longer *terra incognita* – on which it rested its weight
to find the impetus for its upward leap.

Now just how seriously Schopenhauer had proposed to raise that flag
of victory has been one of the most vexed interpretative questions surrounding his philosophy, and readers have not ceased to contest it. For

Schopenhauer, on the one hand, had made central to his philosophical project the discovery that a "subterranean passage" (*WWR* II:195) exists that allows us to take the castle of the phenomena, handing us the key for unlocking the script of the phenomenal world. And this passage, of course, was the one available to us from within, which reveals the will as the key of our own phenomenon and thus of all others. Yet throughout Schopenhauer's writings there are then numerous notes of caution to be heard calling attention to the limitations of this philosophical achievement. For there are "limits inseparable from our finite nature," Schopenhauer remarks in one passage, which entail that our understanding of the world can never be "conclusive," providing "all further problems" with a satisfactory resolution (*WWR* I:428). "Whatever torch we kindle," Schopenhauer states poignantly elsewhere, "and whatever space it may illuminate, our horizon will always remain encircled by the depth of night." His continuation makes the reason for this plain:

> For the ultimate solution of the riddle of the world would necessarily have to speak merely of things-in-themselves, no longer of phenomena … Therefore the actual, positive solution to the riddle of the world must be something that the human intellect is wholly incapable of grasping and conceiving. (*WWR* II:185)

The "in-itself" is always condemned to be a "for-us"; the relation to the knower can never be abolished. The project to know the thing-in-itself would thus appear to be a contradiction in terms, as Nietzsche would later point out. The thing-in-itself – Schopenhauer would qualify his statement of achievement accordingly – cannot be said to be "absolutely and completely knowable," but is accessible to us "only conditionally." Although it has "to a great extent cast off its veils," it does not appear to us "quite naked" but still partly obscured by the "veil of the forms of perception" (*WWR* II:182, 196–97). For the gaze we turn inward is one that *ipso facto* separates us from whatever our gaze discovers; the space of an in-between in which knowledge is possible renders knowledge impossible. Magee had statements such as these in mind when he remarked that there are passages in Schopenhauer's work that seem to "rule out any interpretation of Schopenhauer to the effect that he taught that we have direct knowledge of the noumenon."[7] Julian Young gave voice to a similar conclusion when

---

[7] Magee, *The Philosophy of Schopenhauer*, 447, and see the whole chapter. These remarks are in great part directed against the view taken by Hamlyn, who criticised Schopenhauer on the assumption that he had argued for the identification of the will as the thing-in-itself – an argument Hamlyn found invalid. See ch. 5 of Hamlyn's *Schopenhauer*, and also his "Schopenhauer on action and the will," in G. Vesey, ed., *Idealism Past and Present* (Cambridge University Press, 1982).

he wrote that Schopenhauer "does not, in fact, claim the world in itself to be will at all. Rather, he agrees with Kant that it is, to the rational mind at least, unknowable."[8]

Yet it is hard to decide how to relate these guarded statements to a rather more expansive set of sounds coexisting in Schopenhauer's work, in which the claim of philosophical success appears to register with far less ambivalence. "The whole phenomenon," Schopenhauer writes elsewhere, "can be deciphered according to its continuity and connexion, and I believe I have succeeded in doing this" (*WWR* II:642). It has been "fully discussed and demonstrated" that if we turn to the phenomenon accessible to us from within "we quite definitely find in this the will as the ultimate thing and the kernel of reality" (*WWR* II:494). And again: "Every glance at the world ... confirms and establishes that the *will-to-live* ... is the only true description of the world's innermost nature" (*WWR* II:350). It is significant, in fact, that even while averring the conditional access we have to the thing-in-itself, Schopenhauer would nevertheless allow himself to conclude in the very same context that "the event thus intimately known is simply and solely calculated to become the interpreter of every other" (*WWR* II:197).

Confronted with such competing sounds, readers may feel duty-bound to hesitate about which ones to privilege.[9] And yet it is important to note that it is the second that Schopenhauer would repeatedly privilege outside his philosophical works when reflecting on his own achievement. It is not the spirit of caution and circumspection, but a very different spirit – the spirit of a numinous, almost messianic occasion – that had breathed through his words as he prepared to compose his major work, when he

---

[8] Young, *Willing and Unwilling*, ix, and also ch. 3. Young's thesis has been heavily criticised; see for example Nicholls' "Schopenhauer, Young, and the Will" – though Nicholls acknowledges the difficulties attaching to the traditional view that Schopenhauer identifies the thing-in-itself as the will. Another critical view is given by Atwell (*Schopenhauer on the Character of the World*, ch. 5), who argues that Schopenhauer never claimed we could attain knowledge of the thing-in-itself apart from its appearance in the phenomenal world. Our knowledge of the thing-in-itself is always of the thing-in-itself-in-appearance, though this does not entail we lack grounds for interpreting the appearing world as being will – and here Atwell's emphasis falls on the distinction between knowledge and interpretation. (Cf. Simmel: we are always "thinking about the absolute within the confines of the relative," *Schopenhauer and Nietzsche*, 25.) Compare Wicks' discussion in ch. 6 of his *Schopenhauer*, which appropriates Schopenhauer's somewhat poetic notion of a "veil" in suggesting that our apprehension of the thing-in-itself is, if not fully transparent, a "translucent" one that "approaches transparency" (79). And see Janaway's careful discussion and survey of existing interpretations, including Young's, in his "Will and nature," esp. 158–65.

[9] One way of settling this issue has been by postulating an intellectual change on Schopenhauer's part; yet see Hübscher, *The Philosophy of Schopenhauer in its Intellectual Context*, 220; cf. Wicks, *Schopenhauer*, 67–69.

had prophesied in biblical tones: "I am blessed with fruit," and anxiously looked to the completion of his term.[10] It was the same sense of ebullient conviction that was present in his tones when writing to his publisher in 1818, when he heralded his philosophy as "a series of thoughts hanging together in the highest degree that up to now has never come into any human head" – thoughts formulated "for the first time ... after thousands of years of philosophising" (*WWR* II:199).[11] And it was a similar tone that would persist years later, asserted all the more emphatically in the face of deepening disappointments vis-à-vis the philosophical world. "Who am I?" he would ask in his private diary. "I am the man who has written the *World as Will and Representation* and has given a solution to the great problem of existence ... I am that man, and what could disturb him in the few years in which he has still to draw breath?"[12] Elsewhere in his diary he would categorically state: I "have solved the problem and have fulfilled my mission."[13]

It is this more expansive conception of achievement, similarly, that would cohere with our understanding of Schopenhauer's intellectual temper, whose acerbic and self-assured edge came into view when considering Schopenhauer's confrontation with the neglect of his contemporaries, in the mixture of sustained invectives and late triumphal cries ("I am read and will be read") that formed the texture of his response. It is a character – the character of a pride progressively made shrill by wounding, and of a self-assurance all the more bombastic for having to assert itself against humiliation – that readers experience throughout Schopenhauer's works, indeed from the very moment Schopenhauer begins to construct us as readers. We are not partners in a conversation but schoolchildren to whom detailed instructions and rules of engagement must be imperiously dictated – "I make the demand," Schopenhauer states, "that whoever wishes to make himself acquainted with my philosophy shall read every line of me" (*WWR* II:461)[14] – and who are often reminded that their dutiful obedience to these instructions is presupposed ("as the reader will recall from my *Ethics*," *PP* II:205). This same character, already expressed in Schopenhauer's grandiose reflections on his achievement above, stands out starkly again on many other occasions. "It was reserved for me to expound the true and only genuine and pure foundation of morality," he

---

[10] Cartwright, *Schopenhauer*, 187.
[11] The first quotation is from Schopenhauer's *Gesammelte Briefe*, quoted in Atwell, *Schopenhauer on the Character of the World*, 1.
[12] Schopenhauer, "Eis Eauton," *Manuscript Remains*, vol. IV, 488.
[13] *Ibid.*, 484.   [14] Cf. the preface to the first edition.

writes in *Parerga and Paralipomena* (II:202). "I know with complete certainty that I have produced the first theory of color, the first in the entire history of science," he has the cheek to say to Goethe when discussing Goethe's own theory of colours; and again: "I know that through me the truth has spoken."[15]

Yet surely one of the clearest signs of the depth and force of Schopenhauer's conviction concerning his philosophical achievement would seem to lie in the consideration that gave us our most recent starting point. For however we might propose to prise apart the "surface" facts from those facts carrying greater metaphysical depth, the assumption that the inner nature of the world has been discovered and the thing-in-itself successfully identified is etched deeply into the fabric of Schopenhauer's pessimistic conclusions – into his understanding of the place of suffering in human life, and his totalistic judgement on the spectacle of existence. And it is on this metaphysical assumption that Schopenhauer's reading of the surface of our experience would ultimately appear to rest. For it may indeed be the case – we may find ourselves surrendering fully to the claim – that life, as Schopenhauer asserts, in fact fails to satisfy us, for all the phenomenological reasons he has enumerated. We may wholeheartedly agree with his declaration of "the emptiness and superficiality of existence" and "life's inadequacy to satisfy the spirit" (*WWR* I:322). Yet between this characterisation of the phenomena and Schopenhauer's proposal for a categorical rejection of the world and wholesale disavowal of existence lies a gulf that is only bridged by deepening a contingent fact into an essential one, converting the prospect of satisfaction into a metaphysical impossibility. It is this deeper modal tone that Schopenhauer presupposes, and that he strikes openly in a remark I have already cited: "no *possible* satisfaction in the world could suffice to still [the will's] craving, set a final goal to its demands, and fill the bottomless pit of its heart" (*WWR* II:573; emphasis added).

It was a statement that I earlier suggested could be heard as a profound expression of spiritual need – of the experience of a need for meaning that surpasses what (we feel or believe) the world can offer, not in quantity, but in intensity and in kind. And heard this way, it allowed us to read Schopenhauer's Archimedean point outside the world as a location of exile, reflecting the spiritual homelessness of one standing in a world newly disenchanted and freshly purged of its gods. Exile, of course, is rarely willingly chosen; and most forms of disenchantment are irreversible

---

[15] Cartwright, *Schopenhauer*, 251–52, 254.

events. Wonder, once lost, cannot easily be retrieved. Yet there is such a thing as we might call a will to wonder, and a will to recover wonder lost. And even homelessness is a condition that can be negotiated in different ways; it is a field in which different choices and ways of responding are possible, which we may call better or worse. It may thus be questioned whether Schopenhauer's decision, having occupied a standpoint outside the whole to survey it – a standpoint grounded in a basic human capacity for transcending the given, whose specific form constitutes a cultivated philosophical possibility, and whose more specific modality reflects a condition and predicament peculiarly modern – whether his decision to retain this position outside – outside suffering, outside vulnerability – was not a decision that could have gone differently. More specifically, it may be wondered whether this decision might not have gone differently if Schopenhauer had not assumed the truth of his vision of the world with such adamantine assurance; if he had shown greater intellectual humility in reading the facts and the phenomena; if he had not closed the door to a redescent by an act of epistemic closure that enshrined the disenchanted world as a certain and essential fact.[16]

Here, it is not, clearly, a matter of holding up Schopenhauer's individual person for moral judgement; had this been our enterprise, our judgement would not have been permitted to proceed without being educated by the insight of compassion, which would place Schopenhauer's pompous self-assurance in relationship to an equally profound sense of anxiety (or indeed self-doubt) palpable in his personal writings. The key question for us is not about correctly interpreting or judging Schopenhauer's character, but rather about deciding what kind of character we would wish to embrace as our own. And this demands recognising in Schopenhauer's philosophical decisions significant temptations to which we ourselves are inescapably exposed, and which derive from the same actuating needs and the same underlying experience of vulnerability with its peculiar possibilities of dramatic resolution.

For the resolution that will no doubt most strongly tempt us is one that places us most decisively beyond it; and in this respect, even an epistemic closure whose content is terrible to confront may seem more

---

[16] Kant's contrasting refusal to cross the boundary into the noumenal and his adherence to the position that we lack knowledge of things-in-themselves has in fact been characterised precisely in such ethical terms: see Rae Langton, *Kantian Humility: Our Ignorance of Things in Themselves* (Oxford: Clarendon Press, 1998). Cf. Nietzsche's related charge of hubris – whose shrapnel, in this and later formulations, hits Schopenhauer's philosophy directly – cited in Cooper, *The Measure of Things*, 159.

tolerable than a decision against closure that leaves us – in the words of Mary-Jane Rubenstein (expounding Heidegger, retrieving Plato) – in the "open sea of endless questioning" and the "frightful indeterminacy" of *aporia* with all the vulnerability this involves.[17] Yet one might instead accept that such closure has not been reached; that given our inherent epistemic limitations, it is indeed unlikely to be reached. And to accept this, to disavow the pretense of epistemic mastery in this manner, will be to rediscover oneself standing at an "outside" that is an open sea instead of a stable point from which, even if at the sacrifice of true location, upheaval can be masterfully and calmly surveyed without affecting its representing subject. Yet having retrieved, through such an act of intellectual humility, the vertigo that Schopenhauer's standpoint had after all never fully expunged, this outside space will have opened up more fully to present itself as a field of uncertainty in which different ways of responding might be possible. And as a field, moreover, in which one could directly raise again the question – broached at the end of the last chapter, when inquiring about the relevance of "greatness of soul" as a language of critique – concerning the possibility of redescent. For acknowledging the open sea within this standpoint will involve reattuning ourselves to that aspect of Schopenhauer's standpoint that we can recognise all too well as an expression of our own predicament – its aspect as a forced ascent produced by the weightless conditions of evaluative dissolution, launching one outside the ordinary world to leave one spinning vertiginously in the absence of a thicker *telos* that might pull one back to the ground with the force of a positive aspiration. In air as thin as this, how might it be possible to envisage a redescent? And what might it mean for the language available to us for ethical critique?

Greatness of soul and the quest for the good

There have been many efforts, to be sure, to imagine or sketch out such a project of redescent, nearly as many as the voices that have concurred in naming the crisis of meaning as the spiritual predicament of modernity. Yet one of the richest, in my view, and the one in which I propose to locate the resources for my own argument, is the one developed by Alasdair

---

[17] Rubenstein, *Strange Wonder*, 5, 7; the remarks come in the context of a critique of wonder – including, most relevantly, the strain of wonder represented by the sublime – in which the dialectic between vulnerability and mastery forms a central theme. My line of thinking is indebted to Rubenstein's luminous discussion in several ways, though I am unsure that she would agree with its full development.

MacIntyre in *After Virtue*, which, as indicated earlier, situates itself precisely against this sense of evaluative breakdown. The double objective of MacIntyre's work lies in offering a diagnosis of this crisis and a documentation of its history; and having done so, in articulating a way out, or way down. It is a way down that presents itself as a self-conscious rejuvenation of the ethical legacy of ancient philosophy, reviving both the ancient concern with the virtues, and the teleological underpinning through which these had been understood in the ancient context. Among the constitutive elements of MacIntyre's proposal is the claim that it is human life as a whole, as against individual actions, that we must relearn to address as the locus of ethical concern; and the related claim that it is through its *telos* that a given life achieves its unity, and more specifically its narrative unity as a story with beginning, middle, and end.

Reflecting the complexity of this teleological horizon, MacIntyre's justification of the virtues turns out to unfold on two separate levels, one more local and one more global in kind. For on the one hand, the virtues stand to be defended with reference to their role in "practices," defined as co-operative activities governed by specific standards of excellence and conceptions of their internal goods, and paradigmatically including artistic activities, scientific and philosophical inquiries, and the development and maintenance of communities. The virtues – notably the virtues of courage, justice, and honesty, on which MacIntyre focuses – are in the first instance those qualities of character that allow us to achieve the internal goods of these practices. And the most significant way in which they do so, as I take it, is by regulating the relationship between those who possess authority in particular practices and those still striving to master them. For we need *justice* to recognise authority ("what is due to whom"); we need *courage* in order to be prepared to take the "self-endangering" risks demanded of us; we need *honesty* to recognise where we stand in these practices and to acknowledge the shortcomings and inadequacies to which authoritative practitioners call our attention.[18] These virtues, in turn, come under a similar demand in relating to the history of practices and engaging the authority of their traditions – this being an engagement, significantly, that involves not merely passive subordination to these traditions, but active effort to revise and extend the conceptions of ends and goods at stake in them. For living traditions, as MacIntyre emphasises, when in good health, "embody continuities of

---

[18] See MacIntyre, *After Virtue*, ch. 14, especially 191ff.

conflict," and are constituted by "an argument precisely in part about the goods which constitute" them.[19]

This justification of the virtues, however, stands to be grounded in a larger horizon. And it is this larger justification that forms the centrepiece in the architecture of MacIntyre's overall argument, and the nucleus of his positive proposal for a redescent – one that would draw us out of the open sea towards a new location characterised by greater closure and stability. For if the virtues are necessary for realising the internal goods of particular practices, they play an equally crucial role in the realisation of the good to which human life as a whole is directed, and from which it derives its narrative unity. Yet what, now, is that good? What *is* that *telos* that can organise and orient our life through the magnetic effects of a positive aspiration? The unity of a human life, it turns out, is given by a question that looks to two closely related directions. It is a question, on the one hand, about my good as an individual: "What is the good for me?" Yet this question is framed by another: "What is the good for man?" It is then "the systematic asking of these two questions and the attempt to answer them in deed as well as in word," MacIntyre proposes, "which provide the moral life with its unity."[20]

The unity of a human life, accordingly, turns out to be "the unity of a narrative quest." Forming the heart of MacIntyre's account, in fact, is a conception of the good life understood as a *quest* for the good life, expressed epigrammatically in his formulation: "the good life for man is the life spent in seeking for the good life for man." And it is this conception that then provides the virtues with their ultimate foothold. For quests meet obstacles; the difficulties we encounter tempt us to abandon our pursuit. In confronting these difficulties our self-understanding and understanding of our aims can be developed and refined, if only we persevere in our efforts. The virtues, thus, are

> to be understood as those dispositions which will not only sustain practices and enable us to achieve the goods internal to practices, but which will also sustain us in the relevant kind of quest for the good, by enabling us to overcome the harms, dangers, temptations and distractions which we encounter, and which will furnish us with increasing self-knowledge and increasing knowledge of the good.[21]

And our pursuit of this larger quest, like our pursuit of particular practices, needs to be understood as one fundamentally bounded by tradition.

---

[19] *Ibid.*, 222.   [20] *Ibid.*, 218–19.   [21] *Ibid.*, 219.

For such a quest does not occur in a void; it is an activity that takes place in the context of particular practices with particular traditions. Of this, the quest for the good represented by philosophical inquiry provides the most brilliant example. MacIntyre's own project, indeed, can be read precisely within these terms: as a quest for the good pursued through critical dialogue with the ancient philosophical tradition, which appropriates by criticising and revitalises by revising.

It is a proposal whose vulnerabilities are closely bound up with the sources of its richness, which concern the balance in which openness and closure are held within it. For if we were looking for a specification of the *telos* that would allow us to replace placelessness with place, and vertiginous spin with regulated motion, the account of the human *telos* that MacIntyre has offered us would only appear to achieve this to a limited degree. In many respects – and without disregarding many of MacIntyre's important specifications, including his insistence on locating this quest within existing practices, bearing particular histories, and expressing particular traditions – it is only a placeholder, not a place, a thin and formal blueprint, not a thick and substantive specification. Yet it is precisely this openness, in my view, that makes for its richness and its most powerful appeal. In particular, it is the openness characterising that end to which we must direct our striving even as it remains a not-yet-known, lending our lives a motion that one naturally reaches for the Platonic notion of *eros* to describe, and unifying them through the magnetic effect of an aspiration the precise content of whose potential realisation eludes us, yet whose substantiveness is attested by the fact that a life governed by such aspiration is different from one that is not. And it differs most strongly in what it dares to hope, and to desire, as a difficult yet possible good: the possibility that this aspiration might be realised, illuminating one's desire with an understanding of what it had taken as its object.

It is in this horizon, I would suggest – the horizon of a good understood as a quest, and carrying the openness of a fundamental epistemic uncertainty – that we can find the resources for responding to Schopenhauer's standpoint and its ethical commendation in the most constructive terms. It is a standpoint, I argued in the last chapter, that invites itself to be ranged with one receiving wide expression in ancient philosophy, where the privilege attaching to notions of altitude and ascent had been enshrined in more or less programmatic ways within imaginaries of flight and practices of cosmic journeying that projected the philosopher into cosmic vistas and infinite expanses. Yet in returning to this broad ancient standpoint with MacIntyre's account in view, it will not be difficult to recognise it as one firmly situated in, and indeed carrying forward, the kind of philosophical inquiries about the good that MacIntyre has in mind, forming a tradition in which a modern resumption of this quest could hope to find its bearings. The cosmic standpoint, as we saw, constituted a location deeply transformative in kind – transforming one's identity, one's vision, and most significantly, one's evaluative vision. The space opened up by the cosmic standpoint was one located within the larger questing horizon that MacIntyre points to. In tying it to the virtue of greatness of soul – with its heightened moral aspiration and ideals of transcendence – the ethical character of this space stood out even more clearly to view.

One calls this space "questing"; yet at the same time, modern readers may feel that this was a space in which what had been presumed found outweighed what was still being sought, in which answers outnumbered questions, and in which certainty and not uncertainty determined the overall pitch – and what uncertainty existed was not the vertiginous spin that is our own. The view from above was not a view from nowhere; it had to await the kinds of transformations MacIntyre and others have plotted before it could become the latter. One's ascent to this transformative space, indeed, manifestly took place in many cases (notably among the Stoics) against the backdrop of existing answers to the quest for the good life for man and substantive views as to how life should be lived – hence the fact that this ascent could be purposefully cultivated as a "spiritual exercise."

With Schopenhauer – and with us as heirs of the same history – matters are otherwise. Hence, I suggested in the last chapter, the different type of character that finds expression in each standpoint. For the ancient philosophers, the cosmic standpoint expressed a sense of human grandeur closely connected to the boldness to claim, to desire, to aspire to what is great. Schopenhauer's standpoint, by contrast, was shaped by a character that had withdrawn his claims from the world and no longer enjoyed the licence to a desire so unbounded in kind. This was a character that had been humbled by life and mortified by suffering, suffering read in the light of a disenchanted universe. And that is to say: read no longer as a sign, or only as a sign that points back to itself, that has ceased to have real signification, for it only points to its own necessity. Thus humbled, one dares to desire only "things necessary for life," or "commensurate with life" – realistic. The possibility that the quest for the good life could find a satisfying fulfilment is neither commensurate nor realistic. It is too "great"; for there is nothing great any longer, neither in the heavens nor on earth. Hence my concluding question: how could a failure of *megalopsychia* come up for critique? Can the terms of ancient ethical critique – with their presupposition of positive aspiration, and thus redescent, as a possibility – be our own?

Yet if we are willing to take on MacIntyre's proposal as schematised above, a way of responding to such questions has become available to us, though it requires extending this proposal in a new direction – or indeed: rejuvenating an old direction, and existing tradition, to revise and appropriate it. I described this as a proposal precisely designed to open the way for a form of redescent, and to supply us with a description of our end that could constitute the object of positive aspiration. It may appear thin – a *telos* defined as a quest for itself – yet the life it spells out is already thicker than what Schopenhauer, and what we as joint heirs, would be disposed to envisage. For the audacity to engage in this quest with a desire and hope for its fulfilment registers the double claim that something great is not only worth striving for, but also capable of being achieved. I speak of a thicker life; yet it seems to me that what this line of thinking has discovered is that particular element of the good life that consists in the virtues; and what we have named is simply one – possibly the most fundamental – virtue necessary for sustaining us in the quest for the good on MacIntyre's terms, and for overcoming the "harms, dangers, temptations and distractions" that this quest encounters.

For one such temptation, as suggested above, is a type of intellectual pride that reflects a deeper intolerance of vulnerability, and that prefers closure to uncertainty, even the closure of an unpalatable truth to an openness that might – or might not – lead to truths potentially more satisfying to human needs and sentiments. Humility, thus, would certainly have to find its way into our understanding of the virtues which the quest requires to be sustained, preventing us from seeking closure too quickly, and determining too confidently the "reality" that makes desires, including the desire for the fulfilment of this quest, appear too "great" and "unrealistic." Yet once this exercise of humility has allowed the epistemic space to be wedged sufficiently open, there is then a different kind of temptation – reflecting yet another encounter with vulnerability – to be faced off; and a different virtue to act as its corrective.

For as Philippa Foot has pointed out, the virtues need to be seen as essentially "*corrective*, each one standing at a point at which there is some temptation to be resisted or deficiency of motivation to be made good."[22]

---

[22] Philippa Foot, *Virtues and Vices* (Berkeley and Los Angeles: University of California Press, 1978), 8. Compare Nussbaum's related remark: "the question about virtue usually arises in areas in which human choice is both non-optional and somewhat problematic" ("Non-relative virtues," 37).

Thus, "it is only because fear and the desire for pleasure often operate as temptations that courage and temperance exist as virtues at all," and "if human nature had been different there would have been no need of a corrective disposition in either place." Foot continues:

> As with courage and temperance so with many other virtues: there is, for instance, a virtue of industriousness only because idleness is a temptation; and of humility only because men tend to think too well of themselves. Hope is a virtue because despair too is a temptation; it might have been that no one cried that all was lost except where he could really see it to be so, and in this case there would have been no virtue of hope.[23]

It is precisely where the facts are unclear, as this remark suggests – where the epistemic field lies open to different possibilities – that the field lies open for different ethical responses, including the temptation to close it up by succumbing to despair.

Given the intimate relationship between hope and vulnerability, the temptation should not seem surprising. Writing on the emotions, Wittgenstein would suggest that hope stands to be distinguished from other emotions, demanding that we handle it differently on important levels. For hope seems to lack the natural expression through which other emotions receive their embodiment (we do not see hope in the face as we see anger, or joy, or fear), and the criteria for predicating it are more complex, extending over time through longer patterns of action and involving deeper forms of linguistic conditioning. "One can imagine an animal angry, fearful, sad, joyful, startled. But hopeful? And why not?" Wittgenstein's answer – albeit one requiring additional work to be fully unpacked – would be partly given in the ensuing remark. "Can only those hope who can talk? Only those who have mastered the use of a language. That is to say, the manifestations of hope are modifications of the complicated form of life."[24]

And yet if hope stands apart from other emotions in several respects, it would seem to be united with them in incorporating the vulnerability that typifies the emotions, in so far as they express an ascription of value to entities and outcomes belonging to an external domain that lies outside one's control and can never be fully secure.[25] It was a vulnerability

---

[23] Foot, *Virtues and Vices*, 9.

[24] Ludwig Wittgenstein, *Philosophy of Psychology – A Fragment*, in *Philosophical Investigations*, §1; and see the index under "hope" for other passages (esp. *Philosophy of Psychology – A Fragment*, §§77–78) that enable this remark to be somewhat, if not entirely, unpacked.

[25] For a clear articulation of the emotions in these ("neo-Stoic") terms, see Martha Nussbaum, *Upheavals of Thought: The Intelligence of Emotions* (Cambridge University Press, 2001).

that Schopenhauer was well aware of when he linked hope to desire, and dismissed it disdainfully as a "fairy tale" the mind tells to the will on command, to pacify it when the object of its desire is in reality out of reach by making this object seem "probable and near."[26] Many ancient philosophers would have concurred, according to Nussbaum, who remarks that "the connection between hope (*elpis*) and human deficiency is a traditional motif in Greek reflection about the human condition."[27] And it is perhaps the passage of Aristotle's *Rhetoric* we considered earlier (2.12–13), limning the character of the young and the old, that made the deeper texture of this vulnerability most clearly palpable. For if the old do not hope, Aristotle had suggested, it is because life has "humbled" them through the repeated disappointments it has dealt to their hopes. It is thus one's sense of dignity, this reveals, that is at stake in the decision to withhold hope and desire from the world, retreating to an inner citadel that may not be capacious, but is at least secure against further diminution. To continue to hope would be to retain the vulnerability of potentially ever-renewed humiliation.

Yet Aristotle's own discussion had contained important resources for approaching these reactions more critically. And it is to these resources that we here do best to look in order to engage hope and despair in ethical terms, and more specifically as possibilities that plot a field whose negotiation allows particular strengths and flaws of character to be expressed. For the notion of hope had appeared in this discussion as a key motif, along with the notions of trust and aspiration; it was indeed the confidence of hope that had given Aristotle's portrait of the young its luminous texture. In Aristotle's remarks, the capacity to hope had been connected with the virtue of courage; yet also, significantly, with greatness of soul. And it is precisely the virtue of greatness of soul, I would suggest at this point, that offers itself as the most illuminating way of specifying the particular strength of character which the quest for the good requires as a corrective if the temptations produced by its very openness are to be withstood, supplying it with the daring to aspire to its own fulfilment as a difficult yet not unattainable good. To articulate greatness of soul in this capacity, however, involves an appropriation of an ethical tradition that, as MacIntyre would also have it, must proceed by way of a dialogue with this tradition that is also partly argument and critique.

---

[26] See the remarks in *WWR* II:216–17; cf. the remark concerning the falsifying effects of hope in *WWR* II:141, and the important reference to hope at the close of the first volume of his work, *WWR* I:411.

[27] Nussbaum, *Fragility of Goodness*, 461, n.37.

For as even the most enthusiastic admirers of the ancient ethical tradition would concede, the virtue of greatness of soul is an element of this tradition that has proved rebarbative to the modern temper, and it is no accident that the recent surge of philosophical interest in the virtues has almost entirely passed it by. Where greatness of soul has been singled out for attention, it has often been to expose it to scathing criticism. Aristotle's portrait of the great-souled man in the *Nicomachean Ethics*, in particular, has often been castigated as the morally repulsive image of supine, ungrateful, arrogant self-satisfaction. It is a virtue, in one view, that failed to leave its heroic genealogy sufficiently behind, remaining a "privileged virtue" that constitutes the "preserve of those who have the wealth and political position to gain great honour and public recognition for their service," and that is to be counted among the "holdovers from an age of Homeric heroism that lay too much emphasis on the lottery of natural and social endowments."[28] Efforts have indeed been made to "defend" greatness of soul against its detractors, but these efforts, in my view, have fallen short of a positive defence of the virtue that might give us reasons to think we should aspire to recover it and cultivate it as our own.[29]

Yet such a recovery could not be accomplished without taking into account that this was a virtue that had formed part of a living tradition in which it had already traced out a pathway of internal dialogue and critique. If we were interested, thus, in an account of greatness of soul that would be responsive to the persistent charge of arrogance levelled against Aristotle's portrait, we could hardly do better than look to the work of Aquinas, who had preoccupied himself directly with an effort to reconcile greatness of soul with the rather different imperatives contained in the Christian ideal of humility. Aquinas would partly achieve this reconciliation, as David Horner has suggested, by introducing the notion of basic respect for all human beings – even while retaining the notion of a differential respect dependent on moral worth – as well as by relativising human worth by considering what is great in a person under its aspect as a given, and more specifically as a gift of God. At the same time, Aquinas would make a typically Aristotelian bid for the middle ground by

---

[28] Nancy Sherman, "Common sense and uncommon virtue," *Midwest Studies in Philosophy*, 13 (1988), 103. For an overview of some of the most oft-made criticisms, see Crisp, "Aristotle on greatness of soul."

[29] I have in mind, for example, Howard J. Curzer's discussion in "Aristotle's much-maligned *megalopsychos*," *Australasian Journal of Philosophy*, 69 (1991), and Pakaluk's in "The meaning of Aristotelian magnanimity" (see especially the concluding remarks, 272–75); compare also the sketch of a reconstructive proposal in Cooper, "Aristotle's crowning virtue," 200–5.

twinning greatness of soul to humility, taking the former as a disposition to regard oneself under the aspect of one's powers or strengths – now read, in turn, as givens or gifts – and the latter as a counterbalancing disposition to regard oneself under the aspect of one's deficiencies.[30]

In this moderating stance, we can see the tradition of the virtues engaged in a process of self-revision, waging a substantive debate as to how this virtue should be specified and where the right attitude lies with regard to honour, or to what Nussbaum calls the "grounding experience" of "attitudes and actions with respect to one's own worth" which greatness of soul proposed to regulate.[31] Yet if Aquinas would take the tradition forward through this proposal, he would do so equally through another, when, pulling together notions that had already been present in the ancient tradition, he would forge a clearer connection between greatness of soul and the passion of hope and cement it through a stronger analysis. It is hope, in Aquinas' account, that forms the immediate object of greatness of soul and the passion that this virtue is responsible for regulating, the way that courage seeks to regulate fear. If greatness of soul is concerned with honour, in fact, this is only "mediately," that is, as the object to which one's hope is directed.[32]

Aquinas would describe greatness of soul as a "stretching forth of the mind to great things." It is a movement of stretching or dilating that would in turn be replicated in his understanding of the passion of hope, which Aquinas would characterise as a passion in the fullest and most full-blooded sense of this word – as a surging or foaming of the blood – one that brings a leap of the soul, an exalting upward swell (*erectio animi*, *elevatio animi*), as it stretches out to seize the great object of aspiration.

---

[30] See Horner, "Aristotle and Aquinas on magnanimity," 433–35. See also the discussion of Aquinas' account in Gauthier, *Magnanimité*, part 1, ch. 5, and part 3, ch. 4, and Jaffa, *Thomism and Aristotelianism*, ch. 6. Aquinas' relevant remarks can be found in *Summa Theologiae*, IIaIIae, q. 129.

[31] Nussbaum, "Non-relative virtues," 35.

[32] *Summa Theologiae*, IIaIIae, q. 129, a. 1 and 2. Hence Horner's description of greatness of soul as "hope management" ("Aristotle and Aquinas on magnanimity," 431). As Horner's discussion reveals, however, there are other important revisions afoot in Aquinas' account, such as the remarkable broadening of the first term of the matrix (the basis of the great-souled man's claims) to include not only virtue but a larger range of capacities and powers that constitute *natural* endowments, and the broadening of the second term (the content of the great-souled man's claims) to include more strongly not only external goods but actions that utilise these capacities. By the end of these transformations, greatness of soul has opened up so far that it has become tantamount to a virtue of self-fulfilment or self-realisation: a capacity to recognise one's specific abilities and cultivate them confidently in fulfilment of one's calling. Cf. Gauthier's remark about greatness of soul as defining a "*style of life*, a personalist style of life, wholly devoted to the flowering of the human personality" (*Magnanimité*, 370).

R. A. Gauthier speaks here of an expansion, a "flight."[33] These notions –
along with the affective tone of an intoxication that Gauthier suggests we
read into them – will certainly carry powerful resonance. It will be hard,
in this connection, not to think of the later articulation of the sublime
with its characteristic affective tonality. And the resonance will be carried again by the next element in Aquinas' structure: for if the soul must
leap in hope, if it must push upwards, it is because there is something
that presents resistance and demands to be overcome. For hope, on the
one hand, is directed to an object under its aspect as a good, and thus as
an object of desire. Yet it is also directed to it more specifically under its
aspect as an elevated, an extraordinary good, a great good whose grandeur
renders it arduous to attain, and requires that it be an object of conquest.
The full characterisation of the object of hope is that of a future good that
is great and difficult yet possible to attain.[34]

Aristotle's account of greatness of soul is thus revised in at least two
related ways, modifying its disposition to arrogance through a new ideal
of humility, and modifying the strong notion of claim or entitlement at
work in it – Aristotle's great-souled man, we will recall, had looked to
the external good of honour as his *due* – through a more aspiring and
less possessive notion of hope.[35] It is against such a richer specification
of greatness of soul that a more persuasive argument could be made for
its recovery, and more particularly, for its recovery as a virtue necessary
for overcoming the peculiar temptations of despair to which a quest for
the good as something not-yet-known – as something that we are at a
loss to know how we might know, and what it might reveal about ourselves and our desires once known; something as great as it seems difficult – is inescapably exposed. It is this virtue, accordingly, as Aquinas'
remarks provide the seeds for suggesting, that might allow the sublime
to complete its life cycle – as Schopenhauer's failed to – launching a

---

[33] Gauthier, *Magnanimité*, 332–34. Note the explicit resumption of the notion of "stretching out" in
Aquinas' discussion of hope and his discussion of greatness of soul: hope is characterised as "a certain stretching out of the appetite towards good" (*Summa Theologiae*, IaIIae, q. 40, a. 2); greatness
of soul as a "stretching forth of the mind to great things" (IIaIIae, q. 129, a. 1).

[34] See the discussion in *Summa Theologiae*, IaIIae, q. 40.

[35] Pakaluk's translation of the relevant passage of the *Nicomachean Ethics* brings out this notion of
entitlement particularly strongly: a great-souled man is one who "claims great things for himself, as
rightfully his, *when they are rightfully his*" (1123b1–5; "The meaning of Aristotelian magnanimity,"
248). Aquinas' change of cadence, at the same time, would seem to be strongly connected to the
additional revisions adumbrated in note 32, particularly the broadening of the second term of the
matrix.

movement of upward expansion that could then be metabolised as a return to *terra firma*.[36]

Yet having specified greatness of soul as a virtue that regulates the attitudes of hope and despair, there will be an immediate question to raise concerning the rational justification that such attitudes admit and demand. Indeed, given this analysis, as Gauthier has suggested, to study greatness of soul comes down to nothing less than "asking what is the rational way to hope."[37] One way in which hope can fail to be rational, as Gauthier points out, is by directing itself to an object that appears to be great yet in fact is not. Another way, more relevant in this context, is by failing to direct itself to a good that is possible to achieve. For if a great and difficult good requires a leap like that of hope to be pursued, the strenuousness of this leap will make one exact stronger prior assurances concerning its wisdom or reason, and more specifically its chances of success. If hope exposes us to vulnerability by investing us in a good whose realisation lies outside our control, what rational justification – we may ask – could be given for this vulnerability to be contracted?[38]

To this, one answer might be: none greater, and none lesser, than the justification to contract any vulnerability, namely, the value of what we make ourselves vulnerable to, and our awareness of the impoverished lives we would lead in its absence. This point, indeed, has formed the content of one the most compelling ways of responding to the Stoic disavowal of the passions and their entailed vulnerability. In this instance, the case could be made more strongly still. For if our lives would be impoverished without love for particular persons, whose fragility exposes us inescapably to the grief of loss, or if our lives would be diminished without the aspiration for complex achievements, whose temporal structure makes them vulnerable to frustration, our attachment to a quest for the good would seem to have an even more fundamental connection to our lives. Taken as reflective creatures capable of considering their actual lives with detachment, whose

---

[36] How such a virtue term – in all its extraordinary and almost improbable grandeur – could then be assimilated into our language as an element of our living ethical vocabulary forms a separate question, which the line of thinking developed in my "Educating virtue as a mastery of language," *Journal of Ethics*, 6 (2012), has hopefully provided some of the resources for addressing.

[37] Gauthier, *Magnanimité*, 346.

[38] Taken in the reverse direction, this a question that Schopenhauer invites directly when discussing the most common way of attaining denial of the will – through the experience of great suffering, which often "produces complete resignation" (*WWR* I:392). Yet talk of "production" should not obscure the fact that such resignation, taken as a capitulation of hope, is produced not by causes but by reasons. And then one might ask: what rational justification could be given for the abandonment of hope?

capacity for such reflective transcendence is tied to an inherent need, as David Cooper has recently put it, for holding their lives answerable to a "measure" – Cooper adds: a measure "beyond the human" – the need to search for such a measure would seem to be internal to who we are.[39]

Yet even if we take this view, it will be important to make an attempt to engage the notion of "possibility" at stake more directly. I take Jonathan Lear to have undertaken such an attempt in his recent work, *Radical Hope*, which locates itself in a horizon that we may recognise as MacIntyre's and our own, to investigate how ethics might be possible in the face of cultural collapse – the collapse of a form of life and its social and evaluative structures that catapults us to a place outside where a thick vision of the good life needs to be freshly achieved. Lear places a particular instance of such collapse – the one experienced by the Native American community of the Crow – at the centre of his discussion. Yet the predicament of the Crow is intended to serve as an image of our broader present, and of a "time when the sense of purpose and meaning that has been bequeathed to us by our culture has collapsed." And Lear's aim is then precisely to establish "what *we* might legitimately hope" in such a time, and to ask "what would it be for such hope to be justified?"[40]

The predicament of the Crow, it must be said, contains significant tensions taken as a paradigm that would accommodate our own, for the pronounced spiritual elements that shape the Crow outlook – above all, their belief in an orderly universe governed by a single god, in which human beings occupy a meaningful place – play an important role in Lear's account of the Crow confrontation of this cultural collapse, and more specifically, in grounding their hopes for a reorientation. For it is, Lear suggests, a "commitment to God's transcendence and goodness" that underlies the defining affirmation that "something good will emerge even if it outstrips my present limited capacity for understanding what that good is."[41] Yet it is clearly Lear's intention to ascribe a broader relevance and reach to this insight, and to accentuate its availability to secular no less than religious readers.

> We do not have to agree with Plato that there is a transcendent source of goodness – that is, a source of goodness that transcends the world – to think that the goodness *of the world* transcends our finite powers to grasp it. The emphasis here is not on some mysterious source of goodness, but on the limited nature of our finite conceptual resources. This, I think

---

[39] See Cooper, *The Measure of Things*, ch. 10.
[40] Lear, *Radical Hope*, 104, 103.   [41] *Ibid.*, 94.

most readers will agree, is an *appropriate* response for finite creatures like ourselves. Indeed, it seems oddly inappropriate – lacking in understanding of oneself as a finite creature – to think that what is good about the world is exhausted by our current understanding of it.[42]

It is thus in an imperative of humility, as this remark suggests, that Lear proposes to ground the hope for a reorientation around a fresh conception of the good. Yet this ethical justification of hope can be seen to reflect another, which is more immediately directed to its intentional content. For to say that what is good about the world is not exhausted by our current understanding is to say that we do not possess sufficient rational grounds for determining what (good) is or is not possible. Hope will then be justified so long as the impossibility of its satisfaction has not been shown; and given our finite epistemic capacities, it is difficult to envisage how this might ever happen.

This way of developing the notion of "possibility" may seem too negative. Aristotle, on his part, had made more positive demands when he had discussed the twofold relationship in which hope stands to the notion of experience. For hope can often be grounded in a *lack* of experience – as it is in young people, whose capacity to hope has not yet been dented by the experience of danger or failure.[43] We might prefer to call this negative ground a "cause" of hope, not a "reason." It is the presence of positive experience, by contrast, that supplies us with what we may more properly call reasons for hope, as when through experience we acquire skills that give us the confidence that we can pull through the difficulty we are currently confronting. Sailors who have faced off storms before and soldiers seasoned in battle possess a confidence supported by experience in this way.[44] Hope, in these terms, will be justified by being based on a belief about our own skills that is based on past experience: we have faced this situation before and know how to handle it. It is thus primarily with reference to our own capacities and powers that hope will receive its justification.

Yet what if the situation being faced was totally new, or new in important respects? The quest for the good, it may be relevantly remarked, has

---

[42] *Ibid.*, 121–22.   [43] *Rhetoric*, 2.12.8.

[44] See the remarks in *Rhetoric*, 2.5.18; Aristotle is referring more specifically to confidence in this context, yet confidence and hope are closely connected in his discussion. See also Gauthier's remarks in connection with Aquinas' development of this point in *Magnanimité*, 327–28. Aquinas in fact distinguishes between two ways in which experience may produce hope: by increasing one's powers, and thus by *making* new things possible, and by increasing one's understanding of what is possible – *Summa Theologiae*, IaIIae, q. 40, a. 5.

been pursued successfully before, but never in the circumstances that are our own, and not as a quest for meaning so totalistic in kind. What this may now call attention to, however, is the peculiar status of the notion of possibility within the attitude of hope, and the singular relationship in which hope must stand to demands of rational justification. Gauthier draws our finger towards this precise issue when, discussing the constraint of possibility, he raises the question whether one might not thereby be led "to set up for oneself an ideal in one's measure, to only seek out a grandeur that fits one's frame [*à sa taille*]" – to end up pursuing, thus, not grandeur, but *mediocrity*.[45] Gauthier's own understanding of this question moves in a different direction; yet the most fruitful way of hearing his question, in my view, is by wondering how, if our judgements of possibility are to be based on a measure of our abilities taken from past experience and conclusively established by it, we could aspire to a future achievement that surpasses and transcends this measure. One might frame the point more broadly and with only an appearance of paradox by saying: if hope was fully justified, hope would not be needed. It is after all precisely the absence of certainty that creates the demand for hope as a strength of character that can enable us to overcome the temptations uncertainty produces. Hope cannot simply follow what has already been proven to be possible; indeed, it rather seeks to extend it. A leap that transcends experience – and the understanding of possibility it sustains – is internal to hope.

Having questioned the very possibility of a "grounding" of hope, what I will propose instead is something that falls short of a grounding, and at most can be offered as a template of self-understanding. And in sketching it out, it will finally be possible for me to state in rather clearer terms how I think Schopenhauer's standpoint may be critically engaged in a mode that constitutes an appropriation. For turning back to our earlier analysis of greatness of soul, we may recall that a movement of justification or grounding had in fact formed a central part of its matrix. In Aristotle's account, I suggested in the last chapter, greatness of soul could be analysed in terms of a pattern of interconnected correspondences: a correspondence between one's judgement of one's worth and one's true worth; and another correspondence between one's true worth and the response of the external world. What one is; what one thinks one is; what the world offers in response to what one is. It was the awareness of certain features of oneself that formed the basis of the expectation that one directed towards

---

[45] Gauthier, *Magnanimité*, 351.

the world. Greatness of soul, thus, was a virtue that presented itself at least in part as a virtue of self-knowledge. And if Aristotle had specified this in predominantly ethical terms, other ancient philosophers had understood the moment of self-knowledge more broadly – as an apprehension of oneself under the aspect of a capacity for transcendence that expressed itself in both the ethical and the intellectual sphere. It was this capacity that was manifested when the philosophical mind swept through the infinite universe and scaled the heavens in moments of vertiginous ascent. And this capacity, in turn, revealed the divinity constituting one's truer nature.

Yet it is now important to note that it was precisely the practice of soaring and scaling – the occupation of the broad standpoint I have called a cosmic view *sub specie aeternitatis* – that afforded the means, or one of the means, by which this self-knowledge was attained. And how – to ask, or ask again – did one come to occupy this standpoint? How did one *learn* to do so? To this question one might respond simply by saying: by reading about the primordial flight of the soul in the *Phaedrus*; by following the transformative dialogical process of philosophy, with its visionary stopping places and its education of the gaze; by responding to Marcus' invitations to the imagination to soar, and sweeping through the vastness of a universe that begins from the end of his pointing finger; by allowing oneself to gaze, with Cicero, upwards until the "upwards" became an "around." And similarly: by responding to the visionary evocations of the cosmic vantage point offered to us by Schopenhauer and allowing ourselves to absorb it in its full aesthetic power; by responding to his invitations to imagine the totality of beings as an oscillating pyramid, the succession of beings as a continuous vibration, or a rainbow, or a string of pearls – by becoming, in short, the kind of reader that Schopenhauer conjures for himself through his narrative acts.

It is through the practised occupation of this standpoint that we are revealed in our character as beings capable of occupying this standpoint; as beings capable of a basic form of transcendence that in this standpoint achieves merely a more cultivated and programmatic form. And this, simply, is the basic transcendence that consists in the act of representing and remarking, which picks out being against the possibility of its non-being, and achieves its highest expression in the capacity – once again enshrined in and enshrining philosophical practice – to be astonished at the being of the world and our own. For we might, as Schopenhauer notes, have been "incapable of thinking anything else than that the world is, and is as it is"; yet the facts are otherwise, as this statement reveals in its very possibility. The world and our own existence within it in fact present "themselves to us as surprising, remarkable, problematical" (*WWR* II:170–71). It is an act of remarking, as Schopenhauer's last qualification suggests, that must be partly situated against an act of desiring to be adequately grasped in its character. For if we possess the eyes that allow us to remark the realities present before us, it is often because of the way these realities cause us to suffer and fail to satisfy, stimulating a powerful desire that these realities might be transcended to something better – to something "incommensurate with life," in Aristotle's words, to a condition in which many of the limiting features of human life could be transcended; ephemerality through permanence; motion by rest; becoming by being. Our desire gives us the mind to transcend present realities and reach out for what our condition should make seem hopeless or impossible or absurd.[46]

We may no longer be able to believe in its divinity; yet perhaps we may still permit ourselves to wonder; and to "wonder" may simply mean: to entertain a possibility; to be prepared to ask. And if we do, if we have this will to wonder, we can allow ourselves to see in this standpoint one that we may want to continue to cultivate as a location for self-knowledge – as a location that tells us who we are, and that reattunes us to what we desire, thus enabling us to seek it: namely, an understanding of ourselves and the world that might respond to this identity and to what we dare to hope or believe of its grandeur, and reveal to us how it could find its truest flourishing and fulfilment. As a location, thus, in which self-knowledge could provoke aspiration.

Schopenhauer may have done away with this particular continuation, with the positive movement of desire *towards* that would complement the transcending movement of desire *away*. The desire for transcendence is here a ladder that leads to nothing – to nothing better; nothing good. Yet the location that Schopenhauer occupies in articulating these movements, I have suggested, is one that we may see reason to value as our own. And it is then with the resources, and more specifically the *ethical* resources, of the tradition to which this standpoint belongs that we can approach Schopenhauer's standpoint, placing it in a dialogue with this longer tradition that enables us to appropriate it through criticism. This is a criticism, indeed, of which the earlier appraisal of the rational force and content of Schopenhauer's pessimism can be taken as a necessary stopping place and ingredient. And to the extent that Schopenhauer's specific way

---

[46] The movement I have in mind is expressed with special distinctness in Schopenhauer's remark, apropos tragedy, that "every tragedy demands an existence of an entirely different kind, a different world, the knowledge of which can always be given to us only indirectly, as here by such a demand" (*WWR* II:433).

of inhabiting the cosmic standpoint serves to express a predicament that is peculiarly our own, criticism of this kind will simultaneously constitute a form of self-criticism, demanding that we directly confront the temptations deriving from this predicament and reflect on the ideals of character that govern the way we respond to it. These temptations, I have been suggesting, are deeply connected to the difficulty of negotiating vulnerability in its different forms, and call for a keen reflective effort to engage the delicate relationship between dependence and transcendence, and to balance it in ways that do not entail loss.

Whether this capacity to aspire and to transcend our condition through desire can be read, as Longinus proposed to read our passion for great things, as a sign of grand vocation[47] – whether this aspect of our identity can "point" or serve as a "ground," whether of the weaker notion of "hope" or the stronger ancient notion of a "claim" or "entitlement" – would seem open to question. But wonder, as our own experience and philosophical history eloquently attest, is rarely sterile.

---

[47] Longinus, "On Sublimity," 494 (35.2): the fact that "nature made man to be no humble or lowly creature," bringing human beings into life "as into a great festival, to be both a spectator and an enthusiastic contestant in its competitions," is made evident in the "irresistible desire for anything which is great" that she implanted in us.

Works cited

Abrams, Meyer H. *Natural Supernaturalism: Tradition and Revolution in Romantic Literature*. New York: W. W. Norton, 1973.

Ackrill, John L. "Aristotle on *eudaimonia*," in A. O. Rorty, ed., *Essays on Aristotle's Ethics*. Berkeley and Los Angeles: University of California Press, 1980.

Annas, Julia. "Aristotle on pleasure and goodness," in A. O. Rorty, ed., *Essays on Aristotle's Ethics*. Berkeley and Los Angeles: University of California Press, 1980.

An Introduction to Plato's "Republic." Oxford: Clarendon Press, 1981.

Platonic Ethics, Old and New. Ithaca, NY: Cornell University Press, 1999.

Anscombe, G. E. M. "Modern moral philosophy." *Philosophy*, 33 (1958).

Aristotle. *Metaphysics*, trans. W. D. Ross. Oxford: Clarendon Press, 1928.

Nicomachean Ethics, trans. C. Rowe, introduction and commentary S. Broadie. Oxford University Press, 2002.

Nicomachean Ethics, trans. R. C. Bartlett and S. D. Collins. University of Chicago Press, 2011.

On Rhetoric: A Theory of Civic Discourse, trans. G. A. Kennedy. Oxford University Press, 2007.

Atwell, John E. *Schopenhauer on the Character of the World: The Metaphysics of Will*. Berkeley and Los Angeles: University of California Press, 1995.

Budd, Malcolm. *Music and the Emotions*. London: Routledge & Kegan Paul, 1985.

"The sublime in nature," in P. Guyer, ed., *Kant's "Critique of the Power of Judgment."* Lanham, MD and Oxford: Rowman & Littlefield, 2003.

Cartwright, David E. *Historical Dictionary of Schopenhauer's Philosophy*. Lanham, MD: Scarecrow Press, 2005.

"Nietzsche's use and abuse of Schopenhauer's moral philosophy for life," in C. Janaway, ed., *Willing and Nothingness: Schopenhauer as Nietzsche's Educator*. Oxford: Clarendon Press, 1998.

Schopenhauer: A Biography. Cambridge University Press, 2010.

"Schopenhauer on suffering, death, guilt, and the consolation of metaphysics," in E. von der Luft, ed., *Schopenhauer: New Essays in Honor of His 200th Birthday*. Lewiston, NY: Edwin Mellen Press, 1988.

"Schopenhauerian optimism and an alternative to resignation?" *Schopenhauer-Jahrbuch*, 66 (1985).

Cavell, Stanley. *The Claim of Reason: Wittgenstein, Skepticism, Morality, and Tragedy*. Oxford University Press, 1979.

Chansky, James D. "Schopenhauer and Platonic Ideas: a groundwork for an aesthetic metaphysics," in E. von der Luft, ed., *Schopenhauer: New Essays in Honor of His 200th Birthday*. Lewiston, NY: Edwin Mellen Press, 1988.

Chrysakopoulou, Sylvana. "Wonder and the beginning of philosophy in Plato," in S. Vasalou, ed., *Practices of Wonder: Cross-Disciplinary Perspectives*. Eugene, OR: Pickwick, 2012.

Cicero. *Tusculan Disputations*, trans. J. E. King. London: W. Heinemann; New York: G. P. Putnam's Sons, 1927.

Cioran, Emile M. *Tears and Saints*, trans. I. Zarifopol-Johnston. University of Chicago Press, 1995.

Clegg, Jerry S. "Schopenhauer and Wittgenstein on lonely languages and criterialess claims," in E. von der Luft, ed., *Schopenhauer: New Essays in Honor of His 200th Birthday*. Lewiston, NY: Edwin Mellen Press, 1988.

Cooper, David E. *The Measure of Things: Humanism, Humility, and Mystery*. Oxford University Press, 2002.

Cooper, Neil. "Aristotle's crowning virtue." *Apeiron*, 22 (1989).

Copleston, Frederick. *Arthur Schopenhauer, Philosopher of Pessimism*, rev. edn. London: Search Press; New York: Barnes & Noble Books, 1975.

Crisp, Roger. "Aristotle on greatness of soul," in R. Kraut, ed., *The Blackwell Guide to Aristotle's "Nicomachean Ethics."* Oxford: Blackwell, 2006.

Crosby, Donald A. *The Specter of the Absurd: Sources and Criticisms of Modern Nihilism*. Albany, NY: State University of New York Press, 1988.

Curzer, Howard J. "Aristotle's much-maligned *megalopsychos*." *Australasian Journal of Philosophy*, 69 (1991).

Danto, Arthur C. "Philosophy and/as/of literature," in G. L. Hagberg and W. Jost, eds., *A Companion to the Philosophy of Literature*. Oxford: Wiley-Blackwell, 2010.

Daston, Lorraine, and Katharine Park. *Wonders and the Order of Nature, 1150–1750*. New York: Zone Books, 1998.

Dienstag, Joshua F. *Pessimism: Philosophy, Ethic, Spirit*. Princeton University Press, 2006.

Doron, Claude-Olivier. "The microscopic glance: spiritual exercises, the microscope and the practice of wonder in early modern science," in S. Vasalou, ed., *Practices of Wonder: Cross-Disciplinary Perspectives*. Eugene, OR: Pickwick, 2012.

Eagleton, Terry. *The Ideology of the Aesthetic*. Oxford: Blackwell, 1990.

Engberg-Pedersen, Troels. "Marcus Aurelius on emotions," in J. Shivols and Engberg-Pedersen, eds., *The Emotions in Hellenistic Philosophy*. Dordrecht: Kluwer Academic Publishers, 1998.

Fischer, John M., ed. *The Metaphysics of Death*. Stanford University Press, 1993.

Foot, Philippa. *Virtues and Vices*. Berkeley and Los Angeles: University of California Press, 1978.

Foster, Cheryl. "Ideas and imagination: Schopenhauer on the proper foundation of art," in C. Janaway, ed., *The Cambridge Companion to Schopenhauer*. Cambridge University Press, 1999.

Fox, Michael A. "Schopenhauer on death, suicide and self-renunciation," in Fox, ed., *Schopenhauer: His Philosophical Achievement*. Brighton: Harvester, 1980.

"Schopenhauer on the need for metaphysics," in E. von der Luft, ed., *Schopenhauer: New Essays in Honor of His 200th Birthday*. Lewiston, NY: Edwin Mellen Press, 1988.

Gardiner, Patrick. *Schopenhauer*. Harmondsworth: Penguin Books, 1963.

Gauthier, René A. *Magnanimité: l'idéal de la grandeur dans la philosophie païenne et dans la théologie chrétienne*. Paris: J. Vrin, 1951.

Gillespie, Michael A. *Nihilism before Nietzsche*. University of Chicago Press, 1995.

Gordon, Jill. *Turning toward Philosophy: Literary Device and Dramatic Structure in Plato's Dialogues*. University Park, PA: Pennsylvania State University Press, 1999.

Guyer, Paul. "Pleasure and knowledge in Schopenhauer's aesthetics," in D. Jacquette, ed., *Schopenhauer, Philosophy, and the Arts*. Cambridge University Press, 1996.

Hadot, Pierre. *La philosophie comme manière de vivre: entretiens avec Jeannie Carlier et Arnold I. Davidson*. Paris: Albin Michel, 2001.

Philosophy as a Way of Life: Spiritual Exercises from Socrates to Foucault, trans. M. Chase. Malden, MA: Blackwell Publishing, 1995.

Hamlyn, D. W. *Schopenhauer: The Arguments of the Philosophers*. London: Routledge & Kegan Paul, 1980.

"Schopenhauer on action and the will," in G. Vesey, ed., *Idealism Past and Present*. Cambridge University Press, 1982.

Hammermeister, Kai. *The German Aesthetic Tradition*. Cambridge University Press, 2002.

Hardie, W. F. R. "'Magnanimity' in Aristotle's *Ethics*." *Phronesis*, 23 (1978).

Hein, Hilde. "Schopenhauer and Platonic Ideas." *Journal of the History of Philosophy*, 4 (1966).

Holmes, Richard. *The Age of Wonder*. London: HarperPress, 2008.

Horkheimer, Max. "Schopenhauer today," in M. Fox, ed., *Schopenhauer: His Philosophical Achievement*. Brighton: Harvester, 1980.

Horner, David. "What it takes to be great: Aristotle and Aquinas on magnanimity." *Faith and Philosophy*, 15 (1998).

Hübscher, Arthur. *The Philosophy of Schopenhauer in its Intellectual Context: Thinker against the Tide*, trans. J. T. Baer and D. E. Cartwright. Lampeter: Edwin Mellen Press, 1989.

Inwood, Brad. "Why physics?" in R. Salles, ed., *God and Cosmos in Stoicism*. Oxford University Press, 2009.

Irwin, Terence H. "Ethics in the *Rhetoric* and in the *Ethics*," in A. O. Rorty, ed., *Essays on Aristotle's "Rhetoric."* Berkeley and Los Angeles: University of California Press, 1996.

Jacquette, Dale. *The Philosophy of Schopenhauer.* Montreal: McGill-Queen's University Press, 2005.

"Schopenhauer on death," in C. Janaway, ed., *The Cambridge Companion to Schopenhauer.* Cambridge University Press, 1999.

"Schopenhauer's metaphysics of appearance and Will in the philosophy of art," in D. Jacquette, ed., *Schopenhauer, Philosophy, and the Arts.* Cambridge University Press, 1996.

Jaffa, Harry V. *Thomism and Aristotelianism: A Study of the Commentary by Thomas Aquinas on the "Nicomachean Ethics."* University of Chicago Press, 1952.

Janaway, Christopher. "Knowledge and tranquillity: Schopenhauer on the value of art," in D. Jacquette, ed., *Schopenhauer, Philosophy, and the Arts.* Cambridge University Press, 1996.

Schopenhauer. Oxford University Press, 1994.

"Schopenhauer as Nietzsche's educator," in C. Janaway, ed., *Willing and Nothingness: Schopenhauer as Nietzsche's Educator.* Oxford: Clarendon Press, 1998.

"Schopenhauer's pessimism," in Janaway, ed., *The Cambridge Companion to Schopenhauer.* Cambridge University Press, 1999.

Self and World in Schopenhauer's Philosophy. Oxford: Clarendon Press, 1989.

"Will and nature," in Janaway, ed., *The Cambridge Companion to Schopenhauer.* Cambridge University Press, 1999.

Jedan, Christoph. *Stoic Virtues: Chrysippus and the Religious Character of Stoic Ethics.* London and New York: Continuum, 2009.

Kant, Immanuel. *Critique of the Power of Judgment*, trans. P. Guyer and E. Matthews. Cambridge University Press, 2000.

Critique of Pure Reason, trans. N. K. Smith. Basingstoke: Palgrave, 1929.

Knox, Israel. *The Aesthetic Theories of Kant, Hegel, and Schopenhauer.* London: Thames and Hudson, 1958.

Kołakowski, Leszek. *Metaphysical Horror.* Oxford: Blackwell, 1988.

Langton, Rae. *Kantian Humility: Our Ignorance of Things in Themselves.* Oxford: Clarendon Press, 1998.

Lear, Jonathan. *Radical Hope: Ethics in the Face of Cultural Devastation.* Cambridge, MA and London: Harvard University Press, 2006.

Longinus. "On Sublimity," trans. D. A. Russell, in Russell and M. Winterbottom, eds., *Ancient Literary Criticism.* Oxford University Press, 1972.

Lucretius. *On the Nature of Things*, trans. M. F. Smith. Indianapolis: Hackett Publishing, 2001.

Lukács, Georg. *The Destruction of Reason*, trans. P. Palmer. London: Merlin Press, 1980.

MacIntyre, Alasdair. *After Virtue*, 3rd edn. London: Duckworth, 2007.

"The relationship of philosophy to its past," in R. Rorty, J. B. Schneewind, and Q. Skinner, eds., *Philosophy in History: Essays on the Historiography of Philosophy.* Cambridge University Press, 1984.

McLaughlin, Sigrid. "Some aspects of Tolstoy's intellectual development: Tolstoy and Schopenhauer." *California Slavic Studies*, 5 (1970).

Magee, Bryan. *The Philosophy of Schopenhauer*, rev. edn. Oxford: Clarendon Press, 1997.

Mann, Thomas. "Schopenhauer," in *Essays of Three Decades*, trans. H. T. Lowe-Porter. London: Secker & Warburg, 1947.

Marcus Aurelius. *The Meditations of the Emperor Marcus Antoninus*, vol. I, trans. A. S. L. Farquharson. Oxford: Clarendon Press, 1944.

Michel, Alain. "Rhétorique et poétique: la théorie du sublime de Platon aux modernes." *Revue des Études Latines*, 54 (1976).

Monk, Ray. *Wittgenstein: The Duty of Genius*. London: Vintage, 1991.

Monk, Samuel H. *The Sublime: A Study of Critical Theories in XVIII-Century England*. Ann Arbor: University of Michigan Press, 1960.

Mulhall, Stephen. "Wonder, perplexity, sublimity: philosophy as the self-overcoming of self-exile in Heidegger and Wittgenstein," in S. Vasalou, ed., *Practices of Wonder: Cross-Disciplinary Perspectives*. Eugene, OR: Pickwick, 2012.

Murdoch, Iris. *Metaphysics as a Guide to Morals*. London: Penguin Books, 1993.

Nagel, Thomas. *The View from Nowhere*. Oxford University Press, 1986.

Neeley, G. Steven. *Schopenhauer: A Consistent Reading*. Lewiston, NY: Edwin Mellen Press, 2003.

Nehamas, Alexander. *The Art of Living*. Berkeley and Los Angeles: University of California Press, 1998.

Neill, Alex. "Aesthetic experience in Schopenhauer's metaphysics of will," in Neill and C. Janaway, eds., *Better Consciousness: Schopenhauer's Philosophy of Value*. Oxford: Wiley-Blackwell, 2009.

Nicholls, Moira. "Schopenhauer, feeling and the noumenon." *Schopenhauer-Jahrbuch*, 76 (1995).

"Schopenhauer, Young, and the Will." *Schopenhauer-Jahrbuch*, 72 (1991).

Nicolson, Marjorie H. *Mountain Gloom, Mountain Glory: The Development of the Aesthetics of the Infinite*. Ithaca, NY: Cornell University Press, 1959.

Nietzsche, Friedrich. *Beyond Good and Evil*, trans. M. Faber. Oxford University Press, 1998.

The Gay Science, trans. J. Nauckhoff and A. del Caro. Cambridge University Press, 2001.

Human, All Too Human, trans. R. J. Hollingdale. Cambridge University Press, 1996.

On the Genealogy of Morals, trans. D. Smith. Oxford University Press, 1996.

"On Schopenhauer," trans. in C. Janaway, ed., *Willing and Nothingness: Schopenhauer as Nietzsche's Educator*. Oxford: Clarendon Press, 1998.

Twilight of the Idols, trans. R. J. Hollingdale. London: Penguin Books, 2003.

Untimely Meditations, trans. R. J. Hollingdale. Cambridge University Press, 1997.

Nightingale, Andrea W. *Spectacles of Truth in Classical Greek Philosophy*. Cambridge University Press, 2004.

Nussbaum, Martha C. *The Fragility of Goodness: Luck and Ethics in Greek Tragedy and Philosophy,* rev. edn. Cambridge University Press, 2001.

"Non-relative virtues: an Aristotelian approach." *Midwest Studies in Philosophy*, 13 (1988).

The Therapy of Desire: Theory and Practice in Hellenistic Ethics. Princeton University Press, 2009.

Upheavals of Thought: The Intelligence of Emotions. Cambridge University Press, 2001.

Pakaluk, Michael. "The meaning of Aristotelian magnanimity." *Oxford Studies in Ancient Philosophy*, 26 (2004).

"Socratic magnanimity in the *Phaedo*." *Ancient Philosophy*, 24 (2004).

Philonenko, Alexis. *Schopenhauer*. Paris: Vrin, 1980.

Plato. *Euthyphro, Apology, Crito, Phaedo, Phaedrus*, trans. H. N. Fowler. Cambridge, MA and London: Harvard University Press, 1914.

The Republic, trans. T. Griffith, ed. G. R. F. Ferrari. Cambridge University Press, 2000.

Theaetetus, trans. R. A. H. Waterfield. London: Penguin Books, 2004.

Theaetetus, Sophist, trans. H. N. Fowler. London: Heinemann, 1921.

Ray, Matthew A. *Subjectivity and Irreligion: Atheism and Agnosticism in Kant, Schopenhauer and Nietzsche*. Aldershot: Ashgate, 2003.

Rorty, Richard. "The historiography of philosophy: four genres," in Rorty, J. B. Schneewind, and Q. Skinner, eds., *Philosophy in History: Essays on the Historiography of Philosophy*. Cambridge University Press, 1984.

Rubenstein, Mary-Jane. *Strange Wonder: The Closure of Metaphysics and the Opening of Awe*. New York: Columbia University Press, 2008.

Russell, Donald A. "Greek criticism of the Empire," in G. A. Kennedy, ed., *The Cambridge History of Literary Criticism*, vol. I, *Classical Criticism*. Cambridge University Press, 1989.

Safranski, Rüdiger. *Schopenhauer and the Wild Years of Philosophy*, trans. E. Osers. Cambridge, MA: Harvard University Press, 1991.

Schaeffer, Jean-Marie. *Art of the Modern Age*, trans. S. Rendall. Princeton University Press, 2000.

Schopenhauer, Arthur. *Manuscript Remains*, 4 vols., ed. A. Hübscher, trans. E. F. J. Payne. Oxford: Berg, 1988–90.

On the Basis of Morality, trans. E. F. J. Payne. Indianapolis and Cambridge: Hackett Publishing, 1995.

On the Will in Nature, trans. E. F. J. Payne, ed. D. E. Cartwright. New York and Oxford: Berg, 1992.

Parerga and Paralipomena, 2 vols., trans. E. F. J. Payne. Oxford: Clarendon Press, 1974.

The World as Will and Representation, 2 vols., trans. E. F. J. Payne. New York: Dover Publications, 1966.

The World as Will and Representation, vol. I, ed. and trans. J. Norman, A. Welchman, and C. Janaway. Cambridge University Press, 2010.

Sedley, David. "The ideal of godlikeness," in G. Fine, ed., *Plato 2: Ethics, Politics, Religion, and the Soul*. Oxford University Press, 1999.

Segal, Charles. "Writer as hero: the heroic ethos in Longinus, *On the Sublime*," in J. Servais, T. Hackens, and B. Servais-Soyez, eds., *Stemmata: mélanges de philologie, d'histoire et d'archéologie grecques offerts à Jules Labarbe*. Liège and Louvain-la-Neuve: L'Antiquité Classique, 1987.

Sellars, John. "The point of view of the cosmos: Deleuze, Romanticism, Stoicism." *Pli*, 8 (1999).

Seneca. *Ad Lucilium epistulae morales*, vol. III, trans. R. M. Gummere. London: Heinemann; New York: G. P. Putnam's Sons, 1925.

Shapsay, Sandra. "Poetic intuition and the bounds of sense: metaphor and metonymy in Schopenhauer's philosophy," in A. Neill and C. Janaway, eds., *Better Consciousness: Schopenhauer's Philosophy of Value*. Oxford: Wiley-Blackwell, 2009.

Sherman, Nancy. "Common sense and uncommon virtue." *Midwest Studies in Philosophy*, 13 (1988).

Simmel, Georg. *Schopenhauer and Nietzsche*, trans. H. Loiskandl, D. Weinstein, and M. Weinstein. Urbana and Chicago: University of Illinois Press, 1991.

Snow, Dale E., and James J. Snow. "Was Schopenhauer an Idealist?" *Journal of the History of Philosophy*, 29 (1991).

Taylor, Charles. "Philosophy and its history," in R. Rorty, J. B. Schneewind, and Q. Skinner, eds., *Philosophy in History: Essays on the Historiography of Philosophy*. Cambridge University Press, 1984.

Taylor, Terri G. "Platonic Ideas, aesthetic experience, and the resolution of Schopenhauer's 'great contradiction'." *International Studies in Philosophy*, 19 (1987).

Vandenabeele, Bart. "Schopenhauer, Nietzsche and the aesthetically sublime." *Journal of Aesthetic Education*, 37 (2003).

Vasalou, Sophia. "Educating virtue as a mastery of language." *Journal of Ethics*, 6 (2012).

"Wonder: toward grammar a," in Vasalou, ed., *Practices of Wonder: Cross-Disciplinary Perspectives*. Eugene, OR: Pickwick, 2012.

White, Frank C. "Schopenhauer and Platonic Ideas," in B. Vandenabeele, ed., *A Companion to Schopenhauer*. Oxford: Wiley-Blackwell, 2012.

Wicks, Robert. *Schopenhauer*. Oxford: Wiley-Blackwell, 2008.

Wittgenstein, Ludwig. "Lecture on ethics." *Philosophical Review*, 74 (1965).

Philosophical Investigations, trans. G. E. M. Anscombe, P. M. S. Hacker, and J. Schulte, rev. 4th edn by Hacker and Schulte. Oxford: Wiley-Blackwell, 2009.

Young, Julian. *Schopenhauer*. London and New York: Routledge, 2005.

Willing and Unwilling: A Study in the Philosophy of Arthur Schopenhauer. Dordrecht: Martinus Nijhoff, 1987.

Zagzebski, Linda T. *Virtues of the Mind*. Cambridge University Press, 1996.

Index

Made in the USA
Las Vegas, NV
25 September 2021